D1087410

The Large Group

Dynamics and Therapy

Edited by

Lionel Kreeger

F. E. PEACOCK PUBLISHERS, INC.

401 WEST IRVING PARK ROAD

ITASCA, ILLINOIS 60143

First published in Great Britain 1975
by Constable and Company Limited
10 Orange Street London WC2H 7EG
Introductory material © 1975 by Lionel Kreeger

ISBN hardback 0 09 460190 9
ISBN paperback 0 09 460400 2

Set in Monotype Garamond
Printed in Great Britain by The Anchor Press Ltd
and bound by Wm Brendon & Son Ltd
both of Tiptree, Essex

Preface

The value of small-group psychotherapy is now well established, alongside the disciplines of psychoanalysis and individual psychotherapy. The whole field of psychotherapy is enlarging rapidly, including such areas as marital and family therapy, therapeutic communities and, over the past decade, interest in large groups.

As a result of including large-group experience both in therapeutic institutions and training schemes, the potential of this technique begins to emerge. All those who have worked with large groups will acknowledge the fascination and power that they hold, and most would agree that they present a new dimension to our understanding of group dynamics.

This book was conceived as an attempt to collate our present knowledge of large groups, both at a theoretical and practical level. Its intention is to offer experiences from a wide spectrum of disciplines and settings. Roughly half the chapters are psychoanalytic in their orientation; other contributions derive from general psychiatry, sociology, anthropology, and industrial psychology.

The place of large-group therapy is still to be defined, but it is hoped that this book will contribute to the careful and detailed assessment that is necessary to fulfil its evaluation.

Lionel Kreeger
1974

Acknowledgements

I wish to record my indebtedness to my colleague and friend Pat de Maré, with whom I have worked both at Halliwick Hospital, and at the Institute of Group Analysis since 1965, particularly in the field of large groups. I feel that our contact has been mutually enriching, and certainly catalytic for the realisation of this book.

I am most grateful to Malcolm Pines, who, by virtue of his preparing the concluding chapter, read the entire manuscript as it evolved, and gave generously of his reactions and views to its contents.

Many thanks to all contributors to this book for their enthusiasm and unfailing courtesy, which made the task of editing both exciting and pleasurable.

To all patients and staff at Halliwick Hospital, and to all participants and colleagues in the General (Introductory) Group Work Course of the Institute of Group Analysis, my gratitude for the experiences of the large group, which led to the conception of this manuscript.

My thanks to Miss Elfreda Powell and Mrs Rosemary Williams of Constable, for their encouragement and help at all stages of development of this book.

Mrs Pamela Jameson and Miss Una Coogan were both instrumental in reducing the degree of chaos that threatened at times, and, to both of them, many thanks for their cheerful and efficient secretarial services.

Lastly, my thanks to Hamish Hamilton who kindly agreed to my quoting in my introductory chapter 'The Owl who was God', from *Vintage Thurber*, by James Thurber (1965).

L.K.

List of contributors

S.H. FOULKES M.D., F.R.C.PSYCH.

Physician Emeritus to the Bethlem Royal and Maudsley Hospitals. Founder and Hon. President of the Group-Analytic Society, London. Member of the Institute of Group Analysis. Member of the British Psychoanalytic Society, on whose Council he has served. Fellow of the British Psychological Society. Fellow of the American Group Psychotherapy Association. Member of the Council of the International Association of Group Psychotherapy. Editor of *Group Analysis* – International Panel and Correspondence.

EARL HOPPER PH.D.

Lecturer in Sociology, London School of Economics. Member of the British Association of Psychotherapists and of the Group-Analytic Society, London. Member of the Council of the London Centre for Psychotherapy.

MYLES HOPPER PH.D.

Assistant Professor of Social Work and Community Medicine, and Director, Family Life Project, Memorial University of Newfoundland, St John's, Newfoundland. Currently employed as Project Associate, University of Wisconsin Center for Health Sciences, Department of Family Medicine and Practice.

LIONEL KREEGER M.B., M.R.C.P.(ED.), M.R.C.PSYCH.,D.P.M.

Consultant Psychiatrist, Paddington Centre for Psychotherapy, London. Member Group-Analytic Society, London, and Institute of Group Analysis. Associate Member of British Psychoanalytic Society.

TOM MAIN M.D., F.R.C.PSYCH., D.P.M., F.B.PS.S., F.A.N.Z.C.P.

Medical Director, The Cassel Hospital. Vice-President of the Royal College of Psychiatrists. Member of the British Psychoanalytic Society.

PATRICK B. DE MARÉ M.R.C.PSYCH.
Consultant Psychiatrist on the teaching staff of St George's Hospital, and Halliwick House, New Southgate Group of Hospitals. Lately President of the Group-Analytic Society, London.

TREVOR MUMBY Diploma in Psychiatric Social Work
Director of Interface – the Centre for Group Relations Training. Member, Group-Analytic Society, London. Lately Consultant in Organisation Behaviour, Shell Chemicals. Currently engaged in conducting a Self-Development Programme for an international pharmaceutical corporation.

MALCOLM PINES F.R.C.P., F.R.C.PSYCH. D.P.M.
Consultant Psychotherapist, Maudsley Hospital. President, Group-Analytic Society, London. Member, Institute of Group Analysis. Associate Member, British Psychoanalytic Society.

A. C. ROBIN SKYNNER M.B., M.R.C.PSYCH., D.P.M.
Senior Tutor in Psychotherapy, Institute of Psychiatry, London. Hon. Associate Consultant, Bethlem Royal and Maudsley Hospitals. Hon. Secretary to the Council, and Chairman of Training Committee, Institute of Group Analysis. Member, Group-Analytic Society, London.

RAFAEL R. SPRINGMANN M.D.
Deputy Head of Psychiatric Department, The Chaim Sheba Medical Centre, Tel-Hashomer, Israel. Clinical Lecturer in Psychiatry, Tel-Aviv University Medical School. Supervisor of Psychotherapy, Tel-Aviv University School for Psychotherapy.

PIERRE TURQUET M.A., F.R.C.PSYCH.
Consultant, Adult Department, Tavistock Clinic, London, and Tavistock Institute of Human Relations (Centre for Applied Social Research). Associate Member, British Psychoanalytic Society.

ANNE WEYMAN B.SC.(SOC.), A.C.A.
Social Science Research Worker for Queen Mary's Roehampton Hospital. Currently studying the differential burden on families of in-patient and day patient care for the mentally ill.

J. STUART WHITELEY M.B., F.R.C.P.(ED.), M.R.C.PSYCH., D.P.M.
Consultant Psychiatrist and Medical Director, Henderson Hospital, Sutton. Member, Group-Analytic Society, London.

Contents

Introduction

Lionel Kreeger

My interest in large groups was provoked and stimulated through my work at Halliwick Hospital and participation in the various training schemes run by the Institute of Group Analysis. At Halliwick I held the dual posts of Consultant Psychiatrist and Psychotherapist from 1966 to 1972. During most of this time I had charge of a mixed ward of some 32 beds. Intensive group therapy was the basic approach to treatment and a daily ward meeting consisting of as many as 40 to 45 people was a regular procedure. The whole hospital, consisting of four wards together with a day unit, used the principles of the therapeutic community, and as part of that culture community meetings were held regularly. These were attended by anything up to 120 patients together with 20 to 30 staff members. My colleague Pat de Maré also works at Halliwick as a Consultant Psychotherapist, and together we took a keen interest in how these large groups functioned within the hospital setting.

The Institute of Group Analysis has run training schemes in group psychotherapy for a number of years. The Introductory Group Work Course was modified some five years ago to include a large-group experience in the third and final term. All participants met once a week in an unstructured situation over a period of seven weeks. Seven or eight small-group leaders were involved in this large-group experience, including Pat de Maré, Malcolm Pines, Robin Skynner and myself, together with other colleagues from the Institute of Group Analysis. Such was the success of the experiment that it became a standard part of the course. In his chapter, 'The large group in training', Robin

Skynner describes the events of one such year, together with the excitement and involvement that it occasioned.

In May 1972, the Second European Symposium on Group Analysis took place in London. As part of the conference, de Maré[1]* and I[2] introduced a three-hour session of the large group. This experimental session again occasioned much enthusiasm and interest, and it now seems that no conference is considered adequate without some large-group experience. It was through these cumulative stimuli that I conceived the idea of editing a book on the large group, in the hope that it would be possible to offer a wide and deep-searching perspective to this technique.

The importance of large groups
Therapy

Large groups are frequently employed as part of the therapeutic organisation of institutions. It is arguable whether they are most valuable in the realm of sociotherapy or psychotherapy. The majority, in all probability, would place greater emphasis on the large group as part of administration and organisation, but a growing minority feel that useful psychotherapy can be obtained in a large-group situation. These arguments will be explored at greater depth in later chapters in this book, particularly by Stuart Whiteley in 'The large group as a medium for sociotherapy' and by Rafael Springmann in 'Psychotherapy in the large group'. Whatever one's orientation, however, there can be little doubt as to the contribution that the large group can make to any therapeutic régime. In all hospitals or institutions that try to function as therapeutic communities, the large group or community meeting is a *sine qua non* of the culture. It is within such meetings that the totality of experience within the unit may be comprehended, confronted, and analysed.

The current reorganisation of the psychiatric services in Great Britain has much to commend it. The creation of small psychiatric departments in general district hospitals, to replace the old existing mental hospitals often sited many miles from the centre of town, will help towards confronting psychological problems

* References begin on p. 313.

within the community. It will contribute to a changing perspective of mental illness, with the hope of greater acceptance and
less rejection and denial, with which it is so easy to collude by
dumping 'mental patients' in 'lunatic asylums'. There is no doubt
too that physical methods of treatment can be efficiently applied
in such units. The main area for concern, however, is the availability of psychotherapeutic treatment under these circumstances.
There will be intense pressure on bed occupation with a greater
need for rapid turn-over of patients. There may well be shortage
of staff time to devote to the detailed working-through of
psychological problems. At the present time it is clear that the
National Health Service is sadly lacking in psychotherapeutic
facilities. It is impossible to conceive, within the foreseeable
future, that individual psychotherapy or psychoanalysis will be
freely available to all those who require it. Small-group psychotherapy may be the only answer to the service's requirements for
psychotherapy, but even this is lacking in most centres outside
London and a handful of other towns in the country. It is in
this context that large-group therapy may play a most important
part in future developments.

Training
It is desirable that anyone who intends working at a psychotherapeutic level obtain some personal therapeutic experience
for himself. Ideally, psychoanalysis, individual psychotherapy
or small-group psychotherapy should be available to all those
working in the field, but clearly it is just not possible at this
time. It is here that training schemes can make a valuable contribution in providing a situation which can be used for self-
exploration and personal, emotional growth. Training groups
(T-groups, sensitivity groups) encourage the increase of personal
awareness and insight through the techniques of feedback and
the exploration of group dynamics. The degree to which they
may be psychotherapeutic as such will vary from group to
group and with the orientation of the group leader. On the
whole, training groups tend to be larger than therapeutic
groups. The average number of participants in small-group

psychotherapy is 7 or 8, whereas training groups tend towards a total of 12 to 15. For training purposes, therefore, there is already a movement towards larger groups.

Participation in a large-group setting, that is 40 to 100 or more people, is an invaluable experience for people in training, particularly if they are expected to work with large groups in their own treatment centres. Frequently individuals who have hitherto been terrified of large-group situations, and who will, therefore, tend to remain silent, passive and anonymous, find it possible to be articulate and active, and obtain a clearer identity through a short-term large-group experience.

Research

Some would support the view that the manifestations of the large group are a simple development of small-group dynamics. Others would argue that the dynamics of the large group are very different from those of the small group. Without entering into polemics, I think that most would agree that large groups provide a new and wider dimension of personal experience. For example, it does appear that psychotic mechanisms abound in the large group. I have heard it said by many psychoanalysts and psychotherapists that in spite of their own personal analytic treatment, the experience of being in a large group has put them more clearly in touch with the primitive aspects of their own personality development than any other treatment situation. It seems therefore, that participation in a large group can add significantly to a fuller understanding of oneself, and in turn to an increased awareness of personality development and definition of individual psychopathology. Equally, I think that experience of large-group dynamics helps us to a fuller and more sensitive appreciation of the dynamics of the small group. The application of large-group studies in research would appear to provide immense possibilities.

Sociological and political implications

Apart from the first few months of life, when normally there is an intense preoccupation of mother and baby in a dyadic relationship, we spend most of our waking life in groups. We develop in the primary family group, progress to a play group or kindergarten (if we're lucky), from there to a classroom, eventually to a work situation, join social clubs or other institutions such as the church or political organisations, marry and have children and thus recreate the cycle. Although our group involvement is predominantly at the small-group level, there are many occasions when we find ourselves involved in large-group situations. Because of the potentially powerful forces that are invariably present in the large group, it is essential that further clarification of the sociological manifestations be obtained. The application of such work should be of vital importance to society. One has only to think of mob violence following football matches, or watch the old films of the pre-war Nuremberg rallies to become aware of the need for thorough investigation in this area. Equally, political transactions, both nationally and internationally, so often take place in a large-group setting.

Historical review

In 1921 Sigmund Freud wrote his major contribution to social psychology, *Group Psychology and the Analysis of the Ego.*[3] In it he examined Le Bon's *Psychology of Crowds* (1895), in which Le Bon had indicated the similarity of group behaviour to that of the mental lives of primitive peoples and children. Freud considered two artificial groups: those of the church and the army, and in his discussion of leadership pointed to an important difference between these two organisations: the church was held together by an abstract idea; whereas the army was held together by discipline. Among other comments he observed the process of identification with the leader as being at the basis of group formation. For some years, Freud's contribution was virtually ignored, until in the 1930s interest in small-group psychotherapy emerged.

In 1931 Jacob Moreno introduced the term 'group psychotherapy' in the United States, where Trigant Burrow, Paul Schilder and Samuel Slavson, among others, were working with small groups in a variety of settings. Later, Alexander Wolf published his findings on the application of psychoanalytic principles to group psychotherapy, and Kurt Lewin stimulated and led the field of group dynamics, developing the concept of 'T' (Training) groups.

In Britain, it was with the impetus of the Second World War that major advances were achieved. A number of influential psychoanalysts were based at Northfield Military Hospital, a military neurosis centre that was developed as a therapeutic community. At the end of the war, Foulkes was appointed to the Maudsley Hospital, Bion to the Tavistock Clinic, and Main to the Cassel Hospital. Two main streams of group therapy have emerged: Foulkes' approach of group-analytic psychotherapy, which incorporates classical Freudian theory as applied to the group situation, and the Tavistock method, as developed by Bion, Ezriel and others, which utilises many Kleinian concepts. For more details of the evolution of small-group psychotherapy, reference should be made to other works (Foulkes and Anthony,[4] de Maré and Kreeger,[5] and de Maré[6]).

In 1946, Main[7] published his paper 'The Hospital as a Therapeutic Institution' in which he coined the term 'therapeutic community'. Foulkes[8] produced his first book *Introduction to Group-Analytic Psychotherapy* in 1948, which included a chapter on 'treating a ward as a group'. In the course of this he stated: 'I hope it will be evident what importance these experiments have for communities, large and small, wherever they may be found, and also how they link up with the narrower field of the group-analytic approach.'

Robert Rapoport[9] in his book *Community as Doctor* (1960), discussed the daily community meeting (the '8.30') held at the Henderson Hospital, and in considering the function of these large groups, concluded that: 'Whilst it is recognised that treatment occurs here, and that there are powerful social forces at the disposal of treatment aims in such a group, the principal aims are those of social control.' Social control was to be obtained through: (1) data-gathering, (2) confrontation of deviant behaviour, and (3) the essential channel of communication, for staff and patients.

Rice[10] published his book *Learning for Leadership* in 1965, detailing experiences at the Leicester Conferences, sponsored by the Tavistock Institute of Human Relations from 1957. Part of those conferences was concerned with the plenary meetings, large groups consisting of the total conference membership. Pierre Turquet joined him as a consultant, and describes these developments in a later chapter of this book.

Wax[11] (1965), in a paper in the *International Journal of Group Psychotherapy* on 'Analysing a Therapeutic Community Meeting', described a schema for analysing large-group meetings based on the following four categories: (1) institutional context, (2) social transactions, (3) content, and (4) latent content (consciously withheld material, plus unconscious fantasy).

The same journal published a major paper from Andrew Curry[12] in 1967 entitled 'Large Therapeutic Groups: A Critique and Appraisal of Selected Literature'. In this Dr Curry reviewed the most significant contributions to the understanding of large groups up to that time. He described 'ward milieu therapy' as developed by Maxwell Jones[13] and then went on to discuss three main approaches to the large group: concepts of situational analysis, concepts of behaviour systems theory and, thirdly, conformity and reference group behaviour.

Concepts of situational analysis

Curry referred to the work of Goffman[14] and his analysis of 'engagement among the unacquainted', as well as his recognition of two categories involved in large groups: 'participants and bystanders'. Curry summarised the views of Wilmer[15] in which he included the observation that large-number grouping creates the need for small cohesive sub-groups.

Concepts of behaviour systems theory

Curry quoted Herbst[16] who defined a system as 'a set of activity elements, which: (*a*) are independent with respect to functioning, and (*b*) operate as a boundary maintaining unit'. 'The behaviour system theorist is not concerned with the properties of the situation (i.e. rituals, ceremonies, performances), but with types of functioning possible for systems.'

Conformity and reference group behaviour
Curry focused on the conformity produced by group influence in order to neutralise group pressures. Without adequate frames of reference, behaviour in large groups could be ritualistic, or resemble a performance. Trust was almost impossible and the demand for trust might be understood as a staff defence.

In an attempt to give perspective to the subject, Curry discussed whether or not large groups could be used as a vehicle for psychotherapy. While he did not himself believe that psychotherapy could occur satisfactorily in a large-group situation, he acknowledged that others might take a different view (Small and Small[17]). Curry ended his paper as follows: '. . . Work with large number groupings emphasises again our need for unified theories of human behaviour and psychopathology, both intra-psychic and inter-personal. It has been suggested here that this unified theory must be systematic and comprehensive, a conceptualisation of the relationship of ego-psychological theory to the sociology of conduct.'

Schiff and Glassman,[18] in 'Large and Small Group Therapy in a State Mental Health Center' (1969), described their experiences at Fort Logan Mental Health Center. They used two models, that of Maxwell Jones[19] with its emphasis on 'a living-learning experience' and the 'here and now' of group experience; the other that of Edelson[20] with his concept of 'sociotherapeutic function'. Sociotherapy may be defined as 'being concerned specifically with the discovery, exploration, and resolution of intra-group and inter-group tensions'. (As compared with psychotherapy which is concerned with intra-personal tensions.) Schiff and Glassman summarised Edelson's view that community meetings should not be used for group therapy, but instead as 'task-orientated groups designed to examine and resolve conflicts which inhibit optimal organisational effectiveness'. The production and examination of intra-personal elements might be regarded as task-inhibiting.

Schiff and Glassman went on to describe nine variables relating to increasing group size. They include:

1. An increased tendency to sub-grouping, with more rigid hierarchies.
2. Less opportunity for individuals to speak.
3. Dilution of affectional ties.
4. Decreasing familiarity with others as individuals, and, therefore, the tendency to stereotype.
5. Skewing of participation – the leaders being more active and the less active members more silent.
6. The greater threat to the individual.

They recommended therapist activity be directed towards the following goals:

1. Topic selection.
2. The creation and maintenance of a safe group climate.
3. Gate-keeping, that is, leaders properly influencing the flow and direction of communication.
4. Modelling – of the group on the therapist.

They stressed the need for a more active and controlling therapist, at least in the early stages of the group life.

In 1970, Marshall Edelson[21] published his second book, *Sociotherapy and Psychotherapy*. Edelson was concerned with the application of systems theory to the therapeutic community setting at the Austin Riggs Center in Massachusetts. The following quotations from his writings indicate his approach:

> In the community meeting, the sociotherapeutic function (and not the psychotherapeutic function) is performed . . . it is not a form of group therapy.
> The focus is upon the reality of the tasks confronting members of the therapeutic community and the wider hospital organisation, and the reality of the relationships between them, rather than upon the fantasies shared by group members about these tasks and relationships; the fantasies are tested against this reality.

In those organisations where psychotherapy and sociotherapy are differentiated enterprises, psychotherapists *qua*
psychotherapists should probably not attend the community
meeting because there is no psychotherapeutic function to be
performed there.

Edelson went on to discuss the potential difficulties resulting
from such a split, and alternative methods of dealing with it,
but was insistent that the sociotherapist should not make interpretation of individual neurosis or of the group process of the
community meeting itself.

Rafael Springmann[22] in his paper 'A Large Group' published in 1970 in the *International Journal of Group Psychotherapy*
encouraged interest in the psychotherapeutic potential of the
large group. He described experiences at Tel-Hashomer Hospital,
Israel, and the weekly patient-staff meeting that was held there.
Originally the culture was one of 'an atmosphere controlled
by mutual feedback techniques'. Eventually, however, 'the
patients themselves demonstrated to us that this large and mixed
forum could be utilised for approaching personal dynamics'.
'The higher degree of dilution of transference seems to be one
aspect in which the large group, the general meeting, can in
some instances be regarded as a better therapeutic tool than
the regular group, at least in the initial stages of therapy.' He
indicated the value of these large-group meetings as a didactic
experience for students and visitors and went on to describe
the limitations of the large group:

1. They cannot take the place of regular therapeutic groups.
2. They lack continuity and intimacy, never reaching the
   point of maturation and dissolution.
3. A large part of the group remains silent and anonymous.

I well remember reading Dr Springmann's paper when it was
first published for I was at that time struggling with the difficulties and complexity of the large-group situation. What he
referred to as 'a major drawback' was near to my heart: 'The
leader may be left exhausted (comparable with an hour of intensive

personal psychotherapy with a psychotic), through the constant effort of harnessing this vast power to constructive therapeutic ends, of creating harmony in a potentially chaotic atmosphere.'

David Clark and Ken Myers[23] in a paper called 'Themes in a Therapeutic Community', published in the *British Journal of Psychiatry* in 1970, describe their experience at Fulbourn Hospital in the 60-bedded therapeutic community unit. They list the following six themes: (1) rejection, (2) violence, (3) sexuality, (4) staff division, (5) dependence-independence, and (6) relations with outside bodies, for example, other departments of the hospital and management committees. Those of us intimately concerned with large-group functioning will immediately recognise these themes.

Detailed and valuable work has of course also been undertaken in other parts of the world. For example, Professor Didier Anzieu and his colleagues in France have been applying themselves to the task of studying large-group dynamics, using some Kleinian concepts in their formulations. Any attempt to produce a short, concise review of previous literature does of course have limitations. My hope is that I have done reasonable justice to those who have contributed to our knowledge of large-group functioning, and that I have not introduced any major distortion of their work. My purpose has been to give some feeling of the total context of the large-group field, from which the various contributors to this book can elaborate their own conceptual frameworks.

Personal observations
Before ending this Introduction, I would like to offer a few personal observations.

Psychotherapy in the large group
No doubt the argument will continue for many years as to whether effective and valid psychotherapy can be obtained in a large-group situation. My own view is that it can, given the appropriate set of the group leader or leaders. Pat de Maré has often said that 'structure affects process and content'. Of

this I am sure, and if the physical setting of the large group is such that it can allow some degree of intimacy, it becomes much easier for personal and sensitive communications to be made by individuals. Three rows of chairs with as great a degree of compactness as is possible can allow for face-to-face confrontation in the large-group situation, particularly if there is any possibility of tiering.

I respect the view of those who see the function of the large group as being mainly concerned with sociotherapy, but feel that too rigid an approach can be limiting. Flexibility is always a good thing, and to be able to 'tune in' to the needs of a large group is an essential part of one's therapeutic skill.

Sub-grouping

In my experience, it is commonplace for a large group to focus on the presence of sub-groups and consider the need to split into smaller groupings, when tension, conflict and anxiety predominate. So often this split is realised in an attempt to resolve the conflict, rather than face it in the large-group setting. Whether this is essential is arguable. If one can survive the threat to the integrity of the large group and continue to explore and analyse the conflict in the large group itself, this can often lead to working through and resolving the problem. In small-group psychotherapy, I am sure that no group therapist would collude with the demands of the participants to abandon the group in order to resolve their problems individually with the therapist. (Combined treatment, that is, group plus individual psychotherapy, is a valuable technique if planned from the outset of treatment, but that is another matter).

Psychotic mechanisms

Those who have worked with large groups are familiar with the fact that psychotic mechanisms abound in the course of large-group interaction. They seem to be released in the large-group setting in a way which parallels the infant's primitive perception of external reality. The threat to the individual's identity and his sense of self, the difficulty of maintaining his own personal ego-boundary, are commonplace experiences. Paranoid anxieties with massive projective elements are often manifested. Manic flights into gaiety or sexual fantasy frequently occur, particularly as a defence against the deeper depressive preoccupation of the group.

The power of the large group

The powerful forces of the large group must be acknowledged and respected, because of their potential use for either good or evil. The responsibilities of the large-group leader are high, whether the group is concerned with therapy or indeed with some social, economic or political transaction. The problem of creativity is a fascinating one in a large-group context. There are times when it becomes impossible to think in a large-group situation. As a result of the chaos and confusion that may occur, together with the threat of violence if one exposes oneself as an individual thinker, one may 'lose one's wits' (as Turquet would put it). I remember very clearly how at a plenary meeting at the end of a week's workshop in which the large group met daily, I had planned to give some intellectual assessment of the events of the large group during that week. Because some of the emotional problems of the group had remained unresolved, I found it quite impossible to conceptualise or indeed to give any coherent or rational account of the proceedings. During the course of that plenary session, further work was done by the total group, and it became possible for me the following day to undertake the task that I had been set. (In Bion's terms, the basic-assumption group became a work-group.)

On the other hand, the large group can be enormously stimulating and provocative of real, creative, original thought. From my own experience, I know that at times I can return home from a large group exhausted, depleted, and depressed, but on other occasions I have been 'turned on' in an unmistakable way.

Leadership

The capacity of the large group to regress into a dependent relationship necessitates a degree of integrity in the leadership of the group. Battles for leadership in a large group are common-place, and often become a major element in the group process.

As an example of the type of problem that is frequently encountered, the following extract is offered from the excellent account by Isabel Jacobs[24] of the large group during the European Workshop on Group Analysis held in London in January 1973. Mrs Jacobs reported on all five sessions of the large group, which was led by Pat de Maré and myself, and this quotation concerns the events of the meeting on the second day of the Workshop:

'In the *Second Session* we seemed to have put oceanic feelings and fantasy behind us.

'Sitting isolated on one of the cushions, Dr Kreeger was the first target of negative feelings carried over from the previous session and from the same Seminar as before. When he was attacked furiously for refusing a chair in the inner circle vacated for him by someone moving to the outer one, a newcomer demonstrated once more the need for orientation: he was glad, he said, that Dr Kreeger's "stand" had identified the leader for him. The Group's identification of Dr de Maré as a second leader caused the latter to hint at his theory of multiple leadership. Disowning hierarchical authority, he said that we now had three leaders, and named the newcomer as the third. The newcomer, mystified and alarmed by the role ascribed to him, fell silent.

'Then, an invitation to a participant from a distant country to introduce himself, and the question, had he really come from that country?, initiated a very productive episode. The stranger responded with an anger that resonated with that in the Group. He expressed anger on two counts. The norms of his country required front seats to be left for latecomers and above all for the leaders, to whom respect should be shown; aware of cultural differences here, the Group's impoliteness yet angered him.

'Secondly, he had come with expectations of entering a good group, in which he could participate with fellow therapists, but the question made the Group a bad one, in that it distanced him, thereby denying him fellowship.

'Thus a new approach was made to the problem of attitudes to authority, which had already appeared in a primitive form in interaction with Dr Kreeger. It transpired that there were contradictory attitudes: many people felt that deference to, and accepting something from another was to give way to a babyish dependence unworthy of an adult, or would be seen as such.

'The episode focused attention on contradictions and ambivalences. The stranger's response to the question addressed to him illuminated the contradictory effects of categorising people, already apparent at the first session. We discovered a number of ambivalences: on the one hand, gratification that a stranger should join us, on the other, aggressive curiosity; whether to grab spontaneously what one wants (e.g., a good seat), or to earn social approval by leaving the best for others; and so on.

'Ambivalence was personified in our two staff members, who acknowledged their rivalry for leadership. The fact that they recognised their differences as old ones and that Dr Kreeger referred calmly to the possibility of conflict breaking out between them provided us with a model for coming to terms with ambivalence.

'Both agreed that there was was a dependent part of the group; and that, until negative feelings had been expressed, we could not give expression to positive ones (some people questioned this). But each wanted to tilt the Group in a different direction. Dr Kreeger saw our proceedings in terms of pre-Oedipal object relationships, and invited us to explore a number of interpretations at this level. Dr de Maré expounded his distinction between the hierarchical leader, whose interventions bring communication to a full stop, and the spokesman of leading ideas, who appears now from one part of the group, now from another. He urged us to brave the terrors of merging with each other without hierarchy in order to release the explosive power of the large group. He wanted the large group to be tilted towards the investigation of social problems, which could not be dealt with in the small one; and he held out to us the prospect of freeing the individual from the effect of social blows received in other settings (in school, as aliens in a new country), of people from different close hierarchical systems speaking freely with each other, of exploring inter-group areas.

'The session ended, excited and hopeful for the future of the large group.'

Another problem concerning leadership of the large group centres on the capacity of the group for throwing up the bad or mad leader. One of my favourite stories by James Thurber,[25] 'The Owl who was God', satirises this theme, and I would like to conclude this introduction by quoting it verbatim. (Note the election of the leader on totally inadequate grounds, the expulsion of the rational sub-group consisting of the red fox and his friends, the infectivity of the deification of the owl, and the dangers of identification with the blind leader.)

THE OWL WHO WAS GOD

by James Thurber

'Once upon a starless midnight there was an owl who sat on the branch of an oak tree. Two ground moles tried to slip quietly by unnoticed. "You!" said the owl. "Who?" they quavered, in fear and astonishment, for they could not believe it was possible for anyone to see them in that thick darkness. "You two!" said the owl. The moles hurried away and told the other creatures of the field and forest that the owl was the greatest and wisest of all animals because he could see in the dark and because he could answer any question. "I'll see about that," said a secretary bird, and he called on the owl one night when it was again very dark. "How many claws am I holding up?" said the secretary bird. "Two," said the owl, and that was right. "Can you give me another expression for 'that is to say' or 'namely'?" asked the secretary bird. "To wit," said the owl. "Why does a lover call on his love?" asked the secretary bird. "To woo," said the owl.

'The secretary bird hastened back to the other creatures and reported that the owl was indeed the greatest and wisest animal in the world because he could see in the dark and because he could answer any question. "Can he see in the daytime too?" asked a red fox. "Yes," echoed a dormouse and a French poodle. "Can he see in the daytime, too?" All the other creatures laughed loudly at this silly question, and they set upon the red fox and his friends and drove them out of the region. They then sent a messenger to the owl and asked him to be their leader.

'When the owl appeared among the animals it was high noon and the sun was shining brightly. He walked very slowly, which gave him an appearance of great dignity, and he peered about him with large, staring eyes, which gave him an air of tremendous importance. "He's God!" screamed a Plymouth Rock hen. And the others took up the cry "He's God!" So they followed him wherever he went and when he began to bump into things they began to bump into things, too. Finally he came to a concrete highway and he started up the middle of it and all the other creatures followed him. Presently a hawk, who was acting as an outrider, observed a truck coming toward them at fifty miles an hour, and he reported to the secretary bird and the secretary bird reported to the owl. "There's danger ahead," said the secretary bird. "To wit?" said the owl. The secretary bird told him. "Aren't you afraid?" he asked. "Who?" said the owl calmly, for he could not see the truck. "He's God!" cried all the creatures again, and they were still crying "He's God!" when the truck hit them and ran them down. Some of the animals were merely injured, but most of them, including the owl, were killed.

MORAL: YOU CAN FOOL TOO MANY OF THE PEOPLE TOO MUCH OF THE TIME.'

the strained relationship between the individual and the community. In this way its range is as far and as wide as these relationships go: treatment of psychoneuroses, psychoses, crime, etc., rehabilitation problems, industrial management, education – in short, every aspect of life in communities large and small. Perhaps someone taking this broad view will see in it the answer in the spirit of a democratic community to the mass and group handling of totalitarian régimes.'

A year later, addressing the first post-war Congress of European Psycho-Analysts in Amsterdam,[2] I said:

'The present historical situation shows clearly that human problems cannot be solved in isolation but only through a concerted effort of the whole of humanity. The future of the human species may well be made or marred according to whether or not it is able to grasp this fact and act upon it while there is still time.

'Anything we can learn as to the relationships of persons towards each other, and of groups towards each other, is therefore of great therapeutic significance. . . .

' . . . Group analysis is the instrument of choice for the study of the dynamics of the group, a new science in which psychology and sociology meet. In view of the importance of good relations between groups of all kinds, including whole nations, the relevance of such studies need hardly be stressed at the present time. Once again it may be the privilege of psychopathology, through the analysis of disturbances in inter-personal relationships to throw decisive light on the social life of man in all its manifestations.'

In the same paper, in 1947, I also said:

'Group treatment is the resolve to take a larger part of the external world and of a person's associates into the field of direct observation than is the case in individual treatment. Or, you have a group of patients only, you bring them together so that each can be observed and face himself in a group setting; moreover they can now face their problems as a group, including their reactions towards each other. One could say, too, that group treatment means applying *"commonsense"* – the sense of the

Part One

Theory

In this section, the first three chapters are psychoanalytic in their orientation: Dr Foulkes, a Freudian psychoanalyst, who founded the school of group-analytic psychotherapy, offers a perspective of the group-analytic approach to the problems of the large group. Dr Main is a Freudian psychoanalyst of the Independent group. In his chapter on psychodynamics, he deals mainly with the mental mechanism of projection and the further developed concept of projective identification. Dr Turquet belongs to the Kleinian group of the British Psychoanalytic Society. He is concerned with the individual's sense of identity and need for boundaries, and the threat to these in the large group.

Chapters 4 and 5 approach the large group from a more general psychosocial viewpoint: Dr de Maré, an eclectic psychotherapist trained in group-analytic psychotherapy, discusses large-group dynamics in the light of communication theory and information-flow, with an emphasis on psychosocial therapy. Earl Hopper is a sociologist, who has also trained as a psychotherapist. In collaboration with Anne Weyman, their chapter focuses on the application of sociological concepts to the large group.

For the sake of completion, perhaps it may be mentioned here that Dr Kreeger and Dr Pines are both Freudian Pschoanalysts.

Problems of the large group from a group-analytic point of view

S. H. Foulkes

It is the inner working of the human mind as a social, multi-personal phenomenon – transpersonal processes inside a shared mental matrix – with which the method and theory of group analysis are concerned. No particular limits have ever been set regarding the size of the group under consideration, although we rely mostly on the observation of men and women in small groups, conducted over longish periods. The purpose of the groups is to help them dissolve and overcome difficulties in the relationships with other people which are, in the last resort, the root of neurotic or psychotic disturbances, symptom, character formations, of excesses and inhibitions affecting existence and well-being and for which they consult us.

A paper I read to the British Psycho-Analytical Society 3rd April 1946 ended as follows:

'Group treatment can thus be looked upon in a different categories. The narrowest point of view merely a time-saver, perhaps, or a kind of substitute more individual forms of psychotherapy. Possibly that group psychotherapy might have special advantages indications – say, for instance, for the treatment culties. A wider view will see in it a new investigation, information and education. The look upon group therapy as an expression towards the study and improvement of human our time. It may see in it an instrument, perhaps one, for a practicable approach to the key community – to a problem by letting all those openly participate in its attempted solution who are in fact anyhow involved in it; instead of two people grappling with the problem, the one in the role of patient the other of therapist, you have now a number of people confronted with a problem as well as with the task of its solution. They will soon enough know what they can share in this, what prevents them as a whole group from solving it and where, on the other hand, they have to turn their attention to any one member's personal and individual difficulties.'

If I said no more than that now, in 1973, it would sum up the situation quite adequately. However, since that time world-wide progress has been made in this field. One such development is the approach to problems in a relatively much larger group, of say 50 to 100 people. This expansion is welcome. I am happy still to be able to participate in this, though no longer in the front-line of events. I do my best to take part in what is within my reach, to follow the experiences other authors describe and to think about them, perhaps more quietly than one is able to do while one is in the middle of these activities.

Social psychotherapy

The observation of people in groups usually arises when we are concerned with their problems – in a sense with social psycho-pathology. This is opening up and making accessible otherwise concealed areas. These conditions enable us to observe and to analyse behaviour and experience as they occur in action – serious, genuine action, NOT playing games or roles. Above all, we can observe changes in attitude and behaviour, changes which in a wide sense could be called therapeutic. An important ingredient in our procedure is that the group should be an active participant in these processes, should be aware of what is going on and thus eventually become the responsible agent of its own institutions. In this sense we are concerned with socio-therapy. Our special contribution to sociology and social psycho-logy lies in the elucidation of these processes and in their effects on the individual member. Though we cannot, in my opinion, base the total comprehensive science of man on our work,

cannot, as little as can psychoanalysis, produce a general comprehensive psychology or sociology, our contribution is an
essential one for these disciplines and all disciplines which are
concerned with the human being. Sociology studies the roots of
human conduct and interaction in every respect and on the basis
of social relationships, but it is quasi-statistical; it does not
focus on the particular mental events which occur in the members
of the group on each particular occasion. Let me illustrate this
difference by comparing, let us say, the study of traffic accidents.
The people who study traffic and its rules, who build roads,
regulate speed, are concerned with notions such as the particular
frequency of accidents at a certain place – say a roundabout or a
crossroads. The observation that, for instance, at one place
three times as many accidents occur than elsewhere is relevant.
There need be no doubt that these accidents are linked with the
individual drivers concerned, with their mental or physical condition, with their anxieties and worries, or even with unconscious
needs to have an accident just at that time, day and hour, with
accident proneness – but all this complicated network of motivations enters the picture equally everywhere, at other crossroads.
The psychologist or psychopathologist, on the other hand, is
interested in these very motivations, or even the special individual
compelling reasons which brought about the accident, while
appreciating that a particular turn of the road presented a special
hazard. Some sociologists, for example, Norbert Elias, have gone
beyond this point to a more living or more realistic type of
sociology. Elias[3] has long recognised that so-called 'precise
studies' based on objective measurements alone are misleading
and insufficient. He maintains that it is necessary for the sociologist to co-operate with the psychoanalyst and perhaps even
quite particularly with the group analyst. Professor Elias sees
social psychiatry as an interdisciplinary field, a borderland between
psychiatry and sociology, which are two distinct disciplines. As
he sees it, the understanding on two levels at the same time –
namely the individual and the group level – is essential. Such
a two-level approach he would see as of general theoretical
significance. I have myself always felt that group analysis, rightly

understood, furnishes an integrated approach to these problems which is adequate and new.

Human beings always live in groups. Groups in turn cannot be understood except in their relation to other groups and in the context of the conditions in which they exist. We cannot isolate biological, social, cultural and economic factors, except by special abstraction. Mental life is the expression of all these forces, both looked at horizontally, as it were, in the strictly present reality, and vertically, in relation to past inheritance. In the group-analytic view this inheritance is not seen entirely, or even predominantly, as a genetic and biological one, but more as a cultural inheritance, a transmission from generation to generation, from the earliest days onwards. Rather, the distinction between group and individual psychodynamics is meaningless, except again by abstraction. We sometimes talk of group and individual separately, as we focus more on one or other aspect of what is in fact one single and inseparable process.

Mental processes

Normally, groups are more or less institutionalised or organised, but the more we are interested in the inner mental processes, the more we prefer a minimum of structure. These inner mental processes are not conceived as intrapsychic as if they were encapsulated inside the individual's mind. As a result of unprejudiced observation, I assume these inner mental processes to be the shared property of the group or at least shareable.[4] This becomes visible when we reduce the usual structure and organisation of the group as far as possible. The more we do this, the more translation, analysis, interpretation enter the picture. What is usually unconscious or concealed becomes sufficiently noticeable and we can slowly, resolving defences and resistances by steps and stages, make it a conscious notion of the therapeutic group. This applies not only to the repressed unconscious but also to what I have termed the social unconscious. What is meant here by 'translation', by 'analysing', by 'interpretation', by all sorts of interventions, is that in the fully fledged group-analytic approach we slowly (or sometimes even quite

quickly) achieve a culture and tradition, so that the group itself
can do this work with our expert guidance and help. As this analytical component increases, we are likely to want to concentrate
more on the network of interacting processes as these enter into
the nodal points which are represented by the individual members
of the group. If we do wish to observe these processes and the
way in which they become modified in passing through the
individual, we need a situation which allows sufficient time
and intimacy to devote to those processes in adequate detail.
For this purpose, we must reduce the size of the group. If
we mean this intensive form of psychotherapy, the observation that such groups will have to be reasonably small holds
good.

The concept of mental processes *per se* being multi-personal
seems hard to accept. I will try to illustrate it by way of analogy.
Let us assume that we wish to drive from one place 'A', through
the countryside, passing many villages and towns to point 'B'.
We use a map for our orientation. Now the most useful map for
the total journey is one on a small scale, one on which a town
may be indicated only by a dot. Our journey goes towards
and through this or that town, and out again at another point,
and so on towards the next place. But on entering the town –
which may be quite large for our purposes – we enter into a
complicated network of streets, for which purpose we now need
for our orientation a map on a much larger scale. In fact we need
a town plan, in which all the individual streets are clearly indicated. We also rely on the instructions we find for our benefit
at the different turnings. It is the *traffic* with which we are here
concerned. It is the 'traffic' which corresponds to what in group
analysis we call 'transpersonal processes'. The traffic of the town
is not an isolated fact and closed system. The traffic of the town
is the result of all the connections the town has, of all the roads
reaching the town from various directions, which way they
pass through it, etc. Moreover the concept of 'traffic' is also an
abstraction for something which does exist and yet does not
exist. There is no such thing as traffic, there are only moving
cars, lorries, obstacles of all sorts, and people who wish to move

from one point to another. Together they make up what can be looked upon as a dynamic existing total thing called 'traffic'. One can then talk of traffic flowing, traffic coming to a halt, traffic being diverted and so forth. In the same way we use concepts such as 'mental processes' or 'matrix'. It becomes clear that the town modifies the traffic in its own way, and according to its own characteristics, and sends it out again changed in direction and speed from the way it reached the town. Nevertheless, it is not in isolation. It is not as if there was traffic in the country, traffic in the town, traffic in the village, alongside the river, etc., but it is all one flow, one interconnected whole. To our way of thinking the town represents the individual, and is as such a nodal point. Perhaps this makes it clearer what is meant by transpersonal processes. The processes reach the individual, go through him, are influenced by him in turn, and leave the individual – but the largest unit of observation on which we can focus is the total situation, such as the therapeutic group.

In the standard group-analytic group of 8 people, it remains true to say that the individual is in the foreground, the group in the background – the meaning determined by the context of the whole situation. There is a danger that this favours too much emphasis on the individual analytical approach and this is happening in perhaps the majority of group analysts' practice, especially if they come from an individual psychoanalytical tradition. There is therefore a certain neglect of group dynamics. Remember again that we separate these two only artificially for the purpose of making certain observations. Putting this another way, there is a strong tendency in both patients and therapists to approximate the small group to the family. Like anything else, this tendency must of course be accepted as existing and be analysed. Ultimately it is a resistance. It means that the individuals concerned including the therapist wish to establish as far as possible the conditions which have shaped them, made them into what they are, *so that they need not change*. If we accept that as a basic framework and fall in with it, it is wrong, indeed it is a trap by which ultimately the neurosis successfully resists any attempt at its basic resolution. It is of course quite different when we see a real family, a couple with children, who are a natural group. In the same way and by contrast to the small group-analytic group, all problems affecting groups in a real situation should – indeed must – by the principles of a group-analytic approach put the whole large group in the centre. It is likely that the issues raised in that large group are dealt with more or less spontaneously in informal sub-groups and by each individual.

Community problems

This large-group approach has a wide range of application, under the varied conditions of everyday social life and of course in the fields of psychiatry and psychotherapy themselves. Such a group can either be part of an institution or may encompass the whole of a smaller institution. They may be less organised groups devoted to some movement or pursuit wishing to improve their efficiency, their spirit of common concern and co-operation, to reduce conflicts and friction and to liberate creativity. In a recent Dimbleby Lecture[5] Sir Robert Mark, the Commissioner of the Metropolitan Police, spoke of the four stages in our system of criminal justice: 'Politicians make the laws, police enforce them, lawyers run the trials, and the prison or probation services deal with the convicted offenders. None of these groups is obliged to give much thought to the problems of the others, or to consider the working of the system as a whole. This is unfortunate because the different parts of the system are intimately connected.'

I do not know whether Sir Robert has ever heard of group analysis, but the tenets of his argument are very similar to those held by practitioners of group analysis. The media allow us to gain insight into many spheres and issues of ongoing life with which otherwise we would be quite unfamiliar. A psychiatrist can never know enough of all this for his own work, quite apart from his professional qualifications.

Here is an opening for the sociologist or the social psychologist. If he wants to – as he should – deal with problems and get involved with human beings, he needs to have experience and training in group analysis.

In a similar vein, under my Chairmanship of the Psychotherapy and Social Psychiatry Section of the Royal College of Psychiatrists, we showed that psychiatric problems are not essentially different from those encountered in other areas. These findings were published in a volume, edited by G. Stuart Prince and myself, entitled *Psychiatry in a Changing Society*.[6] I will quote only one statement from my 'Summary and Conclusions': 'Is it too much to hope that the Section might consider it one of its future tasks to act not only as a forum for such reports – danger signals for the health of the community as they are – but as consultants if necessary to intervene and to institute further research? Symposia could be organised of groups of participants representing different factions concerning hospitals, industry, education, law and so on.'

Large group therapy
We come now to the large group as a therapeutic instrument, in a wider sense of this term as well as in a more specific sense. I think we will do well to discern three types of these groups:
  Problem-centred.
  Experience-centred.
  Therapy-centred.

The problem-centred large group
As soon as we enter seriously into an analysis of *problems* – with, as always in group analysis, the whole group actively participating – we enter a field which can be rightfully described as social therapy. We are not concerned with 'diseases' but with problems of interrelationships. The principal vehicle of our operations is verbal communication. In such a group we should not, however, penetrate into the disguises by which some extraneous problems appear as symptoms of this group; it is enough if this fact becomes recognisable and occasionally manifest. The guiding rule should be 'stick to the problem which really concerns this group in front of you'. You can 'analyse'

in this context, but only in this context, if you are qualified to do so, but must NOT go too far into 'underlying meaning' or even 'private' personal, individual motivations.

Under such circumstances this large group situation may well be the only organised meeting of the corporate body. As the processes activated continue to influence smaller groups and individuals these may have to be left to them to deal with. The 'therapeutic' effect on all participants and their different groupings would appear to be the more positive the more discreetly and carefully the emotional climate in the large group has been observed.

In principle, I see no reason, however, for not letting these smaller groups and even individuals have the benefit of an experienced and adequately trained guide if he is available. If, for instance, we think of a hospital, the unit would be the hospital-as-a-whole, if it is possible to assemble it as such; if not, a part-whole – such as a ward – could be the boundary of the large group. If the therapy in the sense explained takes place in this large group as a whole – staff, patients, doctors and all – there is no reason why group treatment, or group-analytic discussion, should not be conducted with smaller groups. There is also no reason why staff groups should not take place or mixed groups of representatives of staff and patients, and particularly also spontaneous meetings. The main principle is that everybody should be in contact with everyone else insofar as they affect the large ward group as a whole. It is clear that what happens in therapeutic groups or in individual treatment should be allowed to flow back through the changed behaviour of the patients concerned rather than be publicised.

The experience-centred large group
The purpose of this type of large group is to allow the individual members, otherwise unknown to each other, to experience what it feels like to be a member of a group, and it is devised so as to open up as wide a range of experience as may be possible.

The experience-centred group has been much practised in

various settings following, I think, on our experiences at North-field Military Neurosis Centre during the last war. It has become known as a sensitivity group or, following the American example, as a T group.

The group which one has asked to assemble is left with a minimum of structure, in line with the group-analytic approach. Some advocate that the group be given a minimum of guidance straight from the beginning. This produces certain phenomena which are then ascribed to the group as inherent in it. These reactions, in particular those of panic, fear and bewilderment, are in my view merely the consequence of the situation into which the group is put. By contrast, I have always felt that, having convened the group or having offered treatment to the patients in such a group, I ought to help them, especially at the beginning, to understand what is hoped for or expected of them and why – not by way of lecturing them but by way of experience. In this way one keeps anxiety at a tolerable level.

Otherwise disturbances and upsets often seem to be more noticeable as the result of tensions within the group which can hopefully be resolved. As far as is known to me, such groups meet for a limited period – say daily for a week, and there are no meetings other than in the large group. This can be contrasted with a group of French psychoanalysts who use larger groups solely for educational purposes.[7] The French give psychoanalytic interpretations which refer to the inevitable basic human anxieties which are activated, such as being devoured, cut to pieces, squashed, annihilated, castrated, etc. They supplement the interpretations given in the large group by working through these experiences in smaller groups. Furthermore, they operate as a team. This latter part of the procedure at any rate seems to me recommendable.

When a group which has no other reason to come together is asked to study its own behaviour, it seems to me similar to asking a centipede to study the way it moves, when it has no particular reason to move anywhere. I imagine that it would be very difficult for the centipede to do that, although it uses its feet in a perfectly co-ordinated way under normal circumstances.

I have observed that a group under such conditions becomes overmuch interested in its own functioning as a group. A group never comes together without a reason. If it looked into these reasons and discussed the various members' expectations freely and frankly, it could then from time to time look back on its own moves. In doing this it might learn something of interest concerning the behaviour of groups *per se*. This would seem to me a better way of procedure. It would also spare the members much unnecessary anxiety. Sometimes, however, one gets the impression that some people are hoping to experience anxiety, thinking that makes for a valuable and 'deep' experience, almost as if they were addicted to it.

The therapeutic influence on group members, where it can be observed, is co-incidental, as it is in the problem-centred groups described above.

The therapy-centred large group

Insofar as the psychotherapeutic large group takes place within the framework of a hospital, in particular of a psychiatric hospital, it is not essentially different from the problem-centred group, except that it may be possible to enter more freely into the totality of the human beings involved and into the symbolic and disguised meaning of their contributions. In other words, the analytic element and the analytic attitude of the conductor may enter into the picture in a more marked way. This is particularly the case when the large group meeting is supplemented by more intensive and more individualised treatment in smaller groups. Since the war, many variations of such treatment have been practised and elaborated: for example by Maxwell Jones, who adopted the term 'therapeutic community', and Tom Main at the Cassel Hospital. Interesting accounts have been given by J. Stuart Whitely[8] and by B. A. J. C. Gregory.[9] The latter approached the group-analytic attitude perhaps most closely and resolutely.

The hallmark of this type of large group is that total human beings are involved, that all aspects are open to investigation and discussion in the ongoing situation; they are all relevant and the conductor is entitled to take this therapeutic function as his mandate. I need hardly say to those at all familiar with the group-analytic approach, as understood by myself, that this does not mean that the conductor or therapist treats the group, but on the contrary that he establishes a culture, a tradition, a spirit in which the group feels free to investigate all these things, based on unfettered, frank and spontaneous communication.

More recently, attempts have been made to use this large group as the only method of treatment, under out-patient conditions. These conditions correspond to those established in the so-called small group-analytic group. In this contribution I am particularly concerned with problems raised by these endeavours, and I can make one or two definite statements about this method in the first place. Such an approach is possible and moreover a situation involving an assembly of say 50 to 100 people is a very powerful forum for treatment indeed. The other point is that under these circumstances treatment in this large group is considered to be a very intensive affair of relatively long duration. I do not think that anything like the ideal time proposed for frequency (namely that, say, 80–100 people should meet daily for a period of about two years) has as yet been realised. It is indeed doubtful whether such conditions are realisable. With somewhat modified or modest expectations, it could be envisaged that the group might be as small as 30, and might meet only once a week – but this is considered a minimum. These expectations bring larger group treatment into line with practicable and even with economic considerations.

In the following I shall review some of the problems which seem to await solution and attention. I will do so on the basis of experience in group-analytic psychotherapy and the theoretical concepts which guide us. It is clear that the principle applies: the total situation in which we operate determines the meaning and significance of all communications. I shall look at a number of these elements, never forgetting that they cannot be considered in isolation but only in interdependence with other elements and all of them with the total situation and purpose of the group.

In order to give a bird's eye view of the location of the large group in the total spectrum of psychotherapy, I will reproduce an illustration from my book *Introduction to Group-Analytic Psychotherapy*[10] and point out the place where the large group belongs.

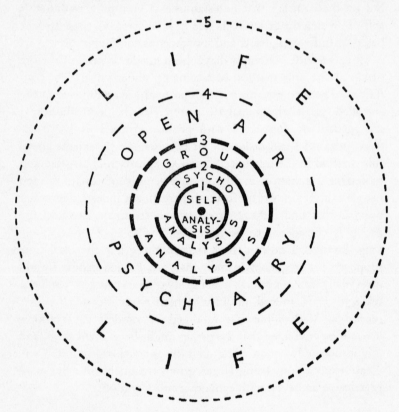

This scheme emphasises the relative degree of concentration of analytic components. They are most concentrated in situations (1) and (2), still fairly concentrated in (3) (group analysis), less so in (4) and (5), at least manifestly. At the same time, we can say conversely that social issues (such as economic circumstances, form of government, the general condition of the community, the laws governing it and so forth), the total conditions of the community, society or nation, come more to the fore the more we approach the periphery of this scheme.

I want to stress that in this schematic representation the different areas are deliberately not represented as watertight compartments, are not shown as closed circles. They are increasingly open as they spread outwards and it is clear that one flow, one life and one mental process, permeates all the spheres in which the human being lives. In real life in our society, the individual lives in his close family and other intimate circles. These different networks of the nuclear family, the present-day circles (plexus) and the newly established network in the treatment situation (matrix) are interdependent. This is not indicated in any way in this illustration.

The place to which group analysis in the stricter sense belongs is clear. One might say that this larger group participates to some extent in the area termed 'group analysis' (3), but spills over as it were into (4) and through that even into (5). The theory we build which ultimately concerns human psychology as a whole must take into consideration all these *loci* of investigation. Indeed it might be best to start from the outermost circle and move from there in order to understand what goes on in the innermost circle, the individual's own mind. In my introductory book, I concluded my brief remarks on this scheme by saying: 'The vantage position of Group Analysis can be well seen, it occupies a central position and is open in both directions.'[11]

Elements of the psychotherapeutic situation

Some of the most important elements of any psychotherapeutic situation are briefly reviewed below in the hope that the problems mentioned may be of help for future developments.

Differences arising from whether the group is open, closed or slow-open[12]
Those engaged in this work would, I think, ideally like a group to be closed – that is, consisting of the same membership throughout – and run over an agreed period. Experience has shown that a group cannot be both closed and indefinite in duration. There is equally great use both for the fully open group, with a free flowing membership, as well as for the compromise solution, which in practice has been found most important –

the slow-open group. In the last case groups would be indeterminate in duration and occasional losses in membership made up.

Problems connected with joining and leaving arise in one type of group and not in the other. Naturally the selection for these types of group differs and the whole manner and range of interpretations and other interventions are modified.

Intensity and duration

Duration has just been mentioned. When intensity is aimed at the duration obviously cannot be too brief.

Intensity does not mean what is usually, and I think erroneously, called 'depth'. Intensity is greatest when the group deals with those issues which are at that moment most strongly cathexed, in a language in which the group or its large majority can approach the immediate issues at that time.

Contra-indications

These are very important to watch. Inevitably, if there is no selection at all, certain individuals will not be able to stand the mental tension, will not have the resilience required and in one way or another will drop out, and be more or less seriously damaged. This raises a special problem in groups within institutions because there should be no exclusions, so there can be no selection, except that which has already taken place in that certain people find themselves members of that institution or of that part of an institution. This whole question is wide open and I can only reiterate that psychiatric labels have a very limited use in deciding contra-indications. Whether there exist special contra-indications for the larger group we will have to see, very likely there might be.

Short-circuiting into life decisions ('realisations')

In the spirit of the large group as conceived, we must assume that no other treatment of any kind is offered, or even tolerated, except perhaps in emergencies. This raises the question of blind sub-grouping, that is to say sub-grouping which takes place outside the sessions and does not adequately come to the notice of the group. A point of even greater importance is that acting out, insofar as it takes place outside the T situation, will be very difficult to notice. The importance of this will lead us to the next point, the question of abstinence. Even if this were accepted and successfully carried out by the group, there is still the almost inevitable occurrence of important changes going on in the patients' lives: changes of serious consequence, decisions which influence the whole future: marriage, divorce, change of job, affiliation to a political or religious organisation and so on. It is very important that such decisions are not made prematurely in a binding form as otherwise problems inevitably arise later in life.

The question of abstinence, including not meeting outside
The question of abstinence in psychoanalysis was originally confined to abstinence from certain sexual activities linked with the current transference situation. The corresponding situation which would seem undesirable in the large group would be intimate intercourse between members, sexual and, as we shall presently see, otherwise. Refraining from meeting outside is partly in order to avoid the temptation of such, as it were, incestuous relationships. There is no question that any fully fledged relationship including those of the most intimate kind have also a very positive side – they help the patients for the time being in the sense of representing the supportive quality of the group.

From an analytical point of view, whether psychoanalytic or group-analytic, the objections to outside relationships are obvious and clear. The forces freed which are engaging the individual in such relationships are better worked through in the transference setting to which they belong. The facilitation of such alliances is counter-indicated not merely for analytical reasons but as a general psychotherapeutic precaution. The cons far outweigh the pros. In addition there is always the risk of precipitating bonds – even lasting ones – on primitive, immature, infantile and, in a sense, transitional grounds.

This raises the question of how such restrictions should be

understood by the group and shared by it since it is contrary to the spirit of our procedures to enforce them by way of punishment, like exclusion, or even to introduce them by way of command and rules. This problem can only be solved with a great deal of tact and understanding. I myself can still think of no better alternative than the method I always practised. When such a situation arises, or threatens to arise, one draws attention to it as soon as possible and makes the participants and the group as a whole aware of the reasons why such precipitate behaviour is damaging. Alas, people may well understand that something is harmful to them, and yet still do it. We need only see increasing evidence of the enormously damaging effects cigarette smoking has been proved to have and compare this to the fact that cigarette consumption has, I believe, doubled in the last few years. Self-destruction is a strong force.

The setting

The setting, really the seating, is a problem by itself. The natural inclination favours a circle or concentric circles, but this does not solve all problems. It would make a decisive difference if each individual were to feel not only comfortable wherever seated but could also see any other speaker. In this way it would remain a face-to-face group. If the group becomes too large or too unfavourably seated so that these conditions are no longer fulfilled it changes its character decisively. The experience of the group becomes that of a mass. We will come back to this point when discussing the size of the group.

Minimal structure – questions of instructions and expectations

Such a group would certainly have a minimal structure. We have already spoken about instructions and the problems connected with this. We would like to think that we can get away with no or minimal instructions, but this is easier said than done. I would rather accept the need to give an instruction than by not doing so foster behaviour which is definitely harmful. About expectations, I will only say here that both the conductors' and the members' expectations play a great part in what happens. If we want to make valid observations of a more universal kind we may well have to examine ourselves continually, question our own expectations, try to remain open-minded and ready to throw them overboard. We may even perhaps deliberately cut across the group's expectations, or at the very least point them out very early on.

Size, numbers

This point is obviously of paramount importance, in that change in size in the large group, with greater numbers participating, is the most decisive new step taken in this form of treatment.

Not much has been established about the optimal size. When does a group become 'large'? At what point does it change its character? The question is of particular importance if we consider that we have not simply a 'large' group and a 'small' group – but that we are moving on a scale on which everything is relative. The essential point to remember is that quantity becomes quality – the point may not always be sharply defined where this switch-over happens but it can be fairly precisely established clinically. A big jump from something like 8 members to 30 or 40 members, not to speak of 100, obviously brings about very different group characteristics. At the same time it must be remembered that all of this is relative. The group-analytic group when first practised provoked very similar reactions in its members, and in a very similar way as now happens in the large group. It is in the hands of the conductor to make this more or less dramatic not to say traumatic. The so-called large group of even 100 is very small and intimate if we think of football crowds of tens of thousands of people – there is a very big jump! – and a lot goes on there and strong emotional experience takes place. Without going to such extremes, if we knew where we were with 100 people, it might be we would find our knowledge not applicable as it stood to 250.

Let me start at the beginning. In the small group-analytic group the individual is in the centre of our attention, though, as I often say, the context, the whole framework which gives the particular meaning to what is going on, lies in that group as a whole. Wishing to be able to follow processes sufficiently as they operate even between two or three individuals, or even what goes on in any one individual alone, I found that a great change occurred as soon as one was in a group of 7, 8 or 9 (conductor always excluded). For practical reasons, e.g., in mixed sex groups, to make the sexes equal, 8 seemed the right number. From 8 or 9 upwards there is a considerable change in character and as a guess this character would hold good up to, say, 14. The zone between 14 and 20 or even 25 is to my knowledge not explored from this point of view; a group of that sort must show quite other characteristics and throw emphasis on different issues and mechanisms than the smaller group does.

Now where does the large group start? Nobody knows. I would have not thought myself that a group under 30 would show the sort of characteristics which we are beginning to observe in a group of say 50 or even 100. Naturally once we are up to, say, 15, it may be that only 5 more or less make an appreciable difference: once we are up to 30 or 40 only 10 or 20 may make a difference. The sort of group which we have in mind here has a membership of at least 30 but more likely between 50 and 100 or even 120.

Under these circumstances the individual participant is confronted with an experience of chaos, with the horror of being overwhelmed by this mass, of losing himself in it; on the other hand, this has a certain fascination also and there is some relief in becoming one of an anonymous powerful mass, not further responsible in any way. We know that this situation produces a pronounced need and longing for a leader who becomes more powerful and imbued ultimately with omnipotent power to whom the individual can turn as a guarantee that somebody or something is in control of the uncontrollable frightening forces released.

Psychotic mechanisms

In continuation of what we have just said we find that psychotic mechanisms (primary mechanisms in Freud's language, very primitive behaviour and experience) are in evidence in such

groups. It is one of their most interesting features and so far as
I am concerned has helped me by throwing light on a number of
clinical observations. The group also reinforces correspondingly
primitive and elementary defence mechanisms, such as identification, projection and splitting. Personally, I think it is a theoretical mistake to build up an understanding of these groups from
such individual mechanisms instead of the other way round. One
should understand these individual mechanisms as emanating
from particular psychological situations which we can experimentally reproduce in groups – and in this particular case even
more clearly in larger groups. The interpretation of these elemen-
ary mechanisms is not difficult or deep as is sometimes thought
but is an easy way out, as long as one thinks that by giving them
names and labels one really understands them. In a theoretical
book which I am hoping to write, I will have more to say on the
bearing this has on the so-called Kleinian type of interpretation
and on the inner-object theory. Suffice it to say here that these
psychotic mechanisms which we know are normally concealed,
except perhaps in dreams, are clearly apparent in this type of
group. Elementary defensive mechanisms to deal with the
common tension are also more obvious.

Consequences for the individual participant
These should be explored by interviewing as many articulate
individuals who have been exposed to this experience as possible.
What we can see relatively easily is that the ego identity, the
sense of self, if at all vulnerable, is liable to be shaken. Any kind
of intimate relationship is made impossible in this large group
situation; one need only think of the space between A and B
if they happen to sit at distant parts of the circle, of the way in
which they would have to shout across the whole room and across
the whole group something which would normally have been
addressed quietly to one another. There is also a very deep
dilemma for the individual as such, for the individuality to emerge.
The individual roots in the group cannot be thought of without
this, but equally well, each individual – like each individual tree,
plant or animal – is unique in himself. The individual's essence

lies in the particular variation in which the common species finds expression through his whole being. The individual is emerging from the group and existing insofar as he or she is in a sense different from the group and unique. This dilemma is enormously enhanced especially as, in addition to other factors, the individual is torn between the mental fear of losing his identity and his very being, and the great fascination this has for him. If we think of a suffering individual with all his cares, worries, anxieties – these are all, as it were, submerged in one go, by diving into the group and disappearing. This is the individual's dilemma.

I believe that the basic process here is a repetition of the ego development in very early stages – a very rapid regression of the ego to these early stages, to its very genesis. I am thinking particularly of the emergence of the individual as a self, as a being of his own, from the total symbiotic unity with the mother. In consonance with this the large group very clearly symbolises this all-embracing, archaic mother who represents his whole world. The dilemma which I have just described can also be understood as a repetition of these early development phases and a re-activation of traumatic scars, of traumatic defects. This has helped me to understand better what I know clinically: that the patients with very deep-going character disturbances, people who of late have been described as narcissistic personalities, or borderline personalities, react especially well to the therapeutic group-analytic group. They are just the same cases who require very long and intensive, skilled psychoanalytic treatment in the individual situation with uncertain results.

Conductor(s)

During the course of this contribution I have touched upon the conductor in the large group. I have mentioned that his whole attitude and the particular way in which he introduces the group to itself and to himself determines very much as to what is set in motion. He should be more than usually aware of the enormous suggestive influence he has, of the more than hypnotic influence he has, and resist the illusion that he can abdicate from this position or that he can easily modify it or that he is in fact not leading or not a leader of the group. It is of course extremely important that the conductor is clear about the situation and his own part.[13] He should indeed not be rigid, but on the contrary ready to react flexibly and to change together with the group – he must as it were be the best patient in the group. I think he must, as always, be careful with interventions and interpretations. As a special point about that: I anticipate that individual interpretations, interpretations directed at any individual, are as a general rule, particularly out of place in the large group. The question of the conductor's involvement and yet detachment is basically subject to the same problems as we have often discussed. One of the decisions he must make is whether he wishes to plunge the group into deep anxiety or act as moderator, as a kind of barometer – the idea being to keep tension and anxiety at a tolerable level for constructive work. It is open to question whether the best answer to the tendency for psychotic mechanisms to be active and manifest is to interpret them, especially in psychoanalytic terms. It would appear that a team of conductors is preferable. They should however meet regularly between themselves, discussing their immediate reactions and adjusting themselves in the light of the progressing treatment situation.

It gives me personal pleasure to note that two workers who are in the forefront of this new expansion of group psychotherapy into larger groups, Drs Pat de Maré and Lionel Kreeger, are prominent members of the Group-Analytic Society (London) and the Institute of Group Analysis respectively. This work has considerable consequences for the theory and practice of group analysis. Not the least benefit would seem to me the light that can be thrown on the smaller group and on the individual's earliest development. As I have already indicated, the problems of early ego development are reactivated[14] and the ego's strengthening, the greater freedom which is expressed in more independence as well as in a better adjustment to the group and the community may well be envisaged as a favourable result. For whom and for how many the more intimate, personal forms of psychotherapy may be necessary instead of, or following, such large group experiences is a question which we cannot answer at this time.

To end with may I express the hope that these remarks and observations will be of some help to the study and progress in the exploration of this new and promising field. I wish to state that while the group-analytic approach has not so far been applied intensively to a larger group of the therapeutic type here envisaged we can only be in support of this development and expect valuable contributions to the understanding of the person and our ability to help him in his troubles.

2. Some psychodynamics of large groups[1]

Tom Main

Projective processes in social settings

Although projective processes are primitive attempts to relieve internal pains by externalising them, assigning or requiring another to contain aspects of the self, the price can be high: for the self is left not only less aware of its whole but, in the case of projective identification, is deplenished by the projective loss of important aspects of itself. Massive projective identification of – for instance – feared aggressive parts of the self leaves the remaining self felt only to be weak and unaggressive. Thereafter, the weakened individual will remain in terror about being over- whelmed by frightening aggressive strength but this will now be felt only as belonging to the other. Depending on the range of this projective fantasy the results will vary from terrified flight, appeasement, wariness and specific anxieties about the other, even psychotic delusions about his intentions.

The above instance concerns only the projector's side of the projective relationship: but projective processes often have a further significance. What about the person on the receiving end of the projection? In simple projection (a mental mechanism) the receiver may notice that he is not being treated as himself but as an aggressive other. In projective identification (an un- conscious fantasy) this other may find himself forced by the projector actually to feel and own projected aggressive qualities and impulses which are otherwise alien to him. He will feel strange and uncomfortable and may resent what is happening, but in the face of the projector's weakness and cowardice it

may be doubly difficult to resist the feelings of superiority and
aggressive power steadily forced into him. Such disturbances
affect all pair relationships more or less. A wife, for instance,
may force her husband to own feared and unwanted aggressive
and dominating aspects of herself and will then fear and respect
him. He in turn may come to feel aggressive and dominating
towards her, not only because of his own resources but of hers
which are forced into him. But more; for reasons of his own he
may despise and disown certain timid aspects of his personality
and by projective identification force these into his wife and
despise her accordingly. She may thus be left not only with timid
unaggressive parts of herself but having in addition to contain
his. Certain pairs come to live in such locked systems, dominated by mutual projective fantasies with each not truly married
to a person, but rather to unwanted, split off and projected parts
of themselves.[2] Both the husband, dominant and cruel, and the
wife, stupidly timid and respectful, may be miserably unhappy
with themselves and with each other, yet such marriages although turbulent are stable, because each partner needs the other
for pathological narcissistic purposes. *Forcible projective processes
and especially projective identification are thus more than an individual
matter: they are object-related and the other will always be affected
more or less.* The results are a variety of joint personality deplenishments and invasions and interpersonal disturbances.

Projective processes are also observable in *group* behaviour.
Half a century ago in *Group Psychology and the Analysis of the Ego*[3]
Freud pointed out that a leader can occupy the role of super-ego
for members of a group, who are thus freed not only of responsibility for decisions but also of burdens of self-criticism and doubt.
But it is a costly freedom; the group members actually lose individual moral sense and the capacity to think and to judge as
individuals. In the light of this observation alone we can understand something of the plight of the Nazi leaders at the Nuremberg Trials who knew themselves only as decent family men and
innocent of responsibility for the criminal acts they had loyally
carried out. Having early projected away and into Hitler their
capacity for moral judgement they (with few exceptions) had

lost the capacity to know that they had behaved viciously and could not understand the present censure. They were psychically impoverished, morally blinded, by projective processes.

Freud's discovery of mental splitting and the projection of the super-ego in group life, coupled with Melanie Klein's later discoveries of projective-identification fantasies have allowed studies of other group-roles than that of leader. It has often been observed in studies of *small-group* life that certain individuals may be unconsciously forced by the group to feel certain things and to carry out particular roles. This one may be unconsciously appointed and required as a sinner, to feel and act accordingly, that one as the giver of wisdom, others as saboteur of the work, buffoon, invalid, etc., with various degrees of personal discomfort.

There is little discomfort for the receiver if he has some capacity which matches the projections fairly well, in a good 'role-fit'.

Example

In a working group one member was observed to be used as the repository of all projected financial meanness. He was kept in this role so that the others could feel safely free not to think about financial matters but he was steadily stimulated to be strict and watchful by their regular financially feckless ideas or behaviour. But he did not mind this *because he actually had character tendencies to be financially strict.*

The unconscious forcing of feelings and abilities into another in a small group will, however, create observable discomfort in the receiver if his relevant character-tendencies are few. He may respond as he is required to yet his loss of freedom to behave otherwise will create strain for him, perhaps breakdown, resignation or illness. Instances of group projection with role comfort and discomfort in the members are easy to observe in play groups, discussion groups and work groups. But whether the role-fit be good or bad the penalty for all in personality restriction loss or invasion should be noted.

In *large* unstructured groups – with memberships of over 20 or so – projective processes may be wide-spread and can lead to baffling, even chaotic situations, which can bring the groups' work to a standstill. The members will sit in long uneasy silences with even the most resourceful apparently lacking the capacity for contributing usefully. It seems that many individuals at such moments actually do not have their full thinking-capacities at their own disposal. For various reasons – which I shall later discuss – they have denied, split off and projected much of their mental vigour outside themselves, occasionally into particular individuals but more often into a vague non-personal creation which they call 'the group'. In the presence of this mysterious powerful 'group' they will actually feel stupid, helpless and afraid of what it may do to them if they speak or move incautiously.

Projection and projective identification as interpersonal concepts have value for the understanding of the behaviour of large unstructured groups as well as small groups, pairs and individuals.

They can also aid the understanding of structured groups, and shed light on how far the procedures, beliefs, organisational structures and activities of an enterprise are reality-orientated and how far they are the result of anxieties, powerful fantasies and defences.[4] Projective processes in the service of relief from intrapersonal pains in industrial situations are powerful factors of major industrial inefficiency and conflicts.[5] Those of us who work in hospitals need, however, look no further than under our noses.

In the literature which has followed my proposition[6] that a total hospital community could be therapeutic or anti-therapeutic, there has been good agreement that one benefit of therapeutic community technique derives from the staff's readiness to offer patients and staff reciprocal adult roles with participant powers and responsibilities for various aspects of institutional life, and further that it can be beneficial if there is open study, by all, of the problems of sustaining these roles. A therapeutic community is one of on-going enquiry about personal and group anxieties and defences and of endeavour to create adaptive thought-out roles, relations, structure and culture geared to reality tasks and relevant to the capacities and needs of the individuals within the community. This is in contrast to the classical medical organisation model in which only roles of health or illness are on offer; staff to be only healthy, knowledgeable, kind, powerful and active, and patients to be only ill, suffering, ignorant, passive, obedient and grateful; and with a corresponding staff structure and a culture of kindness and discipline.

Now to create adult roles for all in a hospital, adaptive to individual capacity and relevant to efficiency, is – quite apart from the time required for on-going studies – easier said than done. Not only is present hospital tradition against this but all of us concerned always carry within ourselves personal attitudes more or less neurotic which hamper such a development. It is of course the insightful laying bare of these very attitudes which allows community therapy to proceed, but this is never easy. In most hospitals the staff are there because they seek to care for others less able than themselves, while the patients hope to find others *more* able than themselves. The helpful and the helpless meet and put pressures on each other to act not only in realistic but also in fantastic collusion and in collusive hierarchical systems. The actively projectively helpful will unconsciously *require* others to be helpless while the helpless will *require* others to be helpful. Staff and patients are thus inevitably to some extent creatures of each other. Therapeutic community technique, which seeks insight for all, is a useful check on institutional collusive projection, but if the mutual projective system is accepted blindly and is institutionalised without reality-testing then it carries dangers to the personality integration of all concerned.

Temporary patient/staff mutual collusive projection of socially split strength and weakness *may* be highly effective, for instance in an acute surgical unit where the illnesses are short and the regression which accompanies illness is temporary and self-limiting; but it is clearly not useful in any psychiatric unit where human behaviour rather than organ performance is under active study and in which regression is not so much the secondary accompaniment of a temporary illness as a primary and permanent part of one.

Requirements of only health for staff and only invalidism for patients are, however, neither socially inevitable nor truly practicable, for human states are never absolute. Stable healthy people contain elements of instability and ill health, and unhealthy unstable people contain elements of health and stability. Indeed there is something strainfully collusive about those psychiatric hospitals which are managed so that one party comes to regard the other as being in an absolute state, either of health or ill health, and they offer us paradigmatic questions for all similar large groups. Why are certain roles (bosses and workers, teachers and pupils, experts and ignoramuses, staff and patients, police and criminals, etc.) so often collusively required to be *absolute*? How does it come about that one party is content to notice its differences from the other but uneasy at recognising the similarities? What are the implications, benefits and dangers when human beings cling to absolute categories?

These questions may in part be answered by a revealing but unpublished study made at the Cassel Hospital by my colleague, Malcolm Pines, of patients who had been nurses. All had had traumatised childhoods with grossly inadequate nurturing and all had developed a similar way of dealing with needy but untended parts of themselves. From childhood onwards they had striven to overcome these by disowning, denying and projecting them into others; and had then sought to nurse these aspects of themselves 'out there' in attempts at vicarious satisfaction. In their adulthood they had done significant work nursing *others*, but in each the projective endeavours to keep suffering 'out there' had eventually failed. All were now unusually humiliated; breakdown was all right for 'patients', but not for 'nurses'. In hospital they presented special problems of which I select one: sometimes each sought to be treated *only* as a resourceless patient but at others *only* as a nursing colleague of the staff, helpful to 'the patients'. One role *or* the other. It was most painful for them to contain both parts of themselves at one time, i.e., to be *sick/nurses*, and any such attempt at integration was quickly followed by further splitting and projection of one or other part. *Absolute states seemed preferable because integrated ones contained unbearable conflict and pain.*

This last finding, well known in individual psycho-analysis, has implications for all social and international situations in which we/they beliefs arise. The common defences against personal mental pain, of denial, splitting and projection into others have immense social consequences when used by whole groups of individuals.

Projective processes and reality-testing

It must be emphasised that externalising defences and fantasies can involve positive as well as negative aspects of the self; and that projection of impulses and projective identification of parts of the self into others are elements in 'normal' mental activity. *When followed by reality-testing* trial externalisations of aspects of the self help an individual to understand himself and others. For instance if we are to *sense* (as distinct from notice the signs of) the distress in a crying child, we can do so only if there is within us a former experience of having been a distressed child ourselves. An experimental projection of this into the child before us, followed by reality testing, can help us decide whether our understanding of the child's distress is more or less appropriate. Similarly, if we are to sense another's joy we can only do so by the experiment of projecting former joyous states of our own, *followed by a reality test* to decide how far our projection fits the facts; i.e., we 'put ourself in his place'.

It is when projective processes are massive and forceful that they are difficult to test or reverse. In malignant projective identification this difficulty arises not only because of the forcefulness of the projection but also because, with the ego impoverished by loss of a major part of the self, reality-testing becomes defective. Thus unchecked and uncheckable pathological judgements may now arise about oneself and the other, quasi-irreversible because of the pains of integration.

Malignant projective processes are to be found in both neurotic and psychotic patients, and may be temporarily observable also in 'normal' people suffering major frustration. Grossly in such delusions as, 'He has stolen the thought-radio and listens to my thoughts' or, 'They whisper filthy accusations that I'm a queer'. Less psychotic but still pathological are such *absolute* judgements as, 'You are an incorrigible thug, without a *single* redeeming feature', or, 'I can *always* count on your help' or, '*As usual*, the boss is thinking only of himself.' 'Dr X will *never* understand this.'

With less forceful projection systems followed by reality-testing the present is usefully tested against the past, and external events against internal ones; the individual maintains his individuation, re-finds out who he is and who he is not, what he feels and thinks, who others are, and who they are not, what they feel and think. Where a reality test confirms that a trial projection fits the other one learns positively about him; and where it shows the projection to be *only* a projection the individual can re-own the projected part, and grow a surer awareness of the distinct identity of himself and the other. Trial projection and *reality-testing* are thus essential preliminaries to real as distinct from narcissistic relationships. By contrast, in malignant projection systems the self is impoverished, reality-testing fails, the other is not recognised for what he is but rather as a container of disowned aspects of the self, to be hated, feared, idealised, etc., and relations are unreal and narcissistically intense up to the point of insanity.

Depersonalisation and personality invasion

When major parts of the personality are subject to compelling fantasies of projective identification the damaged powers of thought and diminished identity-sense in the remnant self lead to various degrees of *depersonalisation* accompanied by bizarre object-relations. When the superstitious person projects into an object (or a person) his own denied areas of, say, malice, he will experience that object not only as malicious but uncannily *alive*, with himself only as magically weakened and in danger. In such nightmarish situations appeasement, flight, warding off the magic by desperate counter-magic, the seeking of allies, or a leader, and so forth, may take place. This is the world of psychosis and of extreme industrial and civil strife.

Where positive aspects of the self are forcefully projected similar degrees of depersonalisation occur, with feelings of personal worthlessness and with dependent worship of the other's contrasting strengths, powers, uncanny sensitivity, marvellous gifts, thoughts, knowledge, undying goodness, etc. This is the world of the devotee, cults and hero-promotion.

But what of the recipient of projection? I have pointed out that in *benign* forms where the projection does not 'fit', the receiver will feel some discomfort at something being inaccurately attributed to him. Sensitivity to this discomfort is an important attribute of all therapists because it is a clue to what is occurring, but this discomfort can be met in daily life. A person may treat us as if we are more clever than we truly are, we may even begin to feel unusually clever, and if we are thoughtless we may try to avoid contention by trying to justify the other's good opinion, by rising to the occasion and straining to be as clever as possible; and so collusively intensify and prolong the 'take-over' that *we* are clever while he is *not*. (He may now actually become stupid and adoring and thus intensify our plight.) Such thoughtless acceptance of a projection means that we are no longer quite ourselves, for we are filled up and dominated by a part of somebody else. If we can recognise the discomfort and think about it we will not however feel unduly clever but simply misjudged or invaded; and so we can remain ourself and indicate by behaviour or protest that the other's beliefs are not justified by fact. In individual *treatment* we would hope to deal with it in another way; show the patient what he is doing and why. My example concerns a positive aspect – cleverness; but similar events can occur with negative aspects – say, confusion, rage or stupidity.

Where projective processes are malignant the recipient always experiences severe discomfort. If rageful confusion is forcibly projected into him he may now feel a strange rage and confusion and may join in ignoring and devaluing his best qualities; and with his rage and confusion preyed upon and stimulated he may

C

over-estimate these and come to feel that they are his essence. Lacking any confirmation of his true self from the other, his own reality-sense will be further threatened. Badly invaded by alien feelings he will have difficulty in thinking calmly, clearly or helpfully. Therapists of severely disturbed patients know well this strain of sorting out inside themselves what belongs to them and what does not. Searles[6] has well described the effort needed to extricate oneself regularly from crazy relationships with schizophrenic people and to regain touch with one's own intra-psychic world and to recover the capacity to think and feel authentically.

Projective processes in groups

The creation of realistic relations in *small groups* depends upon its members being able benignly and regularly to project experimentally their various attributes, and to undertake reality-testing. Thus regularly confirming themselves and each other, they can carry out joint work realistically. If a member is ill-fitted for an attempted projection the group will withdraw it, because of reality-testing, helped by the member who will resist the projection. If the recipient has appropriate properties to make the projection a good enough 'fit' he may by words or behaviour confirm that they exist in reality, he may feel better recognised and can recognise more of himself. His relations with the group may thus be deepened.

With forcible malignant projection where the projectors are depleted and reality-testing is impaired, all recipients will be unhappy, with their *true* selves devalued and in a strain because of having to sort out various confusing projections thrust into themselves. All may become so invaded by projections that reality-testing and judgement become flawed and relations only fantastic.

In *large groups* the multiplicity of relations puts thorough reality-testing at a discount; projection systems and personality invasion may thus run rife in networks of unchecked and uncheckable fantasies. In my experience – mostly limited to hospitals – in any unstructured group of 20 or more members, projective systems alone are liable to produce major difficulties.

Unfantastic recognition of one's self and of others is a dynamic process, not a static once-and-for-all event. Experiments in sensory deprivation have shown vividly that fidelity to one's internal mental life and past experiences are not enough to maintain sanity or the sense of self; the regular confirming of oneself in a continuing relation with the reality-tested external world is essential.

In a group everyone does what he can to understand the many people, to maintain his thinking capacity in the face of many viewpoints and to retain his sense of self. His confirmation of himself by the others is liable to be slow and slight but given fair identity-sense and freedom from mental splitting he can use benign projective processes and reality-testing to confirm who he is and who he is not, and to learn where and where not his projective fantasies fit others. But this takes time, and meanwhile relations with the others are much influenced by the inner world and little by reality-tested sureness.

If he can maintain his own sense of self he can offer his distinctive thinking to any discussion and so can help others to test their fantasies about him. Knowing him better they in turn may offer their more realistic thinking and benign cycles of awareness may thus arise.

In large group discussions it is easy to discern such processes of reality-testing with members responding variously to projections, accepting this one, then that one only after modifying it and now rejecting a third.

Most formal large groups are structured with chairman, agenda, orders of precedence, rituals, rules and procedures which discipline, more or less wisely, spontaneous personal interchange. Such groups keep formal order but at a cost, and they are well known to give ultimate dissatisfaction to their members and to fragment into splinter-groups and factions. They are well worth study but they do not offer the best opportunities for studies of the primitive mechanisms in large-group life. It is in experimental situations, such as total meetings in therapeutic communities, where structuring is at a minimum, that unfettered group behaviour can best be studied.

My own observations were made in such groups at the Cassel Hospital, and I have valued there the most 'difficult' group occasions when phenomena of disturbance were in their crudest form. For reasons of tact alone, I must stress that they were not necessarily typical meetings, that they occurred several years ago and that since then I have had the opportunity of studying less disturbed large group meetings. But the data in the rest of this contribution were observed there.

Large-group meetings

Politicians involved with complex human issues – even at a distance – often escape from the huge problem of trying to understand everybody by resorting to single generalising thought-models – 'the housewife', 'the young', 'the property owner', 'the working man', each of which he invents and endows with more or less plausible stereotyped needs, powers and desires. These may bear little relation to the varieties of the actual people and his statements may reveal more about the politician than about those he attempts to encompass. Something of this escape from human complexity into generalisation and simplification is liable to occur when many people meet together to study each others' contributions; a single entity is liable to be invented – 'the group', 'the meeting', etc. – and to be endowed with various qualities. These group qualities may be plausible but are inevitably much derived from the internal life of the individual, and until reality-tested they contain much projection. They too may tell us more about the speaker than about the various others in the group.

Nonetheless, 'the group', this single invented object, however fictive, no matter how much endowed with projected properties, has an important defensive value for the individual – it allows escape from the danger of being frustrated and overwhelmed by the variety of half-tested interacting others. The simplification allows him to relate to *one* simplified object – 'the group'; to study 'it', to formulate general laws and expectations about 'it' and to make remarks to 'it' and about 'it'. Now he need not think about the many others, nor risk becoming so invaded, occupied and confused by them, that contact with the self might be lost.

By relating to 'the group' the individual of course renounces major attempts to relate to many of the individuals present as well as any prospect that they can make personalised relations with him. This withdrawal from *personal* relations means that the individual is alone in the group and much in resort with his inner world. In this state of increased narcissism he is now liable to use projective processes to rid himself of unwanted aspects of his personality, and because he relates now not to individuals but to 'the group' it is mostly into 'the group' as a single entity that these unwanted and aggressive aspects are projected. 'The group' which is somewhere around but not located in any persons thus becomes endowed with unpleasant aspects of the self. It is felt as uncannily alive and dangerous, while the individual, weakened and depersonalised, is no longer in possession of his full mental resources. The perception of the group can eventually get so distorted by cycles of projective processes that all the *others* may become felt to be the authors of a developing group malignancy, in vague inexplicable fashion. The dreadful belief may arise that in some inexplicable way all have collectively created an intangible monster to be appeased or hidden from.

Many individuals because of projective loss now become 'not themselves'. Awed by 'the group' they are unusually quiet, modest, deferential, and may have noticeable difficulty in thinking or in making unprepared or unwritten statements. The self may now be felt as too ordinary, motives not noble enough, abilities too few. In timid isolation from the others, the behaviour of each is cautious, unspontaneous, conventional. Early contributions tend to be quiet, slow, equivocal or tentative, and are often about those *not* present; perhaps out of envy or in reluctance to engage with those actually present. Discomfort is controlled, disowned or expressed impersonally or indirectly, perhaps disguised as an innocent non-personalised question or generalisation (e.g., 'I wonder if people feel these meetings should

finish earlier?'). Some large groups have initial formalities
which, whatever their other functions, postpone personal commitment or revelation; recruiting an agenda, requesting news
about a former decision or reports from sub-groups, seeking
and making administrative arrangements, etc. Almost any
communication *except* personalised thinking between individuals
and relevant to the *immediate* situation tends to be seized and
dwelt on for initial defensive safety. A member may make a
personal statement. It is less likely to concern his thoughts about
any present individual or the present setting than to be derived
from the past or from outside, but in any event is likely to be made
tentatively. Often the timid others will remain silent and non-
responding, and noticing his fate, other potential contributors may retreat further into narcissism. A second member
may venture another remark, but it is noteworthy how often
this too will be narcissistic, and heedless of and unrelated to the
previous contribution. Individuals are not addressed nor named.
'People', 'members', 'the group' are addressed.

In an on-going group of fair sophistication, someone will
eventually address a remark not to 'people' or 'the group'
but directly to one or more persons, and may be responded to
by that person or persons more or less sincerely. By the institution of other remarks which relate to individuals, dialogue may
grow and others may join in. It usually takes about twenty
minutes, however, before reality-testing is sufficient to show the
majority that 'the group' is a fiction and that the others are not
just collective 'people' but separate individuals comparable with
oneself, singular but mortal. By now others will contribute and
respond more authentically and less fantastically to named
individuals and less to that single unit, the projectively aggressiv-
ised 'group'. An initial period of reality-testing of projective
fantasies and defences seems to be necessary before collaborative
discussion in large unstructured groups can occur. This seems
to be true even for those groups in which members know each
other fairly well, and it has been well, if imprecisely described,
as the 'warming-up' period. Thereafter contributions can be
responsive to individuals, agreement and disagreement can be

less based on fantasy and more on fact, others can be related to for what they are and say and do, and now the fuller exploration of thoughts and reality-testing of the self and the others can proceed.

This is not to say that a group which proceeds fast to reality-tested individuation and to attempts to understand, respect and relate to the complexities of its members will always remain so; depending on events, individuals will tend regularly to withdraw into fantasy viewpoints and to receive these from others.

It is the projection into 'the group' of ego-ideals as well as other personality deplenishments that makes the individual feel that his everyday thinking is not good enough for the group. It may lead him to silent humility, but another individual may try to be only at his best and strive to contribute more profoundly and ably than is his wont. This may result in contributions which are truly useful but, insofar as they are aimed at impressing the ideal-endowed 'group' rather than at relating to individuals, they usually lack the sincerity which furthers relations. Many a group member addressed by another will be embarrassed that his answer is so mundane and will attempt mere rhetoric to match the fantasied high stands of the 'group'. This 'Nobel-Prize thinking' and its effects are in contrast to the warm pleasure felt by all when a member breaks such a cycle by confessing to a thought which is low-level and ordinary.

Some meetings never develop reality-tested relations but remain gripped by an immovable collusive system with contributions and responses so dominated by mutual projective fantasies that good reality-testing is impossible and a general retreat into narcissistic mental models blocks all progress. The anger arising from such frustrating situations is constantly split off and projected into 'the group' and individuals become further involved in cycles of narcissism, projection of rageful aspects of the self into the group, further personality deplenishments, loss of abilities, and fears. Feeling stupid, even badly depleted by such cycles, many individuals may now have serious difficulty in thinking and fear exposure and humiliation about this.

The task of understanding the complicated surrounding reality still remains for the weakened and deplenished individual, as well as the task of finding and reaffirming himself amid the multiple projections forced into him. He may hear others confusedly trying to resist projections, e.g.,

'I did say something like that but not the way you took it. I was thinking of something quite different.' Or,
'When I said "X" activity was useful I meant it honestly not sarcastically.'
'It was only an idea, I thought it might be interesting. I meant it to be helpful, *not* for the reasons *you* seem to think.'
'Why do you treat me as if I was always trying to stop things.'
'I'm all for action'.

The withstanding and sorting of multiple and collusive projections in a fantasy-ridden large group, now very difficult for an integrated person, is impossible if the personality has been depleted in ways described above. The depleted individual may find it impossible to sort out what is truly him and what is being attributed to him and projecting this very confusion into the group will further fear it and hate it. Hopelessly unable to understand what is going on, some may now deliberately cut themselves off from perception and take to day-dreaming; one or two may become explosively hostile and abusive to 'the group'; occasionally one may declare that 'the group' is driving him crazy and will walk out slamming the door: but the majority usually remain in confused silence.

Sometimes everyone may sit silent, withdrawn and motionless for long periods. The longer the silence the more cycles arise of frustration, projected hostility, personality depletion, stupidity and fears of something awful. The loss of the members' capacity to think or relate calmly leads to a dread of everything lest matters get worse. Progress stops and nothing is allowed to occur.

The painful phenomena of long silences are familiar and worrying to all large-group convenors. The general tension, the withdrawals shown by staring out of the window, inspection of shoes or ceiling or fingernails, the occasional cautious looks at other members, one member remarking fearfully that he feels anxious in a voice so unassertive that he cannot easily be heard so that everyone ignores him, the platitudinous comments that get no response, the staff members equally uneasy, stupid and platitudinous, the convenor himself having difficulty in thinking, uneasily waiting and letting sleeping dogs lie but feeling both responsible and confused, many sitting in corners or near the wall or the exit, one member ostentatiously opening a newspaper, another sighing histrionically, another impulsively walking out swearing, the surreptitious glances at the clock, everyone far now from recognising that all are fellow-human beings, all in dread of 'the group' and fearing that the next thing will only be worse; all these are familiar.

On such occasions the projective expectation of being attacked by the others now acquires some validity, because few are now free from the hostility which comes from frustration and many are in addition containing alien hostility projectively forced into them. With stupidity, suspicion and fear of hostility widespread, even such matters as lighting a cigarette or uncrossing legs now become matters of courage in the face of expected attack, and this is not wholly delusional, for anyone who does anything may be treated as hostile. Innocent contributions are now liable to be greeted with inquisitions. Anyone who seeks to understand by asking a question may be challenged and questioned in turn. Here are some actual replies to members of such silent groups who have cautiously voiced discomfort.

'What do you *mean* you're anxious? What are you trying to indicate?'
'*I* don't feel tense, what's wrong with you?'
'You seem to be only drawing attention to yourself.'
'*Everybody* is feeling uncomfortable, what's so special about *you*?'

Anyone who identifies himself as a singular person is liable to be attacked, and pushed back into silent mindlessness. The staff equally depleted, frustrated and projective are equally liable to criticise anyone who moves or speaks.

In endeavours to recover both abilities and intellect certain individuals, especially staff, may seek to assert themselves, but less by making thoughtful personal statements than by ill-aimed and vaguely hostile theoretical generalisations not about themselves but about the difficulties of 'people' or 'the group'. But just as *any* contribution, innocent or critical, personal or general, is now in great danger of being treated only as hostile, such interventions have little chance of being simply received. The staff is always liable to be used by patients as the chief container for projected hostility and when they actually offer lofty interpretations about 'the group' they only make the situation worse. In any event absolute judgements run rife and hostile we/they situations abound. If staff remain silent the patients in turn will attack them for that. Total responsibility for the group's difficulty is liable to be projected into the staff.

'*You* started it.'
'It's *your* meeting.'
'We are only patients.'
'*We* did not arrange this, etc.'

Sections of staff – perhaps all – may be felt by patients to be stern, contemptuous, waiting to pounce, and whatever they do or say may be regarded only as confirming their hostility or duplicity. In turn they may hate the patients or their fellow staff absolutely, as only hostile and destructive. In these we/they situations, judgements are absolute, each side claims innocence and feels the other as wilfully destructive. The recipients of the projections of hostility resent their goodness being ignored. Those accused may become helplessly possessed by the very qualities (e.g. contempt, aggressiveness) attributed to them.

Anonymisation and generalisation

A regular feature of disturbed large-group situations which have not proceeded to terrified silence is the loss of personalisation of relations and the growth of anonymity. Nobody is recognised as a whole person or is addressed by name. Even people who may know each other quite well may address each other only as innominate members of a class, and speak in vague impersonal terms:

'Why doesn't *somebody* say something?'
'Some *people* seem to enjoy making things awkward.'
'The *group* is a waste of time.'
'The *administration* doesn't seem to be interested in people.'
'The *nursing staff* aren't aware that some *people* prefer to be by themselves.'
'I don't agree with the last *speaker*.'

Personal identities are thus not recognised, the very identity of the speaker is veiled, and views are general and unspecific. Vivid personal views, feelings and experiences about actual others are denied, no individuals exist, only 'people' and only moral platitudes or intellectual generalisations remain.

In this anonymous climate individuals often hide behind the class they belong to.

'The medical staff are fairly sure that people are . . . .'
'Many patients have found that the . . . '
'The married people feel that bed-time should be . . . . '
'This is very confusing for the nursing staff.'

Personal viewpoints are concealed in statements from one class about another. This hiding of identity arises especially when an individual imports into the group a personal disagreement with another whom he is afraid to confront directly. In the group it can be made into an impersonal general issue. But it can also arise when personal disagreement arises in the group itself. The result is the same – the group is presented with disembodied general issues of principle and class.

These general class statements allow the individual and his hostility to remain unidentified. The disownment of personal hostility and its projection into one's own class averts personal attack from others (because one is lost in a class) and avoids retaliation from any other because he too is lost in a class. Many remarks in a large group thus appear to come from nobody in particular, to be about nobody in particular and to be addressed to nobody in particular. This avoidance of asserting the self and others' selves in personal interchange, together with the accompanying projective processes, is liable to lead now to paranoid class wars and heated moralisings. These can only be ended if the initiating highly personal issues can be brought to light, and seen as important for certain individuals but irrelevant to the larger group. If they are not brought to light but remain as general matters, the issues may become used as containers for all sorts of other hidden and undeclared personal disagreements. Anonymous class wars over plausible general principles are now seized upon to pay off old personal scores which have not been voiced in the 'dangerous' group. Vehement discussions about abstract principles, and class behaviours thus often develop a baffling unreal quality where the passion, produced by projection and displacement, is out of all proportion to the manifest issues. Certain individuals may usefully identify both the underlying *personal* issues and the few involved; but such meetings often end in high feeling with each class feeling righteous, misunderstood, and angry, while endowing other classes with stupidity and malice.

But even if class wars do not occur, anonymisation creates a 'safe' but stultifying stasis in which nobody exists and nothing much gets done. The gain is that the fantastically 'hostile' group cannot attack anybody for nobody exists as a person or speaks as one. The cost is that personal thought, discussion and interchange are crippled.

Envy and democratisation

If the large group is endowed with projected positive aspects of the self, the projectors will be depleted and relatively ineffective, but will be in awe of and dependent on the abilities now lost and now attributed to the idealised group. But whereas most members actively resist negative aspects being forced into them, so that the invented 'group' is needed and used as the single container of these, the fate of positive aspects is somewhat different. Because of human narcissism some people do not resist positive qualities being attributed or forced into them and do not make appropriate reality tests; some even enjoy being idealised and try to collude with high qualities being attributed to them. A few may even vie prominently for idealising projections and seek to be regarded by the depleted majority as 'the only people who make the group worth while'. Such members usually have some suitability as containers of positive projections but a good 'role fit' is not inevitable and the correspondence of their gifts with those now attributed to them may be indifferent. Those who embark on 'high-level' competition may get admiration and envy of the depleted others; but this leads in turn to the others becoming doubly passive and ineffective so that group discussion is replaced by 'prima donna' displays. The 'prima donnas' in turn project ineffectiveness and invalidism into the group. The single entity of the 'group' may itself become the sole repository of projected positive qualities and itself become idealised and worshipped by its depleted members, and when so endowed with magical status its real activities and its members' functioning may actually be of a low order.

The projection of positive abilities not only leads to mental poverty, awe, tutelage and worship of selected others; more painfully it may result in envy of these others for their abilities, real or fantasied. Those who retain the capacity to think and relate with assurance may thus be privately belittled as too clever, conceited, ambitious and competitive, etc., and at times even attacked in public.

'There we go again. More clever ideas.'
'Why do you try so hard? The group is quite happy being quiet.'
'What gives you the right to think that you know better than the rest of us.'

Envy is a disease of poverty and also of impoverishment by projective identification, but envy is itself often denied and projected, so that others come to be feared as dangerously envious. The resultant *fear of being envied*, as well as the demonstrated attacks on those who retain their individuation and abilities, gives further cause for the hiding of abilities and thoughts from the 'malignant' group and for outbreaks of safe generalisations.

In this overdetermined state of anonymity[8] even talented individuals may be careful to remain undistinguished nonentities; nobody dare be original or unique in thought or capacity. Everybody collusively seeks similarity to others and all are regarded as having identical needs and rights. All patients have the same amount and kind of distress and out of 'fairness' none should be given less or more consideration than others. All staff have the same status and aims, all nurses are equally skilled (or unskilled), all doctors are equally useful (or useless). All treatments are equal in effectiveness, by equal staff to equal patients, and should last an equal time. The rights of minorities are sunk, and the word democracy now acquires magical values and is in common usage. The normal processes of externalisation with subsequent reality-testing which help the individual to find out, differentiate and maintain himself and others come to a stop. The recognition of the variety of talents becomes lost. Truly democratic processes, the creation of a social structure with election to distinct roles of authority and responsibility matched to the special skills of individuals, and with sincere consideration of the different capacities and needs of individuals, are brushed away as 'undemocratic'. Candidates for significant posts and elected positions declare themselves unfit for election or uninterested, so the group loses the benefits of their ambitions and gifts. Indeed the general fear of enviable distinction may lead to the election of harmless nonentities to important posts.

In the face of projectively enhanced fears of group hostility and envy, staff have particular problems because of their inescapable distinct position. Some may now minimise these in placating statements to the group. Others may seek to be on first-name terms with each other and with patients or make other anxious attempts at 'democratic' bonhomie. Others will blur or renounce their roles, authority and responsibilities, and emphasis their powerlessness and goodwill in attempts to escape from envious attack.

Placatory actions of this kind hinder analysis of the fear of envy and prevent the growth of sincere reality-tested relations. Painful problems are evaded in anxious democratic goodwill; and the brake of appeasement is put on discussion, argument and decision-making.

The recovery of the self

After a large unstructured group meeting has ended, no matter whether it has gone 'well' or 'badly', many members gossip with each other. In twos and threes they rapidly seek to recover lost parts of themselves and to re-experience others also as whole personalised individuals, and they no longer act or use these others only as containers of projections. Critical faculties and abilities become re-owned and no longer denied, and simultaneously comes the re-assertion of the self and the capacity to think freely and to relate again to others as asserting individuals. An open shared sense of relief at the break-up of the large group is common in this 'post-mortem'. Many who were silent, paranoid, anonymised, depleted, depersonalised, baffled and and stupid in the large group will now, after a short period of feeling dazed and unsure, begin to chatter and to seek feelings and ideas within themselves and explore and express these with increasing confidence with their fellows; and now interchange with and the exploration of the feelings and views of fellows proceed apace. It seems that in the different, less complex setting the individual can take back into himself much of the aggressive energy he had projected and lost into the larger setting; and can rid himself of elements projected into him by others while he was in the large group. And he will now find others of his kind, also recovering and freer also to *be* again and to allow others to *be*.

In therapeutic communities it is also common now for staff 'after-groups' to meet and discuss with each other the large group events which a few minutes before had perhaps puzzled or confused them. Somewhat formally they do what the patients simultaneously do informally, reviewing the large-group events and recovering and rediscovering themselves and others. These 'after-groups' are not inevitably successful for they too carry the potential anxieties of any sizeable group; and there is an added danger that the 'outsiders' (the patients) may be used as suitable depersonalised receptacles for continued or new projections. Staff after-groups, being relatively small, can usually preserve individual reality-testing but they are not inevitably immune from relational chaos.

A contrast with small groups

Certain differences between small and large groups make for different experiences in the two settings. Benign projective identification, with reality-testing, can certainly proceed faster and more surely in small groups; and the affirming of oneself and the finding of others, and acceptance, modification or rejection of others' projections are faster. The individual has fewer receptacles for his own projections and has fewer others seeking to intrude theirs into him; all are in less danger, both of being overwhelmed and of being seriously depleted by very many others. The individual's ability and need to find himself through relating to others is not so confounded, lost, overlaid or ignored in the simpler matrix of the small group. Retirement from frustrated attempts at relations is therefore less common in the small group, and retreat to personal models, narcissistic experiences, and denial of and projection of self-hatred are less used, and when used are less vigorous. Because the situation is less frustrating, hostility is less, and projective identification is neither so massive nor forced. Because personality depletion is less, the individual has more of his faculties for use in reality-testing.

Some technical observations

How can one help reduce the complex of anxieties which hinder the large group's work task – which in the case of a psychiatric hospital is the examination of the disturbances in working alliances which result from insufficient awareness of the self and of others?

Whereas in personal or small-group psychotherapy interpretation is *sanctioned because sought* it has no such sanction in large groups. Interpretation in large groups is therefore liable to be viewed only as a model of unengaged observer-behaviour and the others may gladly follow this model because of its defensive non-revelatory safety. As a result general talk about what 'the group' is doing may become epidemic. Then nobody is *in* the group, for all become observers of it 'out there', interpreting 'it', exchanging Nobel-Prize thoughts about 'it', and addressing 'it', but not interacting as and with personalised individuals. Moreover, unsanctioned 'group' interpretations are often the result of unease in an interpreter at feeling himself confused, insignificant and lost; they may simply be his attempt to assert a threatened thinking capacity about an 'it' rather than a personal engagement with individuals present. The non-personalised interpreter may thereafter become irrecoverably used as a container for projected positive or negative aspects of others. He may be felt as containing magical abilities to be submitted to in passivity and indeed may continue to be projectively stimulated to be prominent and clever while all others maintain innocence and stupidity; or he may come to be enviously attacked; or be regarded as full of malignities to be feared and hidden from. Many of the complications in large groups outlined earlier may thus be unchanged, and indeed 'group' interpretations may simply confound confusion. The 'therapeutic alliance' of psychoanalysis is not available in work with large groups.

The complexities of large-group life mean that any accurate interpretation about 'it' is at best a part-truth. Large groups rarely behave as wholes moving only in one direction, indeed the individuals in it may be moving in several different directions, and interpretations about group form or content, or themes are therefore almost always incomplete. This is not to say that the understanding of total processes in which many persons are involved can never be attempted, but the interpreter should be fairly sure of his observations, his understanding of these and his motives before he speaks, together with the result he expects. But it remains difficult for the group interpreter to avoid offering a model of me/you-all thinking, with the dangers of ensuing ambivalent dependence on him.

The convenor or convenors cannot of course escape their task which is to listen, understand, intervene and observe the effects of their interventions. But not all interventions need be interpretive, and in large groups *non-interpretive therapeutic interventions* have major merit. Like interpretations in individual treatments, such interventions should be carefully timed and phrased, but, unlike interpretations about 'it' out there, should be highly *personalised* statements about *one's own* sincerely felt position in the face of specific contributions by individuals or groups of individuals; they are distinguished from mere personal revelations, however, in that they are offered only if the declared personal position has been thought out as being revealing also about the situation of others.

Non-interpretive therapeutic interventions are not easy to formulate but are often simple in themselves. They are difficult because they require tolerance of and fidelity to the self and to others in the face of all the group's projective processes, hostilities, confusions, anonymisations, Nobel-Prize thinking, narcissistic withdrawals, generalisations, etc. Of course the better the pathological group-processes are understood the easier it is to remain a whole person relating to well-perceived others and thus to offer models of personalised thinking. Non-interpretive therapeutic interventions rarely concern the whole 'group' however; for they are attempts to help *individuals* recover and rediscover themselves and each other in it and from it. They offer a model of an individual relating not to 'the group' but to individuals present. The following is an example of such an intervention on a not very troubled group. It seems ordinary and elementary *because* it was thoughtful and skilled.

Example

Discussion became taken over by a dozen teenage patients. They addressed only each other and used private slang and nicknames and discussed a complicated set of relations and feelings about an event they had obviously created the previous evening. It was friendly and yet it was private and excluded many present. The older members listened politely but at least some began to feel envious, curious and guilty over being so ignorant, as if they ought to have known about the event. (Staff were able to check this at an after-group.) Afraid of disclosing his remiss ignorance to the large group (and to the other older ones) many an older member sat in uneasy solitude, hiding and trying to disown his uncomfortable feelings from all others. None of this was clear to the members at that time; they took part in it but were not aware of it, only of their various discomforts.

Group interpretations would have been possible perhaps about group splitting, age-rivalries, denial and projection of guilt over enjoyment, denied hatred of younger people, secret delinquency, fear of retaliation, etc. with all the dangers of being both chancy and me/you-all.

One of the staff said, 'I'm feeling left-out of this, and fed up. And I notice I'm ashamed I didn't know about last night and I'm ashamed to say I'm curious. It sounds good – what went on?'

Some older members made immediate noises of agreement. All stopped looking down and looked towards the younger people, who at once began to talk to the older people. Last night they had invented and played a new intelligent game and they explained this. Then one said and the others agreed that they had been disappointed no older people had seen them – 'You'd have been impressed. Honestly, we didn't know we were so good.' Now there was general laughter and much goodwill. A general discussion now took place over details of the evening and then moved on to other incidents in which shyness between older and younger people had limited their relating to each other. Resentments by all at being misunderstood were discussed insightfully and a few plans for the future were made.

It is obviously not possible to make a list of non-interpretive therapeutic interventions for all occasions. It can be said, however, that any which help individuals to feel easier about owning and declaring more of themselves and their situations are therapeutic for all. Not only do they reduce mental splitting and increase personality integration for the individual, but they also allow others to know him (and therefore themselves) less fantastically and more surely. All can therefore better reaffirm themselves and each other, and can grow aware of how, in group settings, personal integration can be maintained.

It is possible, however, to indicate in aphoristic form a few samples of opportunities for non-interpretive therapeutic interventions; they are obvious, even trite, and anyone familiar with large groups will add many more; yet they are difficult to remember and use in the pressures of large-group disturbances. Behind statements of class views is an individual with a recent painful experience with someone in the other class: personal feuds tend to be expressed as a 'group' matter: early generalising statements often indicate a personal carry-over from a particular recent experience; every question conceals personal thoughts and wishes and is never 'innocent': absolute judgements are the result of recent personal pain; statements about 'people' usually hide thoughts about one person: steady presentation of various grumbles are a displacement from one concealed matter – sometimes a good one felt to need protection from others' envy.

The *manner* of intervening is not, however, thus indicated, and it hardly needs stating that aphoristic interventions would be merely non-personal, lofty and generalising. The intervener's manner should be of an ally to those in difficulty and what he says about himself should help them sort out and declare themselves.

Example

A woman patient cautiously asked the group to formulate a view about behaviour at night in the corridors. Perhaps all felt both attacked by this question and glad of the generalising defence it contained, for it was accepted at face value and steadily discussed as a general issue. What *were* the group's views? The group split into those who were and were not in favour of making rules. Ideas and arguments about designating 'quiet' areas arose. Respecting the rights of others and society's needs for defences against anarchy took the topic into abstract levels. Projection processes led to vicious arguments about law-giving and law-breaking with examples. The original speaker and her request became ignored. Many grew silent. Eventually an intervener addressed the first speaker, and said surely hers was not just an academic question. What had happened at night to lead to the question? Could it be spoken about?

Well, the speaker's child had been woken by 'people' talking on the corridor at 10 o'clock last night and it had taken an hour to get him to sleep. People? Could she mention names? Well she didn't want to cause trouble. Others murmured their support of her keeping the issue anonymous. Now several speakers declared their personal innocence and indignant sympathy for the mother. Eventually a pressurising silence arose as if in wait for a sinner to confess. The intervener said if she had been one of the night-time talkers she couldn't possibly say so now, because the group was somehow now making a Federal offence out of a bit of ordinary carelessness. She had herself sometimes forgotten to keep quiet outside a child's room and she couldn't promise to be perfect in future, but she'd try. Was it a hanging matter? One or two others said that they too had sometimes forgotten to be quiet in corridors. Two patients said they thought it must have been them. They'd forgotten about the child and hadn't realised it until this meeting. The mother smiled grimly and said she knew it was them but hadn't liked to say so (although she'd met them that morning). She'd been furious last night. There was some laughter and more apologies. Individuals had emerged. The group's heat about general moral issues vanished and discussion moved on to another topic, with members again in possession of themselves, and relating to others.

Conclusion

Projective processes affect not only individuals but others related to them, and are therefore stuff of multibody psychology. Mutual projective processes not only impoverish and distort experience of the self and the perceived world; they also affect

the behaviour of this world towards the self. Human organisations inevitably create projection systems; some are rife with
them and where they enshrine and perpetuate them they create
personal and interpersonal impoverishments and ineffectiveness.

Therapeutic two-somes and small groups offer the internally
divided individual a chance of resolving in some depth the
anxieties and fantasies observable in those settings. The problems
for the individual of maintaining himself and others in large-
group settings are allied but distinct, and together with the
behaviour of large groups in using collusive projective systems
merit separate study.

At present our best-tested therapeutic technique and most
fruitful observations rest on the classic two-body situation.
Comparatively little is yet known about multibody psychology
and very little about the multi-body psychology of large groups.
Therapeutic communities therefore offer important observational
and technical opportunities.

3. Threats to identity in the large group

A study in the phenomenology of the individual's experiences of changing membership status in a large group[1]

Pierre Turquet

Definition of a large group as a context for study

This paper seeks to describe a consultant's personal experience of working with groups of 40–80 people, and attempts to explicate some of the phenomena which lie behind the structures usually deployed in such groups, such as chairman, rules and procedures, and fixed topics for debate. What I have to say about these experiences is in the nature of a construct and as such is personal.

I have participated in 'large groups' almost from their inception at the Leicester Conferences for the study of group relations, sponsored since 1957 by the Centre for Applied Social Research, Tavistock Institute of Human Relations. In *Learning for Leadership* A. K. Rice[2] recalled how the plenaries (i.e. meetings of the total conference membership and staff called to review and examine the conference as an institution), at these early conferences, were impeded in their work by an upsurge of incomprehensible forces. We decided, therefore, to investigate these forces in specific large-group meetings held for the purpose, comprising the total membership of our conferences. After Rice's solo consultancy with a group of just over 20 members (compared with 10 members in the study groups) he invited me to join him and to develop this area of conference work in still larger groups, as conference memberships increased. I have since acted as consultant also in similar conferences sponsored by related bodies, such as the Grubb Institute for Behavioural Studies and the Department of Education of Bristol University, in Britain, and the A. K. Rice Institute in the United States.

Numbers in these groups have varied from 40 to 80.[3] At first sight such a wide range in numbers might be thought to cast doubt on the universal validity of the phenomena to be described. However, within this range of numbers, I am not aware that these phenomena have varied, or that new phenomena have appeared at the upper limit, or that with smaller numbers they are not to be observed. Any variation has been in intensity. The essential point is that with such numbers the group can no longer be face to face. Attempts to make it so have not alleviated the group's inherent problems and difficulties. Thus the large-group situation cannot be encompassed by any one of its members in a single glance. Seating such numbers automatically provides a different structure from the small group, that of three to five concentric circles. Each individual member is surrounded on all sides, in front, behind, to the left and to the right, except for those in the back row, who have nobody behind them. If, to paraphrase Bales,[4] the small group is one in which each member can give a personal account of each other member, this is certainly not true of large groups, where many a member remains an unknown quantity throughout. Not being face to face, not being encompassable at a glance by any one member, the kind of personal interaction with other members and with the whole, which is characteristic of the individual's experience in small groups, is no longer possible. If the individual member of a small group suffers a dislocation in his sense of familiarity as he goes from a small-group membership of 5-6 to 10-12, so too with these larger numbers he endures further dislocations which, if they are to be mastered, require their own techniques.

Usually such groups have met in a room sufficiently large to leave space outside the seating provided, permitting each member in the outer circle to move, as he wished, either towards or away from the centre of the circle. Such a structure undoubtedly contributes to the member's experience of being in space, surrounded by other members. This heightens inter-member experience and seems to influence and give significance to a member's choice of seat. As a result each circle acquires its own characteristic feeling tone, with a varying range of experiences for each member, depending upon the circle in which he is seated, and with, correspondingly, a varying sense of being in or out, marginally or centrally committed to participation, the object of the group's pressures, or left in peace.

Such groups have been of limited duration, 6 to 12 sessions, the number varying with the length of the conference. On the conference programme each session is allocated one and a half hours, after which the consultants withdraw. Though scattered sub-groups may hang around, I cannot recall any occasion when a large group chose to continue beyond its allotted time, to complete a piece of work, as sometimes happens with small groups. Thus while problems of commitment are prominent, wishes to get out are even more so. However, I am describing the initial stages of large-group life, the first hours of its existence, that period where, at least theoretically, a member's anxiety might be expected to be at its height, and where unfamiliarity, both with the overall situation and with the other members, is maximal. At conferences lasting a fortnight, which have as many as 12 large-group sessions, there has been a growing commitment to the study of large-group processes in their own right, alongside and contrasting with the study of the small group, of 10–12 members.

Thus though my experience in these large groups is restricted in duration, the framework of study is such as to highlight the overt presence of the forces at work, compared with their disguised existence within the various structures deemed necessary for the proper functioning of such large groups in the outside world.

The consultant as a person within a role
The task of the large group as usually set out in the conference brochure and repeated at the opening plenary is 'the study of its

own behaviour in the here and now', this brief applying to all conference events. The study is self-study, in which the consultants' interpretations play their part. The overall context of these conferences, as also of each event within them, is experiential – a self-acquisition of insight from experienced happenings – and is therefore not directly didactic. The model is basically that of Freudian psychoanalysis, with a deliberate and conscious attempt by the consultants to refrain from any form of telling. Thus events are fundamentally allowed to take their own course. The consultants do not propose a subject for discussion, usually remaining silent at the beginning of a session, unless able to make some immediate comment on an aspect of the actual opening, e.g., major chair rearrangements, lateness, and the like. Their task is to take up topics and behaviour as they emerge. Like all free associative situations, though the freedom is conceived of as the members', the topics and behaviour are viewed as being determined by the underlying dynamic of the situation in which both the group and its members, including the consultants, find themselves. The basic notion, then, is the presence of a dynamic interaction between large group and members, an interaction in which all events, whether non-verbal or spoken, are an expression of a process which is there to be understood. Clearly the task of understanding is a difficult one; nor are the consultants always working solely with forces directed at self-understanding, though self-understanding is an essential part of the large group's primary task and *raison d'être*.

Usually two or more consultants are provided to help the members in their task, their numbers being related to the size of the membership and staff availability. The consultant's primary task is to interpret events, not merely describing the group behaviour, but attempting to analyse the dynamic underlying it, that is, its motivation and purpose, in terms of a 'because' clause. Clearly for the consultants all kinds of problems abound, not least how they are able to function and what happens to their interpretative role. Thus one of the consultants may also be the Conference Director, and as a result may find himself treated as the director of the large group, the control man, the voice of authority taking over, and thereby his interpretative role disallowed. To reinforce the situation he may in fact have judged it necessary to step in and exercise his authority as director, usually (or so he believes) with the thought of protecting a member. If in so doing he has stepped out of role as large-group consultant, his behaviour, whether deliberate or unwitting, becomes part of the group dynamic: it certainly becomes an event for further study. The presence of more than one consultant is in part hopefully planned to facilitate inter-consultant processes, though all four have been known not to grasp such nettles or to have otherwise lost their wits.

In this connection it is worth pointing out that a consultant is present in a dual capacity: as an individual person and fulfilling a role. To have a role in itself increases the chances of survival, to survive being an important emergent aim in such a group. His designation as 'consultant to the large group' gives him a special and favoured position from which to come to grips with the behaviour of such a group, the contribution of his 'because' clauses demonstrating an expertise which will have its own development and fate. The study of the fate of this expertise, the fluctuations in facility in finding such a clause, the fluidity or hesitancy with which it is experienced, is not the whole of the consultant's task, but is a vital indicator of the nature of the forces acting on him in his consultancy role. But the consultant also experiences a large group as a person, his capacity to internalise and work on these personal happenings being a basic part of his consultancy. Thus, through events befalling his role and his status as a person, he will also be able to say something about the fate of the individual member in such a situation. Much of what happens to him in his two capacities of role and person also happens to all the other participating members of the large group, as each experiences the group and takes up a role in it. He too will find himself alone, an isolate; he too will lose his wits, be de-skilled, filled up, threatened with annihilation – to mention but a few of the many common personal experiences provided by the large group. As a consultant in a large group my experiences are therefore both common and unique. Because a consultant's experience has this shared quality with other members of the group, the seemingly personal nature of my construct can legitimately be generalised.

I wish to stress this point further. As a consultant, I too, in working with a large group, am involved in a process, a conversion process[5] whose aim is to make me into something other, even something other than my role and function as a consultant. These are powerful forces at work, no respecters of persons, seeking to change my role and status as that of every other individual member of the large group. The struggle to resist them, to remain a consultant, is great. In the harsh terms of large-group life, it is a case of who will dominate whom: will consultant and member dominate the large group or be dominated by it? Participation can lead either way. Only withdrawal can lessen the struggle for the individual. But for a consultant withdrawal is destruction of skills and role, both of which exist and have significance when deployed through participation. Participation and self-exposure is the only way to survive as a consultant. But then the struggle in domination is on. Inevitably in a situation so constantly suffused with the struggle to dominate, survival – if it is to be at a creative level – will have idiosyncratic aspects. The major large-group defence against such forces is by homogenisation, that is, survival by all being alike, sinking or swimming together. But homogenisation is a pure survival mechanism: its creative powers are nil. To be creative in the large group requires standing to be counted, which implies from the point of view of other members idiosyncrasy of self-expression or self-assertion. Necessarily, therefore, the construct I make of my experiences, since it represents my survival as a consultant in this large-group situation, will have this idiosyncratic element, my understanding being the means whereby as a consultant I have creatively come through this conversion process.

It is clear from this that my approach is from the point of view of the individual member experiencing aspects of this conversion process: it is not a sociological one, though hopefully the sociological implications of the individual member's dilemmas and experiences may emerge.

Conference philosophy

Inevitably the structurelessness as to topic, freedom to contribute as and when a member wishes, the offered absence of res-
traints on individual behaviour, contributes to the general
strangeness and unexpectedness of the situation. It reflects the
general conference philosophy of wishing to study what emerges
and to give the joining member as he arrives at the conference
the freedom to examine the conference events in his own particular way. Both tasks – to explorate conference events and to
do so as one wishes – have their difficulties, their development
being a further object for study.

Conference members are recruited from a wide variety of
backgrounds, professions and disciplines, including industrialists
and social workers, psychiatrists and educationalists, clerics and
personnel managers; both sexes and all ages. The aim of the
conferences is equally important and is reflected in its setting
in a university hall of residence: it is designed to be educational
and not therapeutic. Members come for study and learning, not
as patients; any therapeutic gain is a chance though acceptable
by-product. It is true that the overall tone of the meetings is
experiential and teaching in the accepted sense is only occasionally provided, but the aim is through interpretations to help the
membership to come to grips with its own behaviour in the 'here
and now' and hence be insightful about it and possibly change it.
In this sense too the large group is unstructured since no learning
targets are set. Each member is 'free' to experience and determine
his own learning within his relationship both to the total situation
and to the consultants.

The 'I' situation and its interactional nature

Into such a large group there comes a 'conference member'[6] –
an 'I'[7] – who, though he wishes to participate in the group's
activities, and through participation to study the behaviour
of a large group, should at this entry stage be thought of as a
'singleton'.[8] Here at once is one of the major problems in describing large-group experiences: what terms are to be used to
describe the changing states of its members? I have introduced

the term 'singleton' for this person entering into a new experience totally on his or her own, not yet part of a group but attempting both to find himself and to make relations with the other singletons who are in a similar state. As yet within the large group situation no relationships with the other singletons have been established; nor do previous acquaintanceships seem to operate.

One of the characteristics of a large group is that many of its members remain in the singleton state, unable, possibly unwilling, to join in and so to go through a necessary change of state. This conversion process is part of the dislocation every conference member experiences as he takes himself into a world which transcends the usual parameters of his own individuality. I find it necessary also to have a term for the singleton who has established a relationship, not only with the large group as a whole, but also with the other singletons, each and all having thereby evolved out of their singleton states. Such 'converted' singletons I shall refer to as 'individual members' (I.Ms), each singleton having obtained his or her own personal I.M. definition from the kind of relationships established with other singletons as they too struggle in the large group to evolve into I.Ms.

I would like to elaborate further my account of two powerful large-group experiences which give rise to the creation of these terms.

First, there is the conference member's experience of flux and of being part of a process. I hypothesise that this experience is related to a sense of being caught up in a change of state, of becoming an I.M. after having been a singleton. Linked to this sense of flux is the search for a state of equilibrium as between personal needs and roles and group needs and roles. In the large group the experience is of moving from a non-role, the singleton state, to a group role, that of being an individual member. The hope is, and it remains in doubt, that the I.M. state thus found can be maintained over a period – at least the duration of one session; and that the role taken up can be implemented in an individual way (hence the term individual member); and, further, that this will lead to the development of skills within the role.

Any one session of a large group is in itself so kaleidoscopic, however, that any equilibrium appears transitory, with other states ever threatening to take over. In view of these difficulties (and in contrast with small groups), it is perhaps easier not to join but to remain a singleton, despite the isolation that that implies.

Secondly, the large group has to assume some meaning for the singleton, especially if interactions are to occur and if their issue is to be a meaningful state of individual membership. As he tries to interact with the large group and its individual members the singleton seeks to make something of the situation, to give it a meaning, to make a construct of it. Again hopefully the construct will be a positive one, but often it seems to express not only the singleton's destructive feelings, but also, and this is particularly characteristic of the large group – his own experience of being threatened with annihilation as he interacts with the large group and its members. Nor is the experience of the threat of annihilation – in itself part of the more general experience of flux – lessened by the further experience of the large group's attempts to make of him a 'membership individual' (M.I.), where group membership predominates over individual self-definition and needs, and so destroys his I.M. state. Given the size of the large group, the singleton has this special problem how to put his mark on the situation, to become and remain an I.M., but at the same time to resist the large group's attempts at putting its own particular stamp on him by turning him into an M.I. Nor is this problem made easier by the distinctive tone of the large group, especially compared with the very small family group, where the singleton has had his training and where by primary experience he is rooted.

There remains one more important state to be identified: a transitional one, as the individual member in his group life moves between the various states of singleton to I.M., I.M. to M.I., or I.M. back to singleton. The notion of a conversion process adds weight and value to such interim states, however transitory. Theoretically at least, they represent choice opportunities, the choice of the member to be this or that, an I.M. or an

M.I., or to revert to a singleton state, or to opt out. The exercise
of such choice, whether consciously known or not, is the occasion
for the expression of individuality, of 'I-ness'. Assuming, therefore, that there is a struggle within the individual to resist the
conversion process in the group, these transitional states may
allow him, whatever group membership role he may have been
in, to re-assert his own particular individuality, possibly in a
sudden upsurge of idiosyncratic behaviour. It seems reasonable
to refer to the member involved in this transitional moment as
an 'I' and to call that sudden upsurge of 'himselfness' a state
of 'I-ness'. Clearly both terms reflect once again the struggle
between singleton and large group, with the singleton wishing
to interact with the large group and thereby to find an I.M.
role for himself and not to become an M.I.

The I's need for a boundary or skin

The critical difficulty for the singleton on entering a large group
and finding himself in this strange and unfamiliar situation is to
find a point of entry: how to start an interactional relationship
between himself and its members, as also with the total situation? The experience is essentially one of search, the search
for some tool, idea, concept, with which to come to grips with
the experiences he is having and by entering the interactive
process to move from being a singleton to become a 'joiner' – an
I interacting at the interface – and so to establish himself as an
I.M. Essential to this joining process is that the singleton should
find a boundary or skin which both limits and defines him. Of
such skins there are two: external (the skin-of-my-neighbour)
and internal (my own skin).

Through the external skin the singleton can begin to distinguish himself from the other singletons around him who are
also seeking relations. He needs the presence of the other members
in order to say: 'This is me; that is not me'; or 'This is I – that
is the "other" '. Finding and establishing such a skin is a matter
of some urgency if the developing singleton is to find himself
as an I.M. and not to be caught up in the process of becoming
other than himself, for instance, the tool of the group or the

consultants' puppet or zombie, that is part of the M.I. state. This sense of the threat of becoming other than himself, of being in some way altered, pressurised, even diminished, is for the singleton an ever-present experience as he lives in the large group. It is remorseless, to be constantly guarded against, that is, if the 'member' wishes to maintain I.M. status. Without this external boundary, puppetry is a constant possibility, to be fended off by withdrawal. So important is the skin-of-my-neighbour for the singleton in a large group that he will seek to go into a large-group session flanked on either side, i.e., as a threesome. In small groups, by contrast, a member is more easily content with paired relationships. Thus while it might be true of Sartre's world that 'Hell is the other',[9] for the singleton in the large group, any 'other' is better than no 'other' and certainly better than Sartre's 'void', again an ever-present threat.

The second skin, the internal skin, is needed so that the singleton can separate himself out from his background, more specifically from the undifferentiated non-singleton matrix[10] out of which he has developed and to which he might return again, if the I.M. status is not securely established, the various problematical processes having foiled him and the defensive manoeuvres having broken down. In more sophisticated terms, this internal skin includes the creation of a time boundary, of a past and a present so that the 'here and now' can be differentiated from the past, the past becoming a background called the 'past'. From such a background the interacting singleton can say, 'This is me now – that was me then'. The presence of the past as part of a background boundary skin enables the singleton to live and interact in the 'here and now' happenings of the large group (that is, whatever may be emerging or occurring in the large group at any one moment in the present time). This background boundary skin has a further important and special aspect. While the presence of the past gives rise to a sense of continuity of growth out of all our yesterdays, the singleton's immediate experience is nevertheless one of discontinuity, of being different, of being other than he was yesterday, to the extent of his saying: 'I am no longer like that', or even 'I don't want to be like that'.

D

The interdependence of these two boundary aspects in the singleton's 'here and now' experiential life should be stressed. Thus, while the presence of the 'other' as an individual member inherently carries an element of separation and detachment, and even of a forceful pulling away ('That is not me', or, more crudely: 'That's what you think; I think differently'), the background of time-past equally inherently carries a desire to fuse the certainty of yesterday's 'there and then', the uncertainty of today's 'here and now' and the unknownness of tomorrow. On the one hand, the singleton's experience of present living, with its own discrete content of repeated separations from the past, by its very discontinuities may come to reinforce a wish to maintain contact with the 'other', who by his presence seems to offer some experiential assurance of continuous existence in the 'here and now' and hence of survival from a past. Thus the presence of the other member may stimulate the desire to fuse. On the other hand, forceful separations from the other individual members, or difficulties in relating to another I.M., may encourage fusion wishes with the past, which then appears as an attractive proposition – hence the 'Peter Pan' wishes in us all. Fusion/separation is thus an ever-present dynamic, the former leading on to M.I. and the latter leading back to a singleton state.

Other factors play their part in the singleton's urge to fuse with a background, not least the sense of familiarity that the past offers. For the past seems to imply a security and an experience of events that have been lived through and from which there has been survival. Yet this past – the 'what we did yesterday' discussion – is frequently non-adaptive in the face of what is happening to the struggling I.M. in the large group 'here and now'. If, as so often happens, the I.M. cannot recall what he did or what was happening to him yesterday, not only does the past not seem to rescue him and make him feel secure, but it now becomes a threat. What has happened to it? Vanished, like the snows of yesteryear, with a 'who am I now?' feeling. Anxiety surges up with a developing content of annihilation, becoming fear of a void in which to be lost. Since internally nothing can be found, there is nothing there. The move to try to re-establish a 'here and now' contact with the skin-of-my-neighbour can then be very quick. Macneice[11] puts these aspects of the singleton's dilemma very aptly: 'An historical sense is essential, which means that we must know how to be new as contrasted with repetition – psittacosis – on the one hand, and with escape from tradition – aphasia – on the other.' He adds both graphically and dramatically: 'We must sit in the seats of our ancestors, i.e., we must turn our ancestors out of them.' As far as man in a group is concerned, whether it be large or small, that is easier said than done.

While, for the singleton, the first of these two boundary aspects – the skin-of-my-neighbour – involves the play of centrifugal forces, lest loss of self in the other members take place, with the second – the establishment of a past – its creation brings into play centripetal forces, the sense of attraction of the past away from the difficulties of present-day living. True, in both instances it is a question of an equilibrium between the two forces, with the I discovering the extent of his freedom to move in either direction. There is much about the large group to interfere with the I's freedom of movement. Almost immediately on entering the large group the singleton experiences the competing presence of these two forces in terms of whether to belong or whether to pull out. Although this conflict may be true of all relationships, in the large group the polarity as experienced by the interacting but struggling singleton is, in extreme terms, either isolated apartness or a complete fusion with or loss in. The large group reveals the singleton's difficulty in preserving an interactive psychological distance between himself and the 'other', be the 'other' an event, an experience or a member.

In contrast, a major attraction of the small group, particularly a work group when suffused with Basic Assumption activity (as described by Bion[12]), is that it has sufficient generalities and cohesion to further a sense of fusion and hence of belonging while at the same time offering each I.M. a variety of opportunities to implement idiosyncratically the roles such a group provides, especially those concerned with various kinds of leadership.

In other words there are possibilities for separating out, so the I
can be of the group yet separate from it. As a result the crude
anxieties inherent in the large-group polarisation seem to diminish
or at least to become tolerable.

Small groups, as part of their devotion to generalisations as
a means of securing group cohesion and I.M. adherence, like
to employ fusion words such as 'parents', 'siblings', 'families' –
terms where a member is not distinguishable from other members
but is made to belong to a particular category of members
which includes him. At such times too the discussions show much
devotion to 'we' statements, often to be rejected angrily with
terms like 'Speak for yourself!', thereby revealing their capacity
to involve. Equally, on occasions there will be an emphasis on
'You know', as if to make sure that the experience is shared,
and so to procure involvement. The problem with such generalisations is that their use tends to preclude any investigation of
the actual personal way a particular I.M. role is being implemented, such investigations being pictured as likely to be painful,
to disrupt the skin-of-my-neighbour continuity, and hence
to lead to a return to the I state or to some other idiosyncratic
state. Nevertheless there is a sense of security about these 'we',
'you know' phrases, as also in the family terms used, since they
contain within themselves varying degrees of acknowledgement
of I.M. relatedness. The skin-of-my-neighbour is inherently
present in such terms and by that fact they indicate to all that the
I need not fear his loss of I-ness. They also hint at possibilities
of personal idiosyncratic role implementation. The I can breathe
again, in that the state of I.M. seems to be within his grasp.

But not so with the large group, where all seems to conspire
against even the possibility of an idiosyncratic group-related
role while still being a fully paid-up member. The large collectivity in itself hampers the discovery of a discrete role, thereby
encouraging fusion processes. Such a mass hinders the member
from growth and development through trials at personalised
role-implementation: weight overwhelms. In addition, the
large group's fusion words, like the large group, are large,
such as 'care-givers', 'industrialists', or 'the women'. These

are such broad categories that their personalised I implementation is obscured and eventually requires such an effort that the I.M. runs the risk of appearing eccentric. So many are the possibilities within such categories – there being no agreed role of 'psychiatrist', 'personnel manager', 'man' – that the I despairs both of finding his personal implementation and of having it recognised, so that all he can say is: 'I am not like that!' The result is a reduced sense of self, even to the extent of being irrelevant, with a 'Why attempt to develop I-ness?' quality.

In the large group disruption of the skin-of-my-neighbour boundary is an ever-present threat from the action of the centrifugal forces already mentioned which both cause the I to withdraw, but also place him relationally in increasingly idiosyncratic and isolated positions. Continuity with his skin-of-my-neighbour is also in jeopardy because the large group raises many more problems about these neighbours: 'where, who, when, what, are they?' This experience of search and questioning is further aggravated by the almost daily changes in their spatial positioning, at first near, then far, now in front, now behind, now on the left, now on the right, and so on. One day it is a case of 'my small group is around me', the next, 'my small group is scattered'. These repeated and shifting changes of position in space give rise to additional questions: 'Why these changes?'; 'In what way has my neighbour changed?'; 'Into what?'; 'Where has he gone?'; and so forth. One of the characteristics, then, of the large group is an absence of stillness; rather it is a kaleidoscope of experience. The outcome for both the interacting singleton and the I.M. is a sense of skin stretch, based on his neighbour as the last one who spoke but who may be 'out over there'. Such a stretch can reach the proportion of a skin 'burst', to avoid which the I.M. will withdraw and give up. Then he becomes a singleton, and as such a leaver.

The crucial point here is that the I.M's preferred social-response distance for inter-I.M. relations (which facilitates the skin-of-my-neighbour boundary and thus reinforces I.M. status) is constantly being dislocated. Thoreau, in his *Walden*, describes some of the I's problems thus:

One inconvenience I sometimes experienced in so small a house was the difficulty of getting to a sufficient distance from my guest when we began to utter the big thoughts in big words. You want room for your thoughts to get into sailing trim and run a course or two before they make their port. The bullet of your thought must have overcome its lateral and ricochet motion and fallen into its last and steady course before it reaches the ear of the hearer, else it may plough out again through the side of his head. Also our sentences wanted room to unfold and form their columns in the interval . . . . Individuals, like nations, must have suitable broad and natural boundaries, even a considerable neutral ground, between them. I have found it a singular luxury to talk across the pond to a companion on the opposite side. In my house we were so near that we could not begin to hear – we could not speak low enough to be heard; as when you throw two stones into calm water so near that they break each other's undulations. If we are merely loquacious and loud talkers, then we can afford to stand very near together, cheek by jowl, and feel each other's breath; but if we speak reservedly and thoughtfully, we want to be farther apart, that all animal heat and moisture may have a chance to evaporate. If we could enjoy the most intimate society with that in each of us which is without, or above being spoken to, we must not only be silent, but commonly so far apart bodily that we cannot possibly hear each other's voice in any case. Referred to this standard, speech is for the convenience of those who are hard of hearing: but there are many fine things which we cannot say if we have to shout. As the conversation began to assume a loftier and grander tone, we gradually shoved our chairs farther apart till they touched the wall in opposite corners, and then commonly there was not room enough.[13]

The comparatively small social distances of the small group can easily be filled both by the immediacy of the neighbour's presence as also by the use of facile generalisations and clichés. For the large group it has to be massive slogans if the social distances involved are to be covered. Thus the singleton of the large group, in his attempts to establish and then preserve the skin-of-my-neighbour on which his I.M. state depends, is constantly struggling to get in touch with, respond to, and have responses from those other I.Ms, but is for ever experiencing difficulties in the matter, some of which will be discussed below. A further result of his difficulties is that he finds himself more and more forced back into a frame of reference of self-referral, and consequently he becomes less and less neighbour-orientated. As movement away from the other I.Ms starts, so detachment from the skin-of-my-neighbour occurs and two particular states of the I.M. can then be seen to emerge.

The first, an intermediate one, is best described by coining the word 'disarroy'. Here the I.M. finds himself in a state of complete bewilderment accompanied by a sense of an established I.M.-world falling apart from the fracturing of his boundaries as he experiences a widely varied and disturbing range of response impingements. As a person wishing to participate in the large group, for him the world neither stands still nor remains the same, so that the kaleidoscopic bombardment becomes synonymous with and part of change. Hence 'disarroy' becomes the over-whelming experience, including a picture that the world can never be the same again. The word 'disarroy' is used here not only to describe the actual experience of change, with an inherent notion of disintegration and collapse, but also to indicate the presence of a wish to return to the *status quo ante*, with further wishes not to know, never to return and would that he had never been there. At times, this situation of the I.M. in disarroy is defended against as well as mirrored by the emergence in the large group of a paradise myth, the I.M. seeing himself as being expelled from the Garden of Eden, with a loss of innocence and with knowledge as a feared, even unnecessary eruption into what should be a quiet and peaceful existence. At the same time there are present wishes to return to such a state of blissful ignorance, as if ignorance could be recreated.

The second and more extreme state is when the individual member passes through this intermediate state of disarroy into a state of simple idiosyncrasy, expressed in bizarre behaviour. This may take the form of reading a newspaper, doing a cross-word puzzle, sitting at a window with half his body outside and half inside the room, or placing his chair at a distance from the group in some markedly individualistic position. It would seem

that the purpose of such idiosyncratic behaviour is to enable the
individual member to remain of the group and so to be present
at the group. It would be incorrect to describe such a member
as having left the group, because his behaviour acquires its very
meaning, both for him and for the large group, by taking place
within the context of that group and reflecting its own idiosyncratic relationship to the group. By such bizarre modes of
behaviour the I.M. can remain at the group and avoid becoming
a leaver; nor need he revert to the singleton state, as one who
in this situation would have definitely shaken the dust of the
group off his feet. The term 'alienation' appropriately describes
such a member, who has lost his I.M. status through the rupture
of or interference with his boundaries as a result of his interaction with the group, and who is therefore on his way to becoming an isolate, though his behaviour still reflects and is part
of the group dynamic.

This changed state is essentially one of deprivation of the
necessary external boundary, with things – events, noise, people –
pouring into him and continuing to happen to him. It is thus
greatly different from being a singleton, whose state contains
an important dimension of intactness, though intactness may
itself denote self-restrictiveness, inhibition and self-preservation.
On the contrary, the individual member, having now become
thus alienated, experiences no such sense of intactness. Furthermore, this state has an element of estrangement. The sympathy
has broken. Alienation, in its secondary meaning, also fitly
describes the now disrupted I.M. as he seeks to hand over to
other I.Ms or to the large group as a whole those aspects of the
situation which have resulted in interference with his boundaries.
This action of handing over is a vital aspect of self-recovery,
whether it leads to a restoration of the I.M. state or to a definite
reversion to the state of being a singleton.

The nature of the response situation
It is not merely that in the large group the singleton is subjected to
a continuous bombardment of responses – 'There is so much noise
I cannot hear myself think' – and that responses come from

all directions, near and far, but also that the quality of the responses offered is poor. Many an I.M. statement is actively ignored: not only does it not elicit a response but it is cut off at source, ending there in space, treated as a non-event, with the result that much of the discussion is discontinuous, or disjointed and non-syntactical, remaining idiosyncratic to the individual opening speaker. This disjointedness is also expressed in such statements as 'I want to go back to what the last but one speaker said', there being no sense of following on. Following on gets slowed down. Often, too, a statement is answered oppositionally, hence there is no forwarding. Thus A reports that he feels anxious and B responds: 'I feel nothing of the sort', perhaps with a further addition: 'You, A, are exaggerating'. While this interchange may help I.M. differentiation, the response is so clearly blocking that it leads only to isolation on an I.M.-becoming-singleton basis. In the absence of forwarding responses, repetitious statements are likely to abound, leading to rigidly held points of view, which results in non-adaptation both for the I.M. and the group. Under these conditions the singleton state persists: the large-group I.M. state does not develop.

Because responses come from all directions, the initiating singleton who seeks a response is faced with a choice of responses as he tries to establish his I.M. identity. In small face-to-face groups, a member can almost instantaneously discover who made the reply and where it came from. What is more, the response will usually come from the person whom the originating I.M. addressed. This is important when the responding statements contain projective material as: 'Is it that you feel so and so?' or 'I think you are saying such and such', and so on. An acknowledgement makes sense; a contradiction can be immediately corrected. But more often than not this response location does not happen in the large group, where the noise bombardment prevents distinguishability. So the response becomes background noise, not communication, and therefore not only fails to help Is to distinguish between each other but actively weakens the I.M's status. For both the singleton and the I.M. it is not just a matter of not being heard, which may be difficult enough, but, worse, he finds himself lumped together with all the other I.Ms as 'those over there'. Thus the response has probably as much chance of coming from a non-addressed, non-projected-into quarter, as from the member actually addressed. Similarly, not only is the response unexpected, acquiring an 'I was not speaking to you' quality, but it is now more difficult to match the response with the initiating statement, and, if the responding statement contains projective material, to ascertain the degree of fit. In general, when an I.M. projects, he wishes to know if there is fit, and if it relates to the other I.M. whom he is addressing. But if he cannot test congruency, disarray – the disjunction of the socially usual – takes place, with its own consequences, usually in the direction of silence and withdrawal, and so to alienation. Because these and other complications abound it becomes very difficult to establish any sense of familiarity with the situation. Responses from the centre are treated as dangerous. Responses beyond the immediate vicinity seem to come from way-out-there, where 'out there' appears uninvolved or indifferent by reason of physical distance rather than by actual uninvolvedness or real indifference. In any case, because the response is from a distance it makes it difficult to test the projection fit.

Then there is also the problem of the attempting-to-respond I, who sees his I.M. status dependent on giving an appropriate response. If, as is quite often the case in this seeming free-for-all, his contribution is not taken up (whether because of a lack of immediacy, a feeling of distance adding to incomprehension or a sense of doubtful relevance – all causing delays which produce a change in context – or a reply he does not recognise as related to his earlier question), the I.M. thus seeking to communicate, by addressing or replying, feels his responsiveness is not used. The I.M's immediate experience, corresponding with factual reality, is that of being ignored. Because ignored, though still in relation with other I.Ms and the group as a whole, his position inevitably becomes idiosyncratic and bizarre. Disarroy, then threatens. As that state begins to emerge, it requires the use of centripetal strength to overcome the centrifugal forces inherent in disarroy, if there is to be recovery and restoration of I.M. status and skin-of-my-neighbour continuity. In many ways, it is easier for the I.M. to continue idiosyncratic and bizarre, which his subsequent behaviour reflects.

Delays in response cause further difficulty. Only rarely and between members who know each other well is the response immediate, or as the French would say, *'du tic au tac'*. Irrelevant cross-fire occurs and if a topic is to be pursued by 'going back to the last but one speaker' it requires a coordination of resources which is rarely forthcoming. Part of the problem is that the delay is also due to an internal sorting-out process within each I.M. as he experiences what it is like to speak and to take in apparent responses in the large group. Replies from an un-expected direction do not help: 'Was that meant for me?' Delays may additionally occur in taking in – the introjective process – because of the anxieties about the real or seeming massiveness of the large group. Because the large group is perceived as large, the reply is also presumed to be large, perhaps larger than the individual who has to take it in. The fact of distance may lead the respondent to raise his voice or to speak forcefully. Un-expected outbursts – a not infrequent occurrence – also raise the threshold of anxiety about the nature of the reply to be taken in. Therefore at the taking-in stage there is heightened anxiety which contains a fear of being swamped. The sense, too, of being judged, the fantasy that what has just been said in reply is a condemnation, especially when it comes from a consultant, may so increase anxiety that the response is not heard and hence not taken in. Many of the requests to a consultant to repeat what he has said arise not only from such factors as distance, tone, and loudness of voice, etc., but also from this initial belief that some-thing critical and damning has been said and an original assump-tion that it was best not heard. All these factors, especially the last one, contribute to the de-skilling of the I.M. and so promote an M.I. or *Lumpenproletariat* state. The consultants, too, are apt to become part of this de-skilling process through a require-ment to be so simple in their interpretative work as to be banal.

Even when these preliminary anxieties have been overcome

and the response has been taken in, there is the further difficulty of internally relating the now introjected response to what was initially said, the I.M's perspective on this being changed by the intervening period of anxiety and failure to recognise that the response was meant for him. Such is the impact of the internal delay upon him that he may even have difficulty recalling what he said.

Nor do the anonymous references to 'the speaker over there' help. The I.M's preferred behaviour in such circumstances is to withdraw from his skin-of-my-neighbour contact and to sort out the received response within himself quietly and at leisure, foregoing immediacy. For the moment, the threatened return to the singleton state is paramount. Verbal contribution which follows this seems to be defensive in nature, related to the I's needs to assert his distinctive I.M-ness, often by vehement contradiction: 'That is not what I said'. Differentiating himself thus, the I.M. minimises the risk of being taken over by the other. These further interchanges or attempts to define may reveal an even more frightening sense of extension or inflation: 'but that goes beyond what I said', together with an experience of receiving enlarging endowments. It is noticeable that statements of agreement, a simple 'yes' or 'I agree', are rarely heard, perhaps because they carry elements of fusion with the responding I.M., even to the extent of being made into this other I.M. at a time when differentiation is the major requirement.

The I.M's search in his listening to responses is for demarcation, for a response which will strengthen him in his self-differentiation from others and thereby confirm him as an I.M. Moreover, this internal sorting-out presents the I with an awareness of internal depth, of his intrapsychic life having internal extensiveness, with some items being as it were in the foreground of the mind, others part of the background, others loose in the middle-ground, and all with varying degrees of ready accessibility, including his own most recent statements. Hence the problems: 'Will I find?'; 'What will I find?' Perhaps there is nothing, an emptiness, a void.

The I's withdrawal from the immediate current external

large-group situation for these internal sorting-out purposes
has further consequences. For when the I.M., having sorted
things out within himself, and perhaps now knowing what he
wishes to say further, returns to the external scene, the situation
in the large group may have become by then so different that
the I.M. cannot recognise it as having to do with the one he had
just left. His about-to-be-offered further response now seems
irrelevant or, if offered, is apt to fall flat, having through the
time-lag become out-of-context. From his withdrawal he may not
be able to refer to the 'last but one speaker': it may all seem ages
ago. To become silent and to withdraw further may then seem
the best and most relevant behaviour. But his initial withdrawal
for sorting-out purposes and now his silence have tended to
put him in a position of isolation, separated from his neighbour,
whom he now may no longer recognise or know about, and so,
weakened in his I.M. boundaries, he becomes further out of
touch, approaching disarroy, vulnerable to both the group's
attacks and to alienation.

In this area of the I.M's wish to obtain and give responses, his
vulnerability is further increased by his difficulties in the large
group in establishing a sense of 'familiarity'. There are two
fundamental aspects to this: to establish a known picture of the
other, and to test what each other I.M. will tolerate as his contribution. Compared with the small group, where these two events
occur almost simultaneously, it takes much longer for the developing singleton to recognise other separate I.Ms, hopefully in
increasing numbers, and to ascertain the climate of feeling in
the large group, and what it will accept and find relevant to take
up. The greater the singleton's familiarity with the other I.Ms,
the more he can be an I.M. and treat the other I.Ms as distinct,
separate I.Ms. Familiarity, by facilitating differentiation, can thus
help the I.M. in his struggle against homogenisation, which
as we have seen encourages fusion, fosters the M.I. state, and so
contributes to the disappearance of the boundaries of all I.Ms.

On the basis of a known picture of the other I.Ms and a known
climate of feeling in the large group, the singleton-becoming-
I.M. can risk an output, the element of risk being that such an

output carries with it an image of the speaking singleton. Hence the frequent enquiries that occur, more it seems in large groups than in small groups: 'Did I say the right thing?', or, 'How did it sound?' In all groups the singleton needs a confirmatory picture of himself from the group, especially for the establishment and strengthening of I.M. status, and in the large group additionally from a neighbour I.M. Hence the singleton-becoming-I's wish to hear himself quoted either by name or by content or preferably both, to promote his differentiation from other I.Ms: 'Yes, that is what I said'. From this statement, self-evaluation, as an essential part of the establishment of I.M-ness, can begin to take place on a 'This is me, that is you' basis.

In the context of the large group, self-assessment has three basic features: first, a sense of relevance and of sequence with regard to his own contribution in relation to the other's contribution, and hence of being in touch, as part of the process of establishing skin-of-my-neighbour. Secondly, the I.M. hopes that what he has said will add something to the discussion, contribute his part to the construction of a consecutive whole, and thereby strengthen the positive or creative forces within him. Not to be quoted, or, more grossly, to be told that what he has said is 'wrong', implies a negative self-evaluation. Thirdly, if the I.M. has been in touch and relevant, if what he has said is right, built on, and hence appears to be creative, not only is the confirmatory picture of himself positive and good, but also the I has a growing sense of importance, and hence of strength and firmness in his I.M. boundaries.

But in the large group, which by its size creates a sense of so many singletons, the transitional I has the greatest difficulty in establishing any sense of familiarity. There seem to be few possibilities of obtaining such a confirmatory picture of himself. It all remains bewilderingly strange. Furthermore, the absence of quotation, especially quotations linked with names, has a significance beyond the mere ignoring of something said. The lack of quotations not only prevents self-evaluation but also, because the I.M. is identified with what he has said or put out, any absence of reference by other I.Ms underlines the notion of the participant in such a group being part of an inevitable process of annihilation. Thus, in groups, particularly in the large group, silence has not only the meaning of being ignored but also, through the concreteness of the situation, of being eliminated, rendered non-existent. It is not just that an I.M's statement has fallen flat, but that through silence as an activity, it has been made into nothing. Nor at other times is the struggling singleton helped in his strivings to become an I.M. by hearing himself quoted, since the quotation can be such a distortion of what he originally said, needing so much correction and restatement, that he is by no means reassured about his fate. With response-interchanges perceived as distortions, which the originating I.M. dare not let stand unchallenged for fear of losing his identity, he soon becomes immersed with other I.Ms in mutually correc-tive manoeuvres, with the phrase 'being immersed in' revealing the very fear of being lost in each other, with uncertainty of outcome as to who will be who: I-ness is not enabled to develop.

The I.M. in his endeavour to establish familiarity will use the 'search for models' technique to find a model appropriate for the establishment of a suitable familiarity pattern. The model that might seem the most appropriate to use in such a group situation would be that of the family where, as the etymology of the word implies, familiarity of response is fully established, for instance:

'That always upsets mother.'
'That will make father angry; wait until he has had his supper before you tell him.'
'Son, Peter, when upset, always behaves in that way,' and so on.

In a family, given such and such circumstances, each member will play their allotted part or speak their familiar lines. Any change in the pattern comes as a shock and has a significance to be evaluated. On the basis of such familiarity, response-time is of secondary importance. Thus letter-writing in a family can be on a weekly basis, while lovers, who in their complicated mutual projections are as yet unfamiliar with each other, have to write daily. But in the large group the family familiarity model cannot be successfully applied because of all the response disturbances already described. The point is clearly demonstrated in the frequent denials by members such as lecturers, clerics, industrial managers, of having been in a large group before. Its very familiarity cannot be recognised. This further failure contributes to the I's sense of a constantly threatening state of disarroy.

Unable to use the family familiarity model, the I's defensive move (defensive against disarroy and alienation) is to try to establish an 'identical response'. Thus A says he is angry and B immediately says he does not believe it. B is challenged by C and others – 'How can B say such a thing?' B replies that when he is angry he is immediately and behaviourally angry even before he experiences his feelings of anger, let alone before he thinks he is angry and can therefore say he is angry. How therefore can A say so calmly that he is angry? Thus the I has more and more to use a very personal experience or frame of reference as his model, in contrast to the socialised or relational family one. Being a personally idiosyncratic model, it is not an other-I.M.-directed or relational model. In this instance, its use resulted in B being attacked and his contribution rejected. Hence once again the boundary skin-of-my-neighbour is threatened with disruption, and alienation looms once more, though the establishment of an identicality of response would help to restore the weakened boundary and reaffirm a sense of I.M-ness.

Implied in the notion of familiarity is also the experience of a fit or congruency of projections. Because, in the family familiarity model, the projections fit, there is a feeling of relatedness and not of alienation. When congruency of projections does not occur, the I has an experience of strangeness, of something having gone wrong, of dismay, even of being thrown off-balance. The whole situation then needs re-examination and further exploration. Insight, here the awareness of projection, may then hopefully develop.

The central point is that this awareness of incongruity, of something not quite right, secures that there is some move by its original possessor to recover the projection within himself, thus promoting the self-evaluation process and the establishment of I/other boundaries. By implication, it stresses the importance of recovery of a projection as a possibility. However, recoverability in turn depends both on the degree of neighbour proximity and on familiarity. If there is no familiarity, fit or non-fit becomes fortuitous, possibly based on stereotypes such as doctors, clergymen, industrialists etc., thinking so-and-so and behaving thus. Equally, even where familiarity or fit exists, if the familiar neighbour is not in close visible proximity, it may not be promptly recognised. Hence in the large group, because the testing of fit and the recovery of projections by family familiarity model as a social skill is in jeopardy, the possibilities of alienation for the I are increased and his sanity likewise endangered. The breakdown of the I in the large group, with the release of psychotic violence, is thus an ever-present possibility. What the large group constantly demonstrates is that man's sanity in interpersonal relations in part depends upon the fit of projections, in which case they need not be recognised as such, and also on their recovery when they are misfitting or non-congruent for insightful work.

Once again the alternative for the I is to be silent, with all its increased possibilities for alienation or reversion to the singleton state. There is an important preliminary stage to this, which is maladaptive. Since the I cannot recover his projections, self-correction becomes impossible as does consequent responsive behaviour. As an attempt to recover balance and remain an I.M., the threatened I perseverates, either by repetitively stating his point of view or attitude, or by acting out a stereotyped role regardless of the circumstances in which he finds himself. Such tenacious behaviour, however, shows the extremes to which the I feels himself driven in his attempts to preserve his relational boundaries and his essential I-ness.

A significant and appropriate method for coming to grips with this projection-recovery problem is the use of the presence of the four consultants, who amongst other things act as a projection receptacle. Because of their known and identifiable presence and location, and the consistency of their behaviour, projections on to them prove recoverable and hence insights can start to develop. It is highly important therefore that the consultant should keep to the established boundaries, for instance as to the time and accurate representation of what is being said, since he thereby contributes to the creation of an encompassable situation at which each can work for the preservation of his I.M. status. Nor should the importance of the consultants' working amongst themselves on these projections be underestimated: on the contrary, it is imperative that they should do work in this area. Thus for instance, in groups, and to the projecting I.M., the endowment of the other, in this instance the consultants, is in the first place a deprivation of the endowing I.M.: 'You are more intelligent than I', which thereby deprives the endowing I.M. of an appreciation of his own intellectual ability. But in addition it reinforces the singleton's feeling that I activity in a group is only to become lost in the other. The consultants, on the other hand, by sharing their work on the projections with the group are implicitly offering opportunities to the projecting I.M. both to re-acquire what he has projected and so to end the depriving process, and perhaps also to increase his understanding. But even more: by not allowing the received projections to get lost inside them – a possibility when the consultants are either alone or in a pair, but less so when a sub-group – the consultants help by their interpretive discussion to construct a bounded situation, which in turn offers further possibilities for the projection-recovery process. For the I in the large group the fate of his projections is intimately linked with his own fate, whether he can become an I.M. or not, both symbolising it and embodying it. However much he may wish his projections to be unrecognised through disappearance inside the other member or consultant, its complete disappearance implies that this too might be his ultimate fate. Bounding, and hence recoverability, is a very positive reassurance against this ultimate terror. The problem, however, for both I and consultants is that the making-available or handing-back process can very easily acquire a boomerang quality, so that, for instance, the intellectual superiority with which the self-impoverishing I endows the consultants, apparently returns to annihilate him by a display of interpretative brilliance.

The large group and its encompassability

One of the major attractions of the small group is that it is easily encompassable. The eyes can take in the whole situation at a single glance, thereby encouraging some idea that the situation can come under the control of the would-be I.M. But the prospective I.M. in the large group perceives it as larger than he can encompass at one such glance. In addition to anxieties this arouses, the singleton imagines at first sight that the large group is something he may get lost in, unless there are delineating safeguards about, and these are not immediately visible. Its size as 'vast' and 'beyond my grasp' is a matter for comment. A distinction is made between the inner circle – which is described as 'responsible', 'committed', 'involved', to express the core activity of the group: that is, it can be isolated and so made encompassable and to represent encompassability – and the outer circle – where the I feels 'different', 'remote', 'strange', 'uninvolved', 'elsewhere', 'outside, watching, and uncommitted', the whole situation being presumed too vast to be immediately and wholly taken in. So too at the beginning of a meeting the closing of the door seems to have a finality about it, and appears to symbolise an englobement, a having-to-surrender to this big situation. The atmosphere of the large group carries with it a question: will the situation allow for differentiation as to degrees of engrossment in such a large and presumed totally absorbing situation, or will its demands for surrender be total? In a small group there is no such sense of doomed finality: choices seem to be about, and opting-out less menacing. The problem of vastness is also expressed in the felt and often voiced need for concepts with which to understand the large group, which are not to hand. Their absence is also very much a consultant's experience, faced with the problem of what to interpret. This search for concepts expresses a need to find that which will embrace or encompass. The fact that individual members have great difficulty in finding suitable roles for themselves and each other – except for the unenviable role of the victim, the one who might not survive – does not help. Again one of the advantages of the simpler forms of group life described by Bion[14] is that both leader and member roles are relatively simple to establish and to put in practice, as for instance in the Basic Assumption Group devoted to dependency, with its care-giving leader and its 'casualty', or cared-for member. They are clearly and immediately seen as interrelated. But no similar encompassment seems to be immediately available or discoverable in the large group.

Two further factors contribute to make the whole situation seem so difficult to grasp:

First, because many more people are present, there are many more opportunities for the I to project parts of himself into others. But equally thereby he finds himself very severely fractionated into multiple parts. Worse, while the internal splitting within any one member may be constant, the subsequent projection of these parts both as to people and direction develops a gratuitous element. The arc for the projection can be wide and certainly has depth to include a range of potential recipients. Nor is it clear which of the I.Ms, within that segment will pick up the projected part, it being by no means certain that it will be the I.M. spoken to. The search for location then takes on extreme urgency, particularly, for example, if the reply comes from behind, arousing anal fantasies and fears. Focusing on one particular I.M. has a seemingly harsh or overdetermined quality to it: 'go on', 'speak up', 'repeat', ensuring no escape to the designated recipient of the projection, who is not 'to be let off the hook' for fear of what may happen to the projected part. Should a consultant come in at such a moment of fixing, he will be sharply told, 'Let him speak for himself', 'What are you doing, interfering?'.

Because projection-reception is variable, and because it is difficult to know the subsequent fate of the projected parts, again encompassability seems almost out of the question. How can the I, going from singleton to I.M., encompass the now scattered parts of himself if he cannot keep track of them? Thus split into multiple dispersed parts, the I.M. cannot show his positive qualities. The role becomes static and non-creative. This situation in reverse, the experience of being projected into or filled up with the projected parts of others, was described by a member of a large group thus: 'I am not one in the large group; I have to be many things at any one moment in time. It requires coordination to use these many parts together. I may achieve a sense of unity but it takes time. It also takes work to get the parts inside me to work in me and in a unified way.'15 Furthermore this fragmenting of the I in itself seems to facilitate the release of a now unbound destructiveness, which in turn threatens the possibility of any constructive activity. Here the analogy of an atomic explosion within the ego seems relevant.

Secondly, the apparent vastness of the large group seems to give substance to a fantasy of the singleton/I.M's internal world as also vast, unencompassable, or boundless. The singleton requires of external life in groups a bounded experience to take in as an introject on which to build up his own psychic life-notions of internal boundaries or limitations. But the immediate external picture conjured up by the large group is one of vastness if only because the boundaries do not seem to be directly or immediately visible. Not being visible, seeming to be 'out there', they are not encompassable. In the rooms in which these large groups have met, members have sometimes moved the chairs back to the wall, giving expression to centrifugal forces. Such a move, however, makes the large group seem even bigger than it is in reality; so the I's sense of isolation increases. Needless to say, such moves stretch the skin-of-my-neighbour, threatening I.M. intactness.

In either case, and whichever way the singleton turns, the introject is not limited but appears as vast and unlimited. The singleton in this apparently larger-than-life situation searches internally for a suitable model to help him out, and finds himself also casting back into vastness, into remote and far away times, often with the revival of primitive feelings of helplessness, as also perhaps with new fearful experiences of there being nothing there to find. Searching, he has 'here and now' feelings of a fruitless and endless backward hunt 'through the corridors of time'. Hence the introjected vastness of his external world meets a similar internal experience and by their mutual reinforcement the level of anxiety is raised, requiring a further projection into the outer large group of the now reinforced sense of vastness, only to increase the fantasied percept of the large group as now greater than ever before, not only vast but endless. If the singleton continues to strive to interact with the large group, inevitably this further percept of increased vastness is reintrojected to again build up the internal sense of boundlessness and so to result in a constant projection/introjection struggle, with endlessness ever heightened. An end can be put to this process only by leaving, which is what frequently happens. A further characteristic of such a situation is an outburst of 'yes/no' statements, where the 'no' bounds, delimits, puts an end to, though at a cost to furthering work of a relational kind, while the 'yes' plunges the I further on into, so that, though the study of the relational work seems to be maintained, in fact the I feels and becomes increasingly confused and lost with no wits with which to work.

Nor are the singleton's problems finally resolved by the discovered presence of external boundaries between himself and the other I.Ms and between the group as a whole and the world at large in which it is operating. For the presence of such external boundaries inherently contains the further question of their capacity to hold. If they break down, there will be a flowing together of internal and external worlds, and consequently threats to the survival of the I.M., who is now hurled by the dissolution of the boundaries through the state of I into 'disarroy'. Should the boundary between the group and its external environment break, the I.M. sees himself as precipitated into outer space or at least into a cold, harsh, and unfriendly outside world – in part the creation of his own projections and so created in his own hostile image – where he will be left to perish. Hence the 'encystment' phenomenon in groups, which not only fixes a surrounding boundary, but secures its durability. Needless to say, such encystments result in a loss of work efficiency, the lack of permeability precluding access to outside influences and reality-testing. Armies notoriously fight future wars on the basis of the previous one.[16]

Of considerable importance here too is the part played by silences in a group. Often through silences, the silent I is expressing just such a fear of boundlessness, as if to speak were to commit himself to ongoingness which will lead to an endless, unencompassable situation. Thus sentences tend to be short and long statements actively avoided. The one limits; the other prolongs. Some of this fear is also expressed in the anxiety that what the I.M. has said will be subjected to exaggeration from others, to being blown up, to produce a situation larger than himself – as it were – larger than life. So too, at the beginning of a session, it seems as if the member of the large group, no longer singleton, but not yet fully an I.M. – in fact an I – perceives himself as surrounded, therefore bounded, by his own silence. While remaining within his own island of silence he is a singleton. The temptation to remain there is great, since omnipotent mastery seems still within his grasp. To step off into relatedness with others, hence to build up his I.M. status, may be worth attempting, but the move carries the risk of an I turning into an M.I., or worse. The content of this risk is not only to step from the known singleton state into the yet unknown I state, but because the unknown has an unencompassable vastness, there is the further risk of an endless disappearance. On the other hand, the speaking member, whether a singleton or an M.I., as he meets with the silence of the other I.Ms is faced with a dilemma, whether to plunge on – and there will be pressures to do so – or to stay bounded by limiting himself to what he has immediately said, however brief, inconclusive and inadequate an expression of the full range of his thinking and feeling, and then to remain silent. In the main too, the silent singleton would prefer that his silences be treated as non-committal and very strongly resents their being taken as expressing agreement, since to agree is to be involved, perhaps over-involved, and so to be pushed into extremes, and on into boundlessness. Yet if groups are to develop a full sense of responsibility for the consequences of their actions, it is important that silences be treated as expressing commitment, since thereby the positive act of dissent, or withdrawal of responsibility from whatever is happening is recognised and facilitated in its overt expression. At best, on that presumption, the singleton is encouraged to come out of his ambiguous silence and to define himself as an I.M.

This question can be further studied in the following technical problem for the consultants: the length of their interpretations. If an interpretation is too short, it provides limits but will not forward the discussion, nor satisfactorily encompass the total situation, particularly in its evidential aspects; nor will it offer that holding framework which the singleton-becoming-I-becoming-I.M. process requires from the consultants and their interpretations. Condensed summaries tend to be called 'Delphic', their conciseness impeding – so the consultants are told – understanding. On the other hand, if an interpretation is too long it will give rise to anxiety, since it is perceived by the I as not only involving him in some unending situation, mirrored in the interpretation's seeming unendingness – 'When will he stop talking?' 'How long is he going on for?' 'He talks endlessly' – but also as taking him out of his own developing world as an I.M. into the consultant's world, where he may become an M.I. Long interpretations, then, arouse anxiety in terms of a fear of getting lost in them, as well as having, for the listening I, an uncertainty as to which part to latch on to if the whole may not be encompassed. The I.M's requirement is that an interpretation should encompass the situation, thereby bound it, according to his own highly personal limits, leaving him in his original 'here and now' position. Open-endedness, prolongation, a 'What next?' feeling, arouses paranoid anxieties. The I.M's capacity for extension depends on his possession of skills for work in that particular 'here and now' situation, that is, on how secure he is an I.M. If he can work, especially with concepts which themselves extend his understanding of relational experiences he is having, then he is an I.M. If he is still a singleton he may feel discouraged from joining and reaching towards I.M. status, not knowing how to acquire that status. If for what-

ever reason he is an I, that is, a member in transition, he is particularly vulnerable, hence all the more anxious and as such all
the more prone to idiosyncratic behaviour. Driven to extremes,
he must seek to express the idiosyncratic part of himself. His
fear is that in taking in the interpretation he will be taken over,
to find himself elsewhere, with 'elsewhere' pictured as unfamiliar
and fraught with anxiety, and no better off than before the consultant spoke. It may therefore seem easier for him to remain an
unrelating singleton. Why indeed plunge in? Since, however,
the singleton state fails to satisfy his needs for relatedness and
hence for the I.M. state, to be achieved perhaps initially through
relating to the consultant, he now experiences the consultant's
long-winded behaviour as frustrating to both his needs and his
aspirations. Anger is therefore directed at the offending consultant and attempts made, by shaming him, to get him to modify
his behaviour. These procedures also enable the I to draw back
from any fusion process with the consultant's interpretation and
hence with the consultant. Fears of being lost in endlessness are
for the moment diminished. The threatening flux of the I state
recedes: singleton or I.M. status seems once again possible.

Hence, for the consultant, the balance of brevity and length of
interpretation is a delicate one, particularly as the listening
consultant has also been subjected to the bombardment of interchanges in the group and may therefore have some difficulty
in finding precisely what he wishes to say. In group work it is not
an uncommon experience for the consultant to find the 'because'
clause of an interpretation emerging as he delineates the 'here
and now' situation and marshals the relevant evidence. He too,
like the other I.M.s though helped by his consultant role, has a
welter of data inside himself and feels inundated. By putting
distance between himself and this data through talking it out,
he is better able to master it. He may not be able to do the
necessary sorting out in silence and within himself while the
bombardment outside him continues. He may only be able to
do so by talking, as it were 'taking up the cudgels'. As he starts,
so he gets silence, thereby revealing the nature of his authority,
and as he gets under way he begins to get on top of his data, to

underline major themes, and so prepare for his 'because' clause. In all this he shares in the I.M. experience, but averts the I status, though he has experienced its threatening arousal, which may indeed be the prompting of his 'interpretation' and the cause of his initial difficulty in enunciating it. But like all singletons and I.Ms, what else can he do? In retrospect, and as a theoretical proposition, a consultant's best policy would seem to be frequent short interventions rather than biding his time for a more massive, global one, though the latter is very tempting, with its sense of omnipotent control.

There is yet another way of looking at this question of endlessness, namely, in terms of the very great difficulty the I.M. has in the large group in making his past available and bringing forward a model from the past to cope with his 'here and now' situation. The past as a model seems remote in the large group: it is somewhere there, but in the depths. Whereas on occasion in the small group when up against 'here and now' difficulties members readily and exhaustively start on a discussion of their past experiences, searching for something relevant, no such discussion ever seems to take place in the large group. This hopeful interaction between members and the past has its enchanting qualities. That in fact as the discussion proceeds none of the hoped for positive gain emerges from these small-group deliberations is quite another matter! To have held such views seems sufficiently satisfying in itself. The point has been made; the past is immediately available: another world has been re-established and continuity is possible. Also the I.M's exchange of experiences of their common past encourages fusion feelings and strengthens group cohesion. The past here acts as a background both externally to the group as a whole and intra-psychically for the individual members, bounding both the group externally and each individual member within himself internally. But in the large group, past experiences are very rarely discussed. They do not seem to be readily available. Yet despite fears to the contrary, individuals do survive. A sense of the past could prove this. However, this piece of history is not brought forward in evidence for present reassurances.

If there is a past in the large group it is in the sense of tradition: 'We have always done things that way'.[17] Here tradition is revealed as something which has taken place over time rather than as recent events. Time in the large group seems to be experienced as duration, or at least longevity.[18] Thus groups at a moment of change refer to their glorious past and to achievements that almost overnight have taken on solid virtues. If in a more newly formed large group such a tradition cannot be mobilised, myth-making fills the vacuum and promotes in the I increased fears of being taken over by this mythical world, in which he now finds himself and which he cannot check against reality. An ability to mobilise and use his internal models is part of the I.M's skill to survive in the non-historical 'here and now'. Deprived of this skill, he experiences the present as too present or too immediate. Once again the I finds himself driven either to pull out and so go through the states of disarroy and alienation, perhaps even reverting to being a singleton, or to passive surrender to the group M.I. status and thus to homogenisation.

Part of the difficulty in finding a model is that to cast back requires a detachment from the present 'here and now' situation. But this detachment is in the first place impeded by the immediacy of the demands of the present experience, particularly the noise bombardment, which serves to tie the struggling singleton-becoming-I.M. into the 'here and now' behaviour of the group which it is his stated task to study. The experience of the 'here and now' and the novelty of the task set exert a fascination and a powerful curiosity over the singleton, a wish not to miss anything. There is little doubt but that the I does experience a sense of having to use force to tear himself away from this englobing group, which centripetally binds him, so that however open the doors, he cannot leave. He has not the strength to wrench himself centrifugally away; nor is he encouraged by the prospect of the alternative experience of lurching as it were backwards into the boundless depths of his intrapsychic age in search of a model, with the risk that after an exhausting search he may discover that there never was anything there. This fruitless search underlines the singleton's earliest fears of skill inadequacy and hence adds to his general sense of bewilderment on joining the large group. Very often it seems that all the I finds is an unhelpful early family experience of helplessness. If in the face of these difficulties the internal search is abandoned, the I returns to the present in an even more anxious state of mind. It is then, bereft of I.M. skills, that the I is prone to lapse into M.I. status. It would seem that the lesson to be learnt is to stay as close as possible to the present and to survive through unadulterated living-in-the-present, though this is essentially at a cost to learning. The boundary between I.M. and M.I. becomes a tightrope, which it often is, in fact.

On the other hand, because of the anxieties of an external and internal endlessness, because of the constant threats of disruption in the I.M's skin-of-my-neighbour boundary such an internal search for models represents, because of the strangeness of the general external situation, in which there is no immediately discoverable role for the singleton seeking to become an I.M., and because all these factors give rise to a massive sense of inadequacy in each joining singleton or even each participating I, *if* any I.M. should chance to discover a model, a concept or a clue to help in this bewildering and confused 'here and now', he will cling to it most tenaciously as some personal truth, not to be shared. In these situations the I.M's thoughts become so intensely his own even as to endanger his I.M. status, since their personal quality precludes communication and collaboration. Whatever it is that the I.M. may have found within himself is thus preciously kept within himself to become the sole object of his total love, too precious to be tried out in the outside world, which is now perceived as wholly dangerous to, totally destructive of, such discoveries, and hence at all costs not to be engaged with. These are his only remaining possessions, his ultimate confirmation of himself as an I.M., though now as he keeps them to himself and lapses into silence, he becomes less and less an interacting I.M. and so is more and more subjected to disarroy and alienation, and hence reversion to singleton state. This fear of sharing what he has, his inner good, with the world outside is expressed for instance in the common large-group phenomenon where those who agree with the consultants, perceiving them to be right or to have a contribution to make, are silenced or remain silent while those who wish to attack and destroy the consultants are noisily vocal. Clearly the good cannot be revealed to and risked with these I.Ms. Here the splitting and projection of love and hate is at its height and is most clearly seen.

The large group and violence

Let us consider now the phenomenon of violence, which is perhaps one of the major characteristics of the large group, especially in terms of the initial anxiety experienced by its members. As an I.M. of one such large group said: 'The large group is not for the sick, the troubled, or the faint-hearted.' For the control of violence the large group has had to evolve a quite specific and characteristic structure.

The idea of violence is present in many forms, often – especially initially – as a nameless fear, a threat of something that is around, something that is going to happen, voiced in such simple statements as 'I am frightened'. Again it may be expressed through the I's silence, the expression of an unwillingness to talk about this fear and so to give it content, as also in the quiet, lowered, almost inaudible tones adopted by some members. To talk loudly would be to lower the threshold for violence and so almost to provoke it. The motto is that of: 'Let sleeping dogs lie.' On talking, a member may report a sense of 'being dehumanised', 'being made into something animal'. Violence may also find expression as a fantasy directing behaviour: so that search parties are sent for absentees. No piece of behaviour can be treated as innocent, as if all behaviour was both the expression and the result of some present destructive force. The fantasy may be of something going on in the middle, as at a bull-fight, the centre circle therefore to be avoided, and of those in the outer circle as present at a 'bread and circuses' occasion, expressed in almost gleeful wishes that something will happen. The demand for action – itself a characteristic release phenomenon in groups – adds a further impetus, such action to be concrete. This 'bread and circuses' or search for a spectacle theme may refer to the consultants, with the hope that they will quarrel, contradict each other, or otherwise get at each other's throats. Violence finds its chief expression, however, as a myth – myths being the product of inter-member interactions in group situations: the myth of a sacrifice, of the immolation of a victim possibly at Stonehenge, the myth of mob rule, or the myth of errant forces at work, as in Goya's picture of 'Rumour'.

The immediate object of the violence is some I.M., usually one who is seeking to maintain and develop his individuality. Such behaviour or expression of personal feeling, and then of this upsurge of I-ness, is totally unacceptable. Its implied individuality is anathema. It must be crushed. Thus an I.M. remarks 'I nearly burst into tears,' and his statement is greeted with laughter. He is left isolated, almost a figure of fun. Another, who has been note-taking and has made it quite clear that for him note-taking is a vital means of surviving, reports that he has not been able to continue doing so, and the response is again loud, massive laughter. He was on the road to being thrown; his defence was personal; the laughter now completely throws him and nobody protests. An I.M. thinks that he has learned something from the large group and is challenged to explain what it is. He tries to do so, fumblingly tails off, and the group's response is mocking laughter, never help. Or, as a member also tries to express something personal to him as an I.M., some feeling that he has had about the large group, the tension will noticeably rise as he is questioned and in turn strives to explore and explain himself. Hopefully it seems that he may fail; there is relief if he gets through. Often it will be some volunteer who is egged on: 'Why don't you try? Go on, do it', or: 'You say you are frightened, why don't you leave?' At the same time he is filled up with other I.M. statements and there is no let-up: 'You say you are upset. Why don't you tell us some more?' Once the process is on, there is no crying off or stopping.

In such circumstances the I.M. feels threatened in his role: the I state emerges, with the search to express some personal, intimate part of himself – his I-ness – and the large group, by its 'say more' behaviour, seems to encourage this very self-expression. At such a moment this transitional I is at his most vulnerable. To him, it appears that the large group wishes to be present at his annihilation. It seems that the wish is to make him into an I.M., his role and state to be solely defined by the group: 'Tell us – go on – explain more – what do you mean?', and so to become the object of this large group's will. It should also be noted that although on such occasions some members do not go along with such 'hunt' situations, they remain silent and seem unable to exercise any authority over it. Nor does their silence help the endangered I. The I may thereby take the drastic step of withdrawing – though he is not in too good a condition to achieve this – if the imagined breakdown (fantasied too as the group's aim and maybe with some reality) is not to occur. Under such conditions breakdowns are not unknown. It is then that disarroy threatens and alienation can occur.

A further aggravation may arise from the I.M's wish, or his seeming wish, in the eyes of other I.Ms, to support the work of the consultants. By so doing, he may be judged to be thinking for himself, which in itself is heinous. To work with the consultants not only helps to make the I.M. state more secure, it also certainly helps in the struggle not to become an M.I. But with the emergence of violence, the large group – and its members are projectively identified with this aim – seeks to put its mark on all the members. Hence the vulnerability of the fumbling transitional I at such moments. The I's crucial struggle is to seek to re-establish his I.M. role and hence survive. To do so is to escape the large group's imprint. Only if he becomes an M.I. will the large group be satisfied. Participation in large groups is thus fraught with dangerous ambiguities: who to be? what will happen? – ambiguities which as the scent is to the hunt add their quota of danger and hence of violence.

Much of this violence, especially in the early stages of its emergence, is experienced by the consultants as well as directed at them. They will be told not to exaggerate as if, echo-wise, this would bring the felt violence into being. It is stressed that they should be ultra-professional and neutral; all anger, sarcasm, rebukes – these being members' fantasies about their tone of voice – to be kept at bay as if they might give expression to such feelings by their behaviour and reflect the anger that is around, hastening the onset of violence. They are heard as voicing the unmentionable. Furthermore, like the members, the consultants experience the strength of the de-skilling that takes place in these circumstances and which threatens their capacity for effective work. As already mentioned, consultants experience difficulty in working at a description of the situation and at their interpretations. It is borne in on them that there will be pleasure if they fail and that they are struggling with forces which seek to prevent their finding the necessary concepts and holding ideas. *They* are to be homogenised like the rest. They too therefore experience personal needs for self-assertion. To start talking may be a means whereby a consultant recovers his memory. But as he works to put internal distance between his actual experience and his working self, he can never be sure that he will come across his explanation of the underlying dynamic. That too may have disappeared in the welter of internalised cross-talk. It is hard work – touch and go. It would seem then that a consultant's difficulties mirror the members' difficulties. Often these difficulties result in his making more frequent interventions than he might in other situations, for instance in a small group. Technically this may be wise. For increased frequency of interventions has in itself a stabilising and normative effect, though it may encourage the use of the consultants as a projection-receptacle.

In this context of violence the notion of the consultants' acting as a projection-receptacle, especially if there are three to four of them, is very important. It is certainly a dynamic to which they must be sensitive. Each consultant must therefore give an important part of his attention to its study, and seek to include in it not only what is being put into him individually but what is also being put into his colleagues, how they are being used relationally, individually, and as a sub-group, and hence to elucidate the nature of the overall picture that between them they have come to represent. What the consultants experience in this situation becomes more and more a mirror image of the experience and fate of each individual member, and hence may have important foretelling aspects, particularly with regard to the possible presence of violent destructive forces.

A word of technical warning: because very often the anger of the I.M. or of the I caught in such processes as singleton-becoming-I.M. or I.M.-becoming-M.I. or I.M.-becoming-what next? is a projected anger, the recipient being the consultant, and because it rarely comes from one source but from many and hence has a summation quality to it, this anger in transit may be experienced as arising quite suddenly within the introjecting consultant. Additionally, he may be the only consultant to experience it, because as part of a more general splitting process the other consultants are to be split off from him. As part of his work, however, he will start to talk about the experience of being angry, thereby using it constructively. He may then encounter a not unusual response from the I.M's frank disbelief. This disbelief may have two further consequences. First, to leave him with the anger and hence to isolate him. Secondly, to fill him up further with angry reproaches: 'How can he say such a thing?' 'It must be his imagination!' or 'I get really pissed off when I hear the consultants talk like that' – which serves to isolate him further. Now his survival is at stake. To climb back, as it were, or get on top of this situation, he may have to use force, maybe by speaking loudly or emphatically, commanding silence by his weighty entry or personal self-assertiveness; so to be told he is 'obviously angry'. Something of an impasse is reached. To be silent about such experiences originating from the group is to go under. To assert such experiences verbally is to be violent. The technical solution is the interpretation of both aspects – to go under or to survive by domination – where both aspects reflect also the I.M's problems, when he is at risk as an I.

This situation of violence comes about from a number of factors, each reinforcing the other. The size of the large group *is* frightening: violence then is the outcome of the fears and frustrations of expressing oneself in such a large situation. Part of the fear is: what will the vast size of the large group do

E

to the small individual singleton or I.M.? The difficulties in finding roles and the constant threat of loss of skills do not help the
I.M. to have confidence in the potential benevolence of the large
group or the hope of acquiring a stature adequate to its mastery.
The fragmentation of the I, both through response-bombardment
and through multiple projections, serves to weaken his search
for I.M. status, and hence he becomes vulnerable. The frequent
and repeated rupture of the I.M. preferred social response distance means that his boundary at his neighbour's skin is in
constant flux. Nor is his vulnerability reduced by his frequent
periods of abstraction as he breaks off contact from the immediacy
of the large group to take stock of his situation, and thereby
ruptures his contact with his neighbour's skin. It is an impoverished I.M. who is trying to deal with this situation, whose efforts
are directed at keeping his skin intact as best he can though in a
puny way. It is very difficult, if not almost impossible, for an
I.M. to develop the skills requisite for the maintenance of
that role in the absence of an experience of successful work.
Thus the flux of the I state is on him. Whichever way he turns,
disarroy and alienation threaten. Overall, it is as if the I, as he
strives to remain in continuous contact with the rapidly deterior-
ating 'here and now' situation of the large group and seeks to
establish and maintain the I.M. role, becomes the very seat of
an atomic explosion with a consequent release of enormous
destructive forces, directed against all that the situation contains.
Violence emerges. Coming from more than one I.M., it summates.

The problem of violence, especially in its origin, interacts
with the question of the location of responsibility. In groups,
responsibility easily moves away from the level of the uncommitted singleton or even the committed I.M. to a vague and
general level. Detached from a personal responsibility, it manifests itself as free-floating, with doubts and questions as to its
location. In small groups, particularly of the Basic Assumption
type, responsibility for task-implementation and its consequences
can easily be located in the leader and left with him. But since
the large group has difficulties in finding leaders, as also in leader
myth-making, and so in bringing leaders into being, this process

for giving responsibility a location in known or visible leaders is not so readily available. The presence of antipathetic factions does not help. Responsibility is therefore all the more free-floating. It obviously acquires weight from the very presence of large numbers and seems too big for a single I.M. Unlocated, massive, it belongs to no one and hence tends to become a dominant anxiety. Here again the presence of a sub-group of four consultants can greatly help in giving responsibility a location. But then it is all theirs, a thought often expressed in the following terms: 'You set this up. It is up to you. We can do what we like.'

But the problem of responsibility in the large group goes beyond its lack of location and its massiveness. For as it becomes detached from each member, particularly when an I, and so becomes free-floating, it also assumes stern and frightening qualities. It is perceived as threatening and punishing, out to crush the I.M. and certainly the I in disarroy – caught as it were off-base. Thus the consultants are imagined as being able to trump every trick and as always winning, to the I.M's detriment. So authority and responsibility come to be fused, to be part of the consultants' attributes, who on these grounds are now to be opposed and fought. The aggression in each I is consequently mobilised for this fight. It seems that his very I.M. status depends on the successful outcome of this new aspect of his fight with the consultants. To lose is to be taken over as an M.I. under very punitive conditions. Rousseau's primitive '*Volonté Générale* (General Will)' emerges in opposition to authority and thereby violence is fostered: the constructive, integrative '*Volonté de Tous* (the Will of All)' disappears. Inevitably in such conditions it is more and more difficult to mobilise authority for understanding, when it is so suffused with a threatening responsibility, par-ticularly that of the consultants, for constructive work. This new development itself is fraught with consequences, not only for the control of violence but also for the I in his attempts at main-taining his I.M. position through learning, skill-acquisition and role-development, on which his personal boundaries depend.

As has already been hypothesised, when a group member

finds himself in a strange situation he searches for a suitable model derived from his past experience to help in the current 'here and now'. When, for whatever reasons, there is difficulty in finding such a model, an alternative and possibly quicker solution is to identify with the leadership of the group on the basis that 'He, the leader, knows; if I identify with him, I will be safe'. There is a wealth of evidence to show that small groups, in particular when in difficulties, will with fascinating rapidity identify with a near-to-hand authority, taking their group culture from that authority provided that the chosen authority is available and can be observed. This mimetic assumption of the authority's culture acts protectively, but obviously cannot occur if the chosen leader has to be fought or is not available on other grounds. The large group is therefore in difficulties in using this technique. Furthermore, a vital reason for this imitation is the expectation that thereby the authority will be enabled to act as a mediator and interpreter between the I in disarroy and the group in which the disarroy is occurring. But in the large group, since the consultants have to be fought and cannot therefore be used for identification purposes, equally this mediator-role cannot be brought forward, and once more the I finds himself deprived of a familiar means of survival. As a consequence, the fantasy nature of the harsh talionic authority, easily located in the consultant, cannot be worked on and is hence all the more treated as concrete and real, an actuality. It must therefore be continuously fought with increasing violence. Not to fight it is to be overwhelmed by it.

The notion of errancy

Capping the free-floatingness of responsibility and the opposition of the 'General Will' to the consultants' talionic, crushing weight of authority, is the errancy of the massed violence. The notion of errancy is important to our understanding of the large group, being in itself the expression of the diminished powers of functioning of each member. Errancy is expressed in the fears of exaggeration, hence of something getting out of control, as, for instance, in the group myth of the errant mob. Myths are of course in themselves errant, being of the 'thin air', having no location.

The general notion of errancy is taken from Plato. Initially, in the Ion, Plato discusses the magnetic chain of attraction as between the Muses and the audience and how the links in the chain are held together. Thus the Muses inspired Homer as the magnet moves iron. In turn Ion, the reciter, is moved by Homer, and so the audience is moved by Ion. From the Muses to the audience there is a direct, continuous and responsible chain of links, a concatenation. Then, in the *Timaeus*, Plato raises the further question of the consequences of a break in the links of the chain, resulting in an effect becoming detached or errant. In the context of the *Timaeus*, Plato is referring to cosmic events where the effect consequent on a cause is detached from that cause to become a cause in its own right and to have its own other effects. As an effect-cause it is detached, without responsibility, and so errant. And so with violence in the large group, to which accrue its own effects in detachment and errancy. The consequent problem is its re-attachment and the stabilising of its errancy. It is here again that the consultants, as a sub-group, can play a determining part in the control of the errancy of violence, which for each member of the large group is fantasied as cosmic in its effects. Their presence helps to locate it and, being no longer errant but now located, violence becomes aggression, for understanding, hence for further control and mastery.

The notion of errancy may at first sight appear strange, though it is well known to authors who will report that one of their characters in the process of being created took over and consequently assumed a more important role than originally planned. Professor Bradley believes that this is what happened to Shakespeare with Falstaff who as a character got out of hand. He had to be summarily and brutally disposed of at the end of *Henry IV Part 2* by the Lord Chief Justice, lest he spoil the heroics of *Henry V*.[19] Burke uses the theme of errancy in defence of the American Colonies and argued on this basis in favour of their independence. An embryonic form of errancy can be seen in the small group where a member will get excited over some topic and then as it were 'take off'. In the large group, errancy also occurs in the use of massive slogans which seem necessary to bridge the distance between members. But as is well known, though political slogans may win an election, they later fall to pieces at the slightest puff of the wind of reality-testing. So in the large group, the errancy of violence becomes operative through the absence of reality-checks and the free-floatingness of responsibility, from the non-availability of past models for current 'here and now' use and the singleton-becoming-I.M's difficulty in finding an intra-psychic background boundary.

Group/anti-group dichotomy
The large group's first line of defence for the control of such conditions of violence is to attempt to bring into being a situation of stasis by creating a group/anti-group dichotomy. Thus consultants come to hear of:

    'we – the consultants'
    'men – women'
    'The anxious – the indifferent': 'I feel nothing'
    'The feelers – the non feelers': 'I feel nothing'
    'The silent ones – the talkers'
    'The helpers – the industrialists': 'We know nothing'.

As soon as one side of the equation shows signs of coming to the fore the other side too quickly emerges: so the equation becomes balanced. Though there may be complaints that as a result nothing gets done – 'We can never decide upon anything', 'we have done nothing', 'we have taken no decision', and the like – in fact this is the very aim, that nothing should emerge, it being presumed that what will emerge is violence. Hence stasis is the outcome.

As a defence this dichotomy group/anti-group is not very satisfactory, having in the first place a general weakening effect on the I.M's ability to function and hence his sense of security in the group. It is limiting since the presence of the opposition prevents any further exploration of the contained oppositions. Thus the 'anxious' are not encouraged to discover what they might be anxious about by the 'non-feelers'' statement: 'It leaves me cold'. Since in these group situations skill-development basically depends on a forwarding discussion – the content representing insight – at best, skills can only develop very slowly. In some instances – 'men/women' – the I.M. is not in doubt as to which of the antinomies to belong. Though here there may be elements of group solidarity, the terms of reference are so clearcut that nothing further develops as to content. But this may not be so in other cases – 'the interested/bored' – the I.M. being the former at one time and the latter at another. Then there are frequent changes in sub-group membership and hence the I.M. by such changes in allegiance experiences shifts in identification. Furthermore, a sub-group can be exploited by its anti-group. Thus the 'feelers' are lovingly encouraged by the non-feelers to say what it is they are feeling or what it is they are so frightened about. For the feelers their only hope of maintaining their sub-group would be to remain silent. But this proves more and more impossible as they receive the projected hostilities of the non-feelers in terms of: 'Go on, tell us what it is you are feeling'. Thus needled, the feelers' anxiety can be seen to mount to the point of forcing them to speak. But the now speaking, feeling I.M., as he tries to explore his feelings may not be able to say exactly what it is he is feeling except perhaps in general terms, as a pain or as a fear. Hence he becomes the object of ridicule for the non-feelers: 'You are exaggerating, making a lot of fuss about nothing', 'cannot understand you', 'so boring' etc., and so the sub-group gets destroyed and with it the situation of stasis. Additionally, the I, now threatened by ridicule, may feel precipitated into a state of disarray and so on to alienation. Or to take another situation as between the 'interested' and the 'bored' where boredom would be an expression of anger and hostility. The bored will encourage the interested to provide something which could be interesting – 'now if somebody got *really* upset that would be interesting, that would stir something up, why don't you do it?' Thus a bullfight – 'bread and circuses' – situation comes into being. But now the bored are interested and the interested withdrawing interest: so group/anti-group become dissolved. Once again there is no more stasis.

Institutionalisation

A more important and durable defence particularly against these threats of disintegration or annihilation of the I.Ms is by institutionalisation. The presence of this process of institutionalisation of the member constitutes a very fundamental distinction between a small group and a large group. Hence the leadership roles tend to become 'Mr Chairman', 'Mr Secretary', 'Mr Speaker', 'presidents' and 'kings'.[20] It is less a case of consultants and more of 'management'. The emphasis is on professionalism, the I to disappear into rigid professional behaviour and so become impersonal. As was noted above the groups/anti-groups tend to be generic and professionally based. In these circumstances the culture becomes one of conservatism, the central figure is spared, to be treated with pomp and ceremony. His trappings as his chair become more important than he. If his chair is moved there is 'nothing personal about it'. Tradition carries the day. A major benefit of the situation is the sense of continuity: 'The King is dead. Long live the King.'

As a defence it contains problems, notably two:

First, the whole situation gets a further suffusion with the strong feelings of impersonality attributed to institutions, with beliefs that the I will be sacrificed to the needs of the institution, often an acutely painful thought for members of the care-giving professions with their devotion to the succour of the individual. Institutional roles tend also to have great rigidities and cannot be implemented idiosyncratically. Again one of the great attractions of the small-group way of life is that the roles offered can be filled after the member's own individual way. Within fixed but known limits, liberties can be taken. But not so with the institutionalised roles of a large group. Such roles also acquire a hierarchical determination with a sense of leader and servants. But part of the servant/master contract is that the master will protect his servants; thus with Ministers and their civil servants. But since leaders in the large group are institutionalised against their being sacrificed, it is often their 'servants' who are the first for the firing-squad. What then can the I do, since for him survival is by being looked after and results from dependency, a manner which in any case is not to everyone's taste in itself, requiring some self-swallowing, yet it ends at the firing squad?

Secondly, the removal of the leader to a higher position means that he is no longer present in an enabling function. Thus 'promoted', leadership is very much concerned with the provision of boundaries, particularly a background boundary, but in that position is not available for understanding and the development of insights. Hence once again a basic singleton internal model – the required presence of a mediating figure – cannot be used. Furthermore since leadership, in this instance the consultants, are now in the depth of the group as a background boundary, they cannot help the struggling I in his search to be an I.M. For the consultants to have their background boundary position and so to be available as mediators, the group would have to be perceived by the I as including boundaries, as in the case of the small group (as also in the analysand – psycho-analyst, couch, consulting-room) or some other backcloth would have to be found. But this is just what the institutionalised situation prevents. In this matter it is worth contrasting the large group with the small work-group, where in the latter the singleton's initial role-definition comes from the nature of the leadership exercised and from the leader's relation with the group's primary task. As the leader primary-task relation is explored by the singleton, so his own role acquires a clearer definition and thereby his I.M. role receives confirmation. But none of this is possible in the large group by virtue of the group's use of leaders – consultants – by placing them in the depths rather than where their possible mediatory function can be used. Since, however, knowledge that comes down from on high rarely proves to be knowledge that can be worked with, it is a situation for obedience and respect, but not for learning. So that while the I.M. may survive, it will be mere survival and not creativity.

The leader's boundary-in-depth function is expressed in the I.M.'s sense of his being remote and difficult of access, a sense reinforced at times by an actual perception of remoteness. Again this remoteness, whether in fantasy or reality reinforcing fantasy,

not only re-stimulates the violence or summated angers of the
I.Ms at this general situation (which they feel to be intolerably
threatening with all its sense of boundlessness and the void,
and which in the first place was to be controlled by the defence
of institutionalisation), but it also re-endangers the institutionalised person. Thus at such a moment consultant fumblings over
an interpretation are quite unacceptable and lead to a full-blooded
hue and cry.

Conclusion

The greater part of this paper has concerned itself with the experience of dislocation suffered by the singleton as he makes
his way into the activities of the large group. Much of this
experience is frightening, especially as he participates in the
violence either as actor or victim. As already stressed, and a
point to be returned to in conclusion, his survival as an I.M.
depends not only on his ability to work at the task of the large
group (in this instance, the study of its own behaviour), but
also on the presence of the interacting other I.Ms, so that he
may establish his boundary at the-skin-of-his-neighbour. All
fluctuations in I.M. state – and, as has been shown, these abound –
endanger his chances of survival. A dislocation which may in the
first instance appear acceptable all too easily becomes an experience of disarroy and alienation. If secure in his external
boundary he can begin to establish an internal or intrapsychic
boundary which by its very purpose – and hence availability for
content-containing purposes – helps to delimit the seeming
vastness of the large group. Boundlessness is no longer such a
threat to survival. Within the confines of his external and internal
boundaries – and in the large group the I.M. searches for a
confined or limiting experience – an internal world comes into
being, to contain the skills, roles and models for the mastery
of the large group, thereby enabling him to remain an I.M. and
so not to be threatened either by M.I. status or any of the further
dislocation processes. So bounded, he need no longer fear to be
taken beyond himself.

In the singleton's overall experience of dislocation, of threats to his identity, of becoming other than himself, not only must the 'others' be present for boundary establishment but those others must be 'differentiating others'. The singleton, striving to become an I.M., and even more the I.M. struggling to preserve his I.M. status, has to be aware of a difference between himself and the other singletons or I.Ms, and is involved in a creative act, that is, in creating those 'others', and this in two respects: First there is the recognition of difference: 'I am not you; you are not me.' But, secondly, there is a concurrent process of endowing the others with a difference: 'I am not you, you are not me, in this respect: that you are/have such and such which I am/have not.'

It is not only the fact of difference but also the nature of the difference between the singleton/I.M. and those 'others' which is important. The neighbour has first to be located, and then differentiated. Broad classifications – doctors, care-givers, industrialists, teachers – by obliterating discrete boundaries rather than discriminating and focusing on differences, inevitably hamper, even actively prevent this act of creation; while relational words – father, mother, uncle, aunt – because they contain boundaries within themselves, in a relevant context actively foster it. Furthermore, the establishment of differences enables the contributing I.M. to recognise his own particular or unique contribution to the work of the group and hence to assess whether his efforts are worth while.

Deprived of awareness of differences for whatever reason, the I.M. quickly becomes converted into an M.I., part of a group so equal and fused as to resemble a *Lumpenproletariat*, to be treated as such. In this state the M.Is are particularly at the mercy of the quality and integrity of the leadership that is offered, which may for its own purpose wish to keep these converted singletons in such an M.I. state. That does at least offer possibilities of a followership! It is however in the interests of a work-group leadership to foster differentiation on as precise and accurate a basis as possible, and thereby to encourage the singleton/I.M. to explore his position in the field of psycho-social skills. Based on such self-knowledge, the I.M. state is likely to become a reality. The matter may not however end there – for self-know-ledge may be painful, particularly if it points to deficiencies, and may encourage the embracement of M.I. state as a safe refuge. Certainly, as has already been described, there is much about a large group which encourages the search for safe refuges, despite the diminished identity that results.

Mutual endowment is of course common to all interpersonal relations. But the large group highlights special aspects which have their own danger. In order to create something of the 'other' the singleton, as he struggles to establish his I.M. identity, projects a part of himself into the other singleton or I.M. In the large group, however, response-location presents such difficulties that the projections have an unpredictable element for the recipient 'other'. Hence an ambiguous situation comes into being, giving to the overall projection situation a gratuitous tone. Here the consultants can witness the birth of André Gide's *'acte gratuit'*. Now the unexpectedness and ambiguity of the endowment create a hesitancy in the recipient 'other': 'Do I want to receive that and so become like that?' – and hence causes delay in the establishment of the skin-of-my-neighbour boundary. As a result, singleton conversion to I.M. is slowed down. If the endowment is rejected, as too ambiguous perhaps, then the whole conversion process is totally held up and the singleton state predominates. The large group is then all emptiness. The *acte gratuit* is now revealed for what it is – destructive.

Acceptance of the endowment, on the other hand, not only encourages vicarious living but leads to the endowed recipient I.M. finding himself lumbered with a fixed role: for example, the I.M. who is the constant critic of authority, or who can be relied on to introduce a moral note, or who repeatedly knows of enemies who persecute, or of 'poor souls' who need looking after. Such fixed roles have their advantages in securing survival, though they are very limiting. The I.M. is not allowed to imple-ment them idiosyncratically, or if he tries to do so he is more likely than not to be the object of large-group violence for think-ing for himself. In such situations he verges on being an M.I., since he only stands out from the crowd within the limits of the role as endowed by the 'others', and does not know whether he can truly distinguish himself or is but grasping at the shadow of freedom. If he abdicates the role he might as well be a singleton assisting by his presence at events.

Thus role-fixation is strengthened by the presence of a collusive relationship between the I.M. and the group. This process is on occasion overt and implies endowment fit: that is, the recipient 'other' I.M. has already within himself, whether he is aware of it or not, an equivalent to the endowment which he receives. Already an embryonic or *de facto* critic of authority, endowed now with renewed strength to attack authority, thus inflated – the bull-frog phenomenon – the role becomes stereotyped. It is at times doubtful whether these later I.M. certainties are any better than the former singleton uncertainties. Nor should we lose sight of the strength of introjective wishes. So, with an I.M. who sat opposite 'a nice face: it reassures me about myself'. Likewise there are times when the quality of the consultant's voice is the major dynamic rather than the content of what he is saying: his soft, quiet, soothing accents being introjected, the words left outside, to form an inner world of peace. Here again there is survival in the chosen role of receptive listener but at the expense of knowledge.

The projective endowment of those 'others' with positive qualities, especially if there is a major degree of fit – 'You are not me in that you are more intelligent than I' – where in fact the endowed 'other' *is* more intelligent than the endower – can act as a powerful release of envy in the endower towards the now 'richer other'. Many aspects of the large group can be interpreted as exercises in the force of envy towards this presumed 'richer other'. Thus, an I.M. feeling his way into his role – i.e. one bound for survival – his role being perhaps to explicate matters, volunteers to explain. He will be encouraged to try to do so and is thereby endowed with the survival hopes of all the others: 'Please tell us what it is all about!' and later: 'Go on: go on . . .'. Vicariously the others live through him as they watch him explain, seemingly, even hopefully, surviving. Yet he fumbles, cannot quite find the explanation he thought he had and is met with mocking laughter as his wits desert him. Now the projection-endowment situation dramatically changes. This fumbling 'other' is now the recipient of all the singleton/I.Ms' fears of non-survival, to become their individual non-surviving, no longer in fantasy but in actuality. Disarroy and alienation loom again. The only hope is to revert to being singleton with the now added experience of failure and hopelessness of good intentions.

Out of the dramatic element of vicarious living present in such a situation – 'You do it for us and we will see how it comes out' – emerges that one role characteristic of the large group, namely that of the 'victim', though it is not to everyone's taste to offer the necessary sacrificial element. It is here too that the institutionalisation of the I.M. role takes over the I.M. surviving the M.I. fate as victim through his role being institutionalised. As 'Mr Chairman' ,'Mr Secretary', 'Mr Minister', he will survive, but his wings may be permanently clipped. As was said of the hawk who had his beak straightened, his spurs cut and his pinions pruned: '*Now* you look like a bird'. The strength of the ever-threatening annihilation can likewise be very clearly seen in the obsessive characteristics which appertain to the rules of procedure for committees.

Paradoxically, the envy derives its strength from the fact that through his endowment the endower is now weakened. He has not only diminished his own skills and abilities through his recognition of a difference, but has even put himself in an inferior or subordinate position vis-à-vis the richer other whom he has endowed. So, doubly at a loss, he finds the presumed superiority of the recipient intolerable. He must now be attacked, although the attack, if successful, will lead to the destruction in the receiving 'richer other' of a vital part of the endower: the content of the endowment. The import of the superiority, that which constitutes the threat, seems to be: 'He will think while I can't', when to think is to have knowledge and knowledge is perceived as power. This power now attributed to the 'richer other' is threatening because of the general concreteness of the large-group situation, where fears cannot be held in fantasy, but are experienced as actually happening, especially if they have a talion connotation. But on the other hand if there is to be no endowment, no 'richer other', there can be no skin-of-my-neighbour and no conversion from the original entering singleton state. It all seems inescapable.

The characteristic defence adopted by the large group against the machinations of envy, one which also ensures survival from the dislocation and conversion processes, is that of homogenisation. As this term implies, all members are alike, with no differentiation, an 'all in all' with a search for the lowest common factor, or, as an I.M. remarked: 'It seems that the ceiling of this room is falling lower and lower'. For the large group truly all men become equals. Since all are alike, there is no need for envy. Homogenisation may express itself through a culture of conformity where no member is to be quoted or to be distinguished from another. An early stage is the emergence of a situation of stifling devotion to 'fair shares for all', a situation easily recognisable by the development of an orderly discussion, each speaking in turn, for similar lengths of time, in equivalent grey tones, when the act of speaking rather than the content is the point. In such situations no discrimination need be exercised or choices made. Since envy is no longer a problem, the I.M. is safe from immediate annihilation though if afterwards he has any powers of introspective self-assessment left, he may realise, as one I.M. put it: 'he is just part of a glob!'

All too clearly the life of that joining singleton wishing to participate in large-group work is fraught with difficulty, with the despairs almost as common as the dangers. There may be survival but at what level and at what cost? At times the processes seem totally circular, with the end point possibly a notch or two further down the descent towards being nobody. Even his life force, the libido which drove him to explore man's human condition, is of no avail and indeed when it expresses itself in creative endowment, in an *acte gratuit* may only end in disaster. Friedrich Hölderlin poetically summarises this experience in his poem *Lebenslauf* (*Life's Journey*):

Grössers wolltest auch du, aber die Liebe zwingt
All uns nieder, das Leid beuget gewaltiger,
Doch es kehret umsonst nicht
Unser Bogen, woher er kommt . . . .

You yearned after greater things also, but love forces all of us down and suffering humbles us still further. Yet our bow does not return, vainly, to the same position.

For the singleton, like Hölderlin, his struggle in the large group never takes him along a level path: nothing is straight, nothing seems to come right. Hence his flight into homogenisation or M.I. state. The powers that be not only seem dumb, but bizarre, remote, disinterested in his fate. For the singleton, at the end of this course, it requires much strength to accept Hölderlin's conclusion that he can even be free again. Like Prometheus, for his daring he has been tied to his rock. Yet free he must become, through the appropriate structures. *Prometheus Unbound* has been lost; it may never have been written. Either way, that play has to be constantly re-enacted, as Hölderlin accepts:

Alles prüfe der Mensch, sagen die Himmlischen,
Dass er, kräftig genährt, danken für Alles lern,
Und verstehe die Freiheit,
Aufzubrechen, wohin er will.

Let man test everything, say the heavenly powers, so that, fed on such strong meat, he learns gratitude and discovers the freedom to set out in any direction he chooses.

As King Lear discovered, it is the fate of 'unaccommodated man', that 'poor, bare, forked animal', that is in the balance.

4. The politics of large groups

Patrick de Maré

To his very fingerprints each individual is essentially unique. By the same token society inevitably appears alien to him. This constitutes an ever present dilemma that can never be finally resolved. But it gives rise to ongoing processes of communication so that the problem is not so much a matter of authenticity (in any case a value judgment) as one involving the degree to which informational flow can be negotiated. As Jaspers[1] put it, 'Truth is communicability' (rather than as some would have it, a special preserve of madness).

Levi-Strauss[2] has suggested that we cannot, though we will, evade the law of exchange for it is upon exchange that the whole of the cultural structure is built. To enjoy power without sharing it, to separate it from its informational roots, from society and communion, always ends in disaster. Currently, for example, the economic power of bankers bears no relationship to the real wealth and productivity potential of the modern world; as a result mankind itself is being treated as a form of pollution, the 'population explosion' in the constraining ethos of an effete accountancy system, where money, not wealth, is power. Form has become confused with substance. Generative purpose gives way to futile obsessionalism. Humanity is being gelded by guilt.

The conceptual shift from matter-energy to information flow, previously confused, marks a major breakthrough in the history of science. A parallel shift has taken place in psycho-social thinking – from the psycho-biological to the socio-cultural perspective. If we are to survive at all we can no longer put off the day when the psychological, the politico-economic and the socio-cultural contexts must meet operationally in a unified field. What is imperative is large-group thinking. The World Health Organisation in 1959 naively recommends fitting the individual by re-establishing social adequacy and entirely overlooks the total inadequacy of the social structure itself. As Foulkes[3] has put it, social psychiatry is still a discipline in the making. The question is where and how to start? Pious intentions are not enough. Social insight can only emerge in an operational setting. Context is a prime consideration – context which relates to meaningfulness.

The small group by its very nature displays only the most fragmentary evidence of social dynamics. To apply small-group or psychoanalytic models to the large group is like trying to play ludo on a chess-board.

The large group on the other hand offers us a context and a possible tool for exploring the interface between the polarised and split areas of psychotherapy and sociotherapy.[4] This is the area of the inter-group and of the transdisciplinary, where a crossfire between distinct hierarchical structures – viz, the nursing and medical disciplines – can occur.[5] Where these structures have succumbed to the sclerosis of their own 'sanctions from above', they become impervious to each other's 'lateral sanctions'. They become impervious, too, to their own and each other's informational resources.

If we are to progress it is essential we differentiate clearly between this new approach to the large group as distinct from the loosely structured organisations that we are already familiar with, such as therapeutic communities, ward meetings, social club, community and staff meetings, plenary meetings, communes, etc. This is new territory which is relatively unexplored and entails the intensive and extensive exploration of large, face-to-face, 'primary' groups *per se* – a meeting of the same members regularly over a considerable time, and not simply a sudden short burst of meetings, however 'marathon'.

It is proposed these meetings be as rigorous as any psychoanalytic or group-analytic setting – freed of current community ties and of redundant hierarchical strictures. Such a setting could provide a melting pot – an opening of otherwise impervious and closed barriers.

What is needed is a deeper understanding of the phenomena of the large group itself, in its own terms, as a developing and self-regulating system, and this mutual knowing of each other inter-experientially, inter-subjectively, developed to its fullest extent, might lead also to an expanding of consciousness, since consciousness itself is by derivation a process of knowing with others. Within this situation one might gain experience of those ephemeral, and to a great extent ignored, contextual features of climate, ambience, atmosphere, ethos, drama, attitudes and ideologies which are so characteristic of the micropolitics of the large group, and which play such an enormous role in matters of morale, communication and information flow. These characteristics are quite distinct from similar processes taking place in small groups in that for the first time we have a context in which outsight or social insight can develop *per se*, not only into personal social behaviour in the fullest sense, but into a questioning of current social assumptions which are so assumed as to be often totally unconscious, in the manner that a person is often totally unaware of his own accent.

The large group has two very powerful aspects and, given the opportunity, an equally powerful capacity to contain and convey its own power. In the first instance, it has an enormous capacity to generate emotion which can very easily become ungovernable, either in the form of splitting in uncontainable panic or in the form of spilling over emotions which are irrelevant, inappropriate and ephemeral. In the second instance, the large group is above all a highly sensitive thinking apparatus – given the necessary time and place to evolve its matrix or organisation, communication and containment – of which language is a typical example. Each large group can learn to develop its own containing network, can discover its own thinking potential. The 'containing' is of lateral, affiliative, 'on the level' communication when an expansion of consciousness, of mindfulness emerges and grows if given the time and opportunity. The system becomes freed of redundant hierarchy in favour of self-regulation, away from mindless, crushing, machiavellism of manipulations through coercion and power.[6] It has its own currency and styles of control and guidance in the micropolitics of such strategies as silence, ridicule, boycott, ignoring, punctuating, timing, stimulating, promoting, in atmospheres which can on occasion be 'cut with a knife'.

It is these and other manifestations of large-group processes which we are hoping to explore more fully in their own operational setting.

Definition of the large group

For convenience, I would suggest that social systems be broken down into the following categories:[7]

A. Primary (face-to-face) structures

1. Small groups from 3–20 people.
2. Large groups from 20 upwards such that people can directly hear and see each other.

B. Secondary structures

1. Multiple group structures, complex organisations of all sorts, often only very tenuously related, for instance through 'interstitial groups', such as smaller communities.
2. Larger communities – 'the community'.
3. Societies, nations and larger still, total social systems.

It is large groups (A2) that we shall be concerned with here, ranging for purposes of psychotherapy from between 20 to, let us suggest, 100 people seated in a two-tiered circle, the same members meeting at least once a week for $1\frac{1}{2}$ hours.[8] Until recently large groups have been treated very much as secondary, peripheral phenomena and very much less rigorously than small groups, being viewed as supplementary adjuncts in such procedures as social clubs, ward meetings, community meetings, therapeutic committees within extremely haphazard and tenuous networks. The very self-evidence of the background scene of the large group seems to have obscured its significance. However, interest is growing in this topic, which may very well mark an important breakthrough therapeutically and operationally speaking – for instance, as a possible technique in the treatment of psychotic anxiety and in such conditions as phobic states where panic – typically a large-group phenomenon – can be handled within the individuals concerned.

History

Interest in the large primary group in a more general way has, of course, a very long history, using the word primary as primarily face-to-face. Mankind, having progressed through various phases – pagan, religious, philosophical, scientific, psychological – is now at the brink of a growing sociological awareness of socially based insight that might well prove crucial for psychotherapy ('Knowing something in oneself with others') if practised operationally in a large-group setting. It would follow that the construct of the group mind would be a more consistent concept than that of the individual mind. The unconscious mind in that case is the mind that is not shared – presumably conscious to some individuals, but not to others.

The Ancient Greeks with their large face-to-face meetings in the circular amphitheatres of their *poleis*, seating several thousand – any one member of which could be clearly seen and heard – laid stress with remarkable clarity on the principle of *Koinonia*. My Greek friend, Thalia Vergopoulo, tells me that *Koinonia* is a sort of spiritual-cum-human participation and communion (for instance Holy Communion), fellowship generally, and that people who are *Koinonicos* relate truly as distinct from *Cosmicos* who relate superficially and more sentimentally, in a *'mondaine'* manner. The Greek chorus in the centre of the amphitheatre during the plays represented the *Koinonia* feeling ethically – aesthetically, rather than moralistically.

The Greek horror of alienation and exile (which impelled Socrates to choose death) was only equalled by their failure to grasp the significance of inter-group or inter-state relationships which resulted in the final destruction of their civilisation.

Cooley[9] (1902) appreciated the large primary group as the nursery of human nature. Cody Marsh's credo[10] was 'By the crowd they have been broken; by the crowd they shall be healed'.

In 1916 Trotter[11] saw neurosis as a warning signal of pain in a maladjusted society.

More recently Laing and others have described neurosis and psychosis as a measure of social alienation in terms of social oppression and violation.

In latter years communes, therapeutic communities and social clubs have played a highly significant role, but we are not concerned here with therapeutic communities; on the contrary, it is the intensive and relatively more rigorous application of the large-group technique that holds our interest.

Role of the large group

Small psychotherapy groups everywhere have tended to be analytically orientated. Foulkes[12] suggests that 'the small group, the typically psychotherapeutic group, is probably the most interesting apart from being the most valuable tool of psychotherapy, in that it is on the borderline of the two situations – it can easily be tilted towards the individual situation as well as towards the group situation'. My experience, on the other hand, has been that the small group turns more easily towards the psychoanalytic and psychodynamic intra-personal dimension than towards a specifically group-dynamic orientation, and that group dynamics have not yet been utilised to their full extent since it will only be in the larger group that their full potential can be shown. Though Foulkes appreciates the power that a large group might have and cites famous political demagogues, he considers that the new thinking such an enterprise requires already came into being with the creation of the small group, 'each situation emphasises phenomena of a different kind, but the old phenomena are still present in the new setting'.

This I doubt and since these phenomena have never yet been investigated in the new context, I think it is altogether too sweeping. In any case Foulkes considered that the possibility of a large group meeting daily for 2 hours over a period of 2 years as more in the realms of fantasy and doubted whether this would ever be carried out in the rigorous sense I suggested. He also considered that the question of size is a relative one and that one would require to supplement the large-group experiences in smaller groups or individually. He did add, however that it would constitute an interesting experiment. He is aware too that such a large group under these conditions brought psychotic mechanisms and anxiety to the fore – which incidentally already suggests a striking distinction. However, in the course of further discussions he has evinced an interest in the possible implications of the large group *per se*.

Freud was profoundly interested in the psychoses for their relevance to the understanding of the psychoneuroses. Neuroses presuppose a relatively developed ego-structure capable of repression, displacement, rationalisation, reaction formation and sublimation. In psychosis on the other hand the ego-structure is itself undeveloped and resorts to splitting rather than repression, with projection and introjection incapable of the work, the capacity of negotiation evident in neurotic symptoms and dreams. Similarly, in any new large group at an early stage of development, contributions carry some of the character of a schizophrenic thought disorder. Unlike the schizophrenic, however, is the capacity and openness to learning secondary process equivalents, the containing of primary process equivalents by learning how to negotiate communication, how to order and organise through developmental as distinct from magical processes. The schizophrenic is like an arrested large-group process within the individual psyche, like the splinters of the mirror in Hans Andersen's tale, *The Snow Queen*. Perhaps we are indeed on to the fringe of a technique which could shed light on psychotic and phobic anxiety.

I must admit that, in order to make the point, I put the suggestion in caricature form, to the effect that while psycho-analysis delivered us from the limitations of organic psychiatry and group analysis has liberated us from the constraints of psycho-analysis, the large group may do likewise in relieving us of the constrictions of the small group, that the large group is a totally different proposition, and I suggested a situation for large-group therapy entailing 20–100 people seated in a one or two-tiered circle – that the structure of the meetings be arranged as rigorously and intensively as in the psycho-analytic or small-group setting – certainly not less so, and recommended as an example closed daily meetings of $1\frac{1}{2}$–2 hours' duration over a period of two or more years.

In fact, on a much more modest scale at St George's Hospital (London), I am currently collecting a list of predominantly phobic patients who will, I hope, be meeting for $1\frac{1}{2}$ hours once a week for as long as seems feasible, inviting several conductors to join me with the proviso that the group, once started, will be closed and the participants will be expected to attend regularly.

I do see the large group as playing an antithetically distinct role from that of the small group, introducing distinctions which are quite specific to it. While the small group only too readily lends itself to a psycho-dynamic approach, usually psycho-analytic, the large group manifests characteristically group-dynamic features. In the small group the individual self-system is much more actively involved along a time-based, 'vertical' or hierarchical dimension which concerns the personally repressed with transference phenomena from the 'there and then'. In the large group, on the other hand, the lateral or horizontal spatial dimension of the 'here and now' is involved, manifesting 'topological' phenomena such as splitting, projection and displacement, which is transpositional rather than transferential, that is, a transposing of total worlds of contexts, environments, positions and settings as distinct from a transferring of the relationships within these settings. This involves total social situations without regard for present or past, involving total cultures, climates and value systems with specific ideologies and ethos.

The amplifying and totalising effect of the large group is most striking and emotions sweep like a breeze throughout the entire group, altering the atmosphere, rather as biologically 'the energy of a system acts to organise that system'.[13]

While the problem for the member of the small group is how to feel spontaneously, for the large group it is primarily how to think. Freud pointed out the dilemma of having to procure for the group (and he referred to large groups) precisely those features which are characteristic of the individual and which are extinguished by the formation of the group. Similar experiences are described by Bion in referring to the numbing sensation which groups at times create in the therapist. While the problem for the individual and for the small group is the intrusion of unconscious factors (Bion[14] has called them basic assumptions), for the large group it is consciousness itself that is at risk – or the group's equivalent of consciousness, namely communication and organisation. The problem for the large group is its mindlessness.[15]

The technique of large-group psychotherapy, which would seem to be a self-evident procedure, meets with the suspicions once accorded to psychoanalysis and later to small-group psychotherapy; the reasons for this would seem to relate to this very characteristic of the powerful, unpredictable and potentially chaotic emotions stirred up in such a setting, releasing psychotic type anxiety. Once this becomes more contained and organised it can have powerful political repercussions. The impact of the large group on its environment is indeed very much more in evidence than that of the small group or the psychoanalytic situation which takes place behind closed doors; witness the precarious careers of certain therapeutic communities (Henderson, Forest House, Halliwick 'House', and the Paddington Day Hospital), threatened or even destroyed by political and administrative interference.

It is quite clear that an enormous potential of information lies vested in the large group. The tragedy is that its flow only too easily becomes blocked by all sorts of pressures, coerciveness, energy generally in the form of power and authoritarianism. Intelligence succumbs to coercion; hierarchical pyramids, far from being flattened, grow even higher, affiliative communication gives way to hierarchical blocking, leadership of ideas and trends give way to the pressure of personalities in authority and 'leaders', obfuscation rules the day and the large group, rather like a large vulnerable animal, is subjected to all sorts of violations, when it is in fact a most highly sensitive instrument whose enormous potentials we can at present only very dimly envisage. I am reminded of the treble and bass clef in music;

often the bass clef is the carrier of a mechanical rhythm; it is only comparatively recently that it has been considered as a provider of melody in its own right, not simply repetitiously, but contrapuntally in relationship to the treble clef which in turn is able to follow up more readily the implications of the rhythm for the composition as a whole.

While psychoanalysis deals with matters of personal insight with relatively little political ramifications and while group analysis has perhaps special relation to that hierarchy of all hierarchies, namely the family, large-group therapy could have considerable micropolitical significance in providing a new type of insight into factors which remain outside the orbit of psychotherapy, notably that of social insight; in fact most scientific discourse in psychology seems to be designed to ignore the socio-economic context in which psychological factors play their part. In certain countries one feels the group therapists are compelled for political reasons to adopt a stringently psycho-analytic stance, maintaining therefore a strictly neutral 'academic' position, since social insight acts as a two-way mirror – not only into the individual's social behaviour, but into the social situation around us.[16]

There are, too, considerable conceptual implications when one considers the possibility that consciousness itself is a social phenomenon – 'Knowing things with other people' – so that the social context is often so completely assumed as to be completely unconscious. The split between the kindliness of individuals and the callousness of 'the system' is only too frequently seen – let alone society's seemingly psychotic type of behaviour in the sense that an individual behaving in the manner society adopts would be considered insane.

Lacan[17] has put it that the Freudian unconsciousness is the discourse of 'the other' and Wilden has said that information divested of context is so much noise – since all knowledge has politico-economic bearings. To leave out the social context leads to a logical flatness and to the loss of the all-important factor of ethos, in which attitudes and ideologies make themselves evident not as cloudy idealistic non-sequiturs, but as crucial and clearly definable climates which either impair or promote the flow of communication and information. While in the individual setting it is the intrusion of unconscious factors that are the problem, for the large group it is the equivalent of consciousness, namely communication and organisation, that is threatened; the communicational network or social matrix can either block or contain information flow and the problem is the mindlessness of inadequately evolved hierarchies where rudimentarily developed networks (affiliative, lateral, on the level) have succumbed to over-developed, inappropriately evolved hierarchies (vertically structured to prevent violent collisions and unfortunately communication as well).

Control and structuring are the group's equivalent to mentation and become organised as a response to frustration, hate and aggression occasioned by the situation. The large group, through lack of opportunity, may have to resort to an overly-developed control by hierarchy. This easily becomes an abuse of hierarchy resulting in mindless and dehumanised organisations. Oppression as distinct from negotiation provokes hate, anxiety and then depression in the individual. The interface at the boundaries of these hierarchical or compartmentalised areas become split or closed to information flow instead of negotiable and open. In this context, Levi-Strauss's nature and culture could be seen as a dialectic between hate and hierarchy. Given the time and opportunity a group culture can develop. It is this cultural (thoughtful) potential of the large group that should be our concern and which we should aim to nurture in setting up a large group. It is this too which is incidentally psychotherapeutic.

The social matrix is a useful construct because it refers to the ongoing processes of a growing communicational network. Where it is only at a rudimentary stage, spilling over and splitting in violence and panic occur, but this is only evident in the early phases. 'Where chaos was, there shall matrix be'! While panic fragments and stampedes intelligence, hate unites and constitutes the group's driving power for organising, communicating and thinking, provided it does not become crushed by reactive hierarchical strictures. The hierarchy to end all hierarchies is that of the family. Unfortunately, the tendency to repeat this setting at certain stages in large groups is enormous, structures which are neither realistic nor gratifying. The members are then faced with the task of reshaping it. This is an example of the changing shapes which are so characteristic a feature of large groups and which Buckley[18] has called morphogenesis. Invisible intrapersonal barriers are projected as more tangible constellations which the members, having imposed them, have therefore to reshape. In the large group this differs from the small group in being so much more amplified, so much more manifest. What has to be maintained if growth and therapy are to occur is a permeability at the interface of the hierarchical levels – the intrapersonal hierarchies of ego, super-ego and id can thereby undergo an active process of revision and redefinition through the group members' work of re-organising the structure of the large group itself. A better word for it would be metastructure or culture, since it refers to factors other than time-space and number.

A typical and often repeated phenomenon is the manner of talking in large groups. What occurs is that in the first meeting only a minority speak as if the anxiety of talking in such a large assembly could not be contained – an anxiety which for many people is so acute as to border on panic. As the meetings proceed, more and more members take part and gradually the silent majority becomes a silent minority, till even they participate. This constitutes a very active exercising of the ego to handle and contain anxiety which, since it is a situation which provokes anxiety rather than represses it, is a form of learning therapy. The repressive force is externalised into the presence of the large group as such – so that in learning to cope with this and with the often overpowering emotions stirred up by this setting, the individual ego learns gradually to talk and think spontaneously which, in turn, creates and exercises an enormously enriched and thought-provoking situation in the large group itself. In staff groups, for instance, the members are able to jump the hierarchical barriers within and between the disciplines, and the informational gold mine which lies vested in the nursing staff can be shared.[19]

The following are verbatim comments by a severely phobic patient and are worth quoting as an illustrative example of primarily large-group feeling:

'It seems that you withdraw into your body and feel so intensely your feelings that you appear to be overwound inside and cannot cope with anything outside of yourself, the eyes and ears are outlets to a strange, frightening place overpowering your feelings, something you try to escape from, yet desperately want to belong to. I long to remember how it was to be outside of myself, living outside of my body, not wondering how my body is going to react to outside pressure, but for my body to accept living outside of myself as normal. It is like being locked up in a cell and being punished while, outside through the window, I can see people happy, normal and, better still, contented, making a success of life, and I have a key to my cell somewhere, but it's very hard to find. Sometimes I find the key and escape for a while, it seems so perfect, but then I realise that when I'm outside I do not belong there – I am still on my own, I try to get among the people and sometimes I become part of the crowd, but I cannot find anyone amongst them who seems to care whether I'm there or not, I just seem to stay an outside member of the crowd and so, against my will, I return to my self-made cell to die a little more inside, and also to start looking for the key so that I can try once more outside. I do not know if the pain of going outside is worth it, but I feel I must for three reasons. The first is that perhaps things might alter outside for the better, secondly I detest myself as I am, and thirdly, if I remain locked up inside for too long I feel I shall mentally die. If you know of anybody who needs affection and thus can help me stay outside I deeply stress, please help me to get to know them, but please don't ask me to join any clubs because I will still be on the outside looking in.'

There seem, then, to be three ways of thinking. First there is a process of finding out what the general opinion appears to be and 'thinking it', a form of posturing; secondly, experiencing one's own impressions exclusively as half-formulated thoughts which leads to idiosyncrasies and insularity; thirdly, expressing

these and testing them out against what other people are thinking
through mutual exchange, and constituting an extension of
consciousness.

The large group, in its early phases of existence and thinking,
appears to be experienced as a persecutory environment which is
oppressive to the individual members who do not feel free
enough to breathe ('spiritual') nor inspired enough to express
their half-thoughts spontaneously. This suffocating oppression
leads to a depressive state or alternatively to an unthinking
euphoria of evasiveness, the price of involvement with and
'belonging' to the group at that particular time. The alternative
is not to belong at all – 'Every man for himself!' and 'Panic
stations!'. So which is it to be? Security and depression? Or
freedom and panic? Claustrophobia or agoraphobia?

The negotiation of a way across this gap, the working through
and the infiltration by the delicate filaments of communication
between the interface of these two worlds constitutes, amongst
many other factors, psycho-social therapy.

The large-group situation needs to be set up, and the time,
the regularity, the encouragement and a suitable locus established.
Alas! too often this does not occur. Individuals in themselves
repeatedly break away and never succeed in passing through
these early phases, never experience anything further, but move
to another setting which is then repeated, and their problems
fail to be worked through. The repeated groups remain non-
living immutable constellations, unproductive, unrealistic and
closed to both the personal exchange or environmental influences.

5. A sociological view of large groups

Earl Hopper and Anne Weyman

This article has several purposes: to introduce certain elements of the sociological perspective which may clarify the nature, or ontological status, of social phenomena and processes, to isolate several properties of large groups as distinct from their members, to provide concepts for their denotation and to discuss their interrelationships. The fact that the present volume includes articles on the large group from many related disciplines makes these tasks both easier and more difficult. They are easier because it is possible to exclude certain topics which are covered elsewhere, but they are more difficult because even this limited approach requires consideration of the most central and vexing problems of sociological theory, which still lacks an adequate language for their discussion. These problems are the focus of the shifting paradigms of competing schools of sociological analysis. In fact, sociology is a large, amorphous, rapidly developing discipline, entertaining many specialities and competing perspectives (it is rather like a large group). From our point of view, it will be sufficient to state what sociology is in principle and to show what it has to offer on this basis for the study of large groups.

What is sociology and the sociological perspective?
No two sociologists would answer this question in the same way, and even if their answers were similar in substance, their terminology would differ. Nor should any two sociologists who are on reasonably good terms be asked to agree, for if they had to do so they would undoubtedly never speak to each other again. However, most sociologists would recognise what they usually get

paid to do in the following: sociology is the scientific[1] study of social systems which results in public, communicable, systematic, reliable and valid knowledge about them.

The application of a systems perspective to the study of human collectivities is not an imposition of order upon chaos. Evidence shows that human collectivities possess systemic properties and the development of the concept 'system' is part of an attempt to understand them. It enables us to see beyond the ostensibly random activities of individuals and to discover patterns of social order and conflict.

A system exists if a set of elements within an environment relate to one another in such a way that changes in them can be predicted without reference to that environment. The actual relationships among the elements of a system and between the system and its environment are always problematic. Perfect systems do not exist in the social world; their imperfections often constitute their most interesting and relevant properties, especially in connection with social change.

Although this definition is formulated in a highly abstract way, it may be applied to any empirical reality which has systemic properties, regardless of its size or complexity. For example, it might be used to study a dyadic relationship, a small group, a formal organisation, an economy or a society. Sociology would have little to contribute to the understanding of large groups if they were not social systems.

A social system is a specific kind of system. The term 'social' refers to two interrelated properties of human collectivities, the recognition of which is axiomatic to sociology. The first of these essential properties is that human beings cannot exist except within a society of some kind, no matter how simple, and that society cannot exist without human beings. Human organisms might be born and survive for a while in the wild, but would not be recognised as human beings. They would not be able to speak, reason or feel in the way that human beings do; they would not have the needs and responses acquired through socialisation, not only in infancy, but also throughout life. The dichotomy between society and the individual is an abstraction. This does not mean that society and the individual are in complete harmony but that, although social constraints on some human beings may derive from external coercion and force, society is maintained primarily through internal volition.[3] Social forces require a high degree of participation from both those who force and those who are forced.

The second essential property to which the term social refers is that much of society is made up of emotional or mental phenomena. These exist in the minds of men and are a product of interactions between human beings. The existence and maintenance of all social phenomena, except in so far as they rely on material inventions like technology, are an expression of meaningful 'human action' (as distinct from behaviour) based on a body of shared understandings and a common intellectual and emotional discourse.

It follows that the understanding of social phenomena demands the recognition that the essence of the social is that it is human and the essence of the human is that it is social.[4] Thus, the properties of any social system cannot be distinguished fully from the properties of the human beings who are its members. However, the properties of social phenomena also transcend the properties of the members of social systems and their actions. Therefore, the properties of social systems may be studied independently of the individuals within them and the properties of individuals may be studied independently of their social context, within reason. For example, it is possible to study the structure of authority within a particular group without taking into account the personalities of its members. It is known that groups of a certain size faced with certain types of tasks tend to develop specific kinds of authority structure, despite the existence of a variety of personality characteristics amongst their members. Similarly, it is possible to study an individual's personal styles concerning authority without taking account of the basic authority structures to which he has been exposed and in which he will have to participate. Although these essential aspects of his social context are important, they may be less important in the first instance than knowledge about many of

F

his other personality characteristics such as how frightened he is of helplessness and dependency.

The study of any problem requires the choice of its boundaries. These are set by the resources available and the kind of solution sought. However, if all the elements of the system are not taken into account, by definition, the solution to the problem will be partial. Sociologists are particularly aware of the partial nature of such explanations, and stress the importance of the context within which the boundary is drawn. For example, they argue that although interaction between individuals in a group can be understood, to an extent, by considering processes within the group, the group exists in a social environment which cannot be ignored completely. It is impossible to consider everything at once, but it is essential to realise that every study involves a choice to concentrate on certain aspects and not others.

This stress on the social context of all interaction is often ignored. Many people are unable to see that to find explanations for human action it is necessary to go beyond the individual.[5] However, their 'individualism' is misleading. Human action is affected by social phenomena, and it must be recognised that when the consequences of social phenomena are identifiable and, hence, 'real', the phenomena themselves are real.[6]

The sociological perspective is based on the acknowledgement of the social as real and that it affects human action. The concept 'social system' is a particularly valuable tool for this work. It enables us to establish the systemic properties of social forms and to analyse the various relationships among them and their effects on individuals' actions. Furthermore, we can examine the relationship of any particular system to its environment. The categories obtained from the analysis of one system can be used to compare different types of social systems, whether these are different societies or parts of any one society. Thus, our knowledge of the social system 'society' can help to extend our knowledge of the social system 'large group'. It can do so in two ways: first, by disclosing similarities and differences in structure, and, secondly, by clarifying the nature of the interaction between them. This latter process is extremely important because society is the environment in which the large group exists and, hence, forms its social context, the vital focus of the sociological perspective.

Elements of the social system
The attempt to extend knowledge in this way requires the description of some of the elements of a social system. We can define the elements of a social system as those roles, relationships and norms which are primarily concerned with the attempted solution of fundamental problems. We will first consider the concept of a fundamental problem and then will examine the notions of roles, relationships and norms.

Fundamental problems
The term fundamental problem describes any problem which people must attempt to solve if they are to survive. There are two kinds of fundamental problem. The first arise from the nature of the human organism[7], and the second from the structure of any organisation through which people attempt to solve the first type of problem.[8]

Although it is possible to have different forms of social organisation within which people attempt to solve organism specific problems, once a particular form of social organisation exists, it presents fundamental problems of its own. These problems are in a sense derivative from organismic ones, but they are nonetheless constraining. For example, if people did not have to eat to live, they would not have an economy, but because they have an economy they are almost as much constrained by the development and maintenance of its particular form as they are by their need to eat. Equally, the solution of the organism specific problem of coordination requires that leaders be selected and trained. The provision of suitable succession demands that this must be a continuous process. However, it may be accomplished in various ways, two of the most familiar being hereditary succession and election. Both assure succession, but each presents the society with an additional set of fundamental problems which must be dealt with if the arrangement is to work.

The idea that fundamental problems can be related to particular institutions leads us to the concept of *sub-system*. Each sub-system is related to activities which are concerned primarily with a specific fundamental problem. Such sub-systems are not always easily distinguished empirically, especially in the case of simple societies. However, they can always be distinguished analytically no matter how simple the society under consideration. Thus in the case of the social system 'society', the elements of the system are equivalent to the sub-systems which are themselves related to particular problems.

Many sociologists have tried to classify fundamental problems as a basis for the comparison of all social systems.[9] However, such schemes have proved of little help in efforts to understand actual social systems. The difficulty is not their level of abstraction, but their lack of theoretical and logical justification. They are primarily *ad hoc* lists which seem adequate only because they are so general. Such schemes may facilitate the presentation of data but should not be held in too much esteem by those in search of conceptual order. In fact, sociologists are only able to indicate that there are fundamental problems and to suggest which of these are shown by current evidence to be universal. These insights can be used in constructing testable propositions.

Although the list of problems which have been treated in this way pertains to societies, any social system which has sufficient social stability for it to have recognisable boundaries and, therefore, which is identifiable as a social system, contains sets of activities which are concerned with their attempted solution. However, some social systems are specialised. They depend on other social systems in their environment for the attempted solution of one or more of their own problems. For example, one organisation may rely on another to provide it with already socialised human beings. Equally, a large group may specialise in the maintenance and production of core values and may depend on other agencies for everything else. However, a specialised social system of any kind is likely to have some arrangements which contribute to its own maintenance, if only to provide for the receipt and distribution of goods and services it receives from other systems.

So far, we have concentrated on those similarities among people which are the result of the human condition and which enable us to analyse society into its constituent sub-systems, such as the educational sub-system or the economic sub-system. We must now look at the actual activities which go on within social systems. To do so we must return to the notions of roles, relationships and norms.

Roles, relationships and norms: social structure
When we say that social phenomena are structured we mean that in all relationships people do not just meet as people. Instead, they meet as the incumbents of various roles which are attached to certain positions. There are many varied roles and positions in a society and people occupy and act in more than one. All social action involves positions and roles and is comprised of two interrelated components of social structure which we will call *interaction patterns* and *normative patterns*.[10] Interaction patterns are the actual affiliations and relationships between people, and normative patterns are the rules which specify the form and content which these interactions should take. Consider, for example, the social structure of the relationships between a subordinate and his boss: the boss usually initiates verbal interaction, and has control over the basic framework of the relationship; the normative patterns pertaining to this relationship concern the manner in which orders should be given, received and accepted or rejected. The interaction and normative patterns of this relationship may not concur; although the boss may usually initiate the verbal exchange, both he and his subordinate may share the norm that they should be equal in their initiation of verbal exchanges.

Five types of interaction patterns are particularly important: the exchange of goods and services, cooperation towards a common goal, voluntary conformity to social norms, involuntary conformity resulting from coercion and the struggle which results from conflict.[11] Any particular interaction may contain more than one of these types of pattern. For example, marriage may be seen as an exchange of goods and services, cooperation towards a common goal (happiness, social prestige) or conformity to the norm that people ought to get married. In this case, the interaction could be considered in terms of any of the categories, depending on your attitude to marriage. Another example which involves more than one type of interaction is that of the low-paid worker like a nurse who receives a socially unfair exchange because he or she has no bargaining power to counteract the employer's coercion. This situation is reinforced by a norm which says that nurses should not strike.

The causal connections between interaction patterns and normative patterns are always problematic. When a new behaviour pattern is established coercion may be required to impose it; if those who coerce have control over the socialisation process, they can ensure that future generations will accept the pattern as 'natural'. Thus, an interaction pattern based on differences in power may impose a normative pattern which reinforces it. Although the interaction pattern is usually primary, under some conditions the normative patterns may initiate or preclude certain interaction patterns. For example, if it is felt that people should not express their feelings readily then they will not necessarily behave aggressively even though they may feel aggressive, and this will influence the way others behave towards them.

'Social structure' is not a sub-system of the society. It is a term which refers to the interaction and normative patterns which pervade an entire social system, and occur in endless forms throughout it. As a consequence of the fact that all social phenomena are structured, people in different positions tend to have different views, interests and attitudes. Surtax, for example, is not a problem the poor have to face and supplementary benefits do not play a large part in the lives of the rich. As a result, these two groups tend to differ in their attitudes towards tax policy. It is not just that rich and poor experience a different reality, but that in any structured relationship there are differences of interest which engender different views.[12] Differentiation need not always involve stratification.[13] However, when a relationship is characterised by an unequal distribution of rewards, it will almost always involve a conflict of interest. Even though the norms may say that the differences are just, such conflicts will reduce the possibility of cooperation.

Hence, structural arrangements have important consequences for social action. In particular, we know that great differences of access to the good things in life exist and that these affect the whole pattern of activity in society. Indeed, nearly all societies have sufficient social surplus for the struggle for survival of any individual member to be due to the system of distribution and not to a lack of production. The term 'social stratification' describes the fact that social positions are hierarchically ordered so that some people own more than others, some have more political power and some have more social status. An individual's positions in all these hierarchies are likely to be congruent, but discrepancies do exist. A poorly paid profession such as the clergy may have high social status, whereas a bookmaker who earns large amounts may have low status. Status is a more problematic basis for a hierarchy than the other two dimensions because it is more of a social construct, and different groups in society may differ violently in their assessment of the social prestige of different occupations.[14] The more concrete basis of economic and political stratification is reflected in the fact that it is unusual for those without economic power to have political power. It may appear that a politician without economic power may nonetheless have political power. However, he is constrained by the economic power of others, and can further their interests without being rich himself.

Various types of structural arrangements are possible in all social systems ranging from societies to large or small groups. The sociologist attempts to understand these variations. Dimensions of comparison are required for this task and we will now discuss some of them.

Some important dimensions of social systems

All social systems may be compared with respect to a number of basic properties, which may be conceptualised in terms of dimensions or continua. Although this constitutes an elementary analysis of social systems, it is surprising how much information is offered by locating a social system on a number of these dimensions simultaneously. The following are a few fundamental properties which can be treated in this way, but the list is far from exhaustive.

Complexity

Societies vary in their degree of complexity with respect to the differentiation and specialisation of their parts. Differentiation and specialisation refer to the number of more or less empirically discrete elements with distinct boundaries within a social system which relate to the attempted solution of its various fundamental problems. Thus, the ease with which sub-systems can be identified empirically and the degree to which they are concerned primarily with one fundamental problem, and with that problem alone, is a function of the social system's complexity. A continuum from 'ideal complexity' to 'ideal simplicity' can be envisaged. A society may become more or less complex, and this increasing or decreasing complexity may be manifest in either the interaction system or the normative system, but usually in both.

As societies become more complex, their sub-systems come to consist of specific roles which are combined in distinct structural units. Less complex societies have more diffuse roles which are less distinctly grouped. The concepts of specificity and diffuseness are very important. A specific role requires action, thought and feelings from its holder which are circumscribed and bounded, and does not require a full personal involvement. A relationship between two such roles is like two billiard balls touching. For example, a bank manager and his client have a highly specific relationship. On the other hand, a role characterised by diffuseness requires a full personal involvement in its tasks. Even though the tasks themselves may be clearly defined, they are usually exceedingly complex, and it is difficult to formulate standards for assessing their performance. A relationship which is structurally diffuse may be compared with two warm wet sponges pressed together. A good teacher and his pupil, a therapist and his patient, a parent and his child, and siblings all have diffuse relationships.

Social systems that are complex will have sub-systems which are primarily made up of structural units in the form of sets of specific roles, but they will also contain some structural patterns which are more diffuse. Less complex societies will consist primarily of structural units which contain diffuse roles, but they will also have some specific roles. Thus, increasing and decreasing complexity does not necessarily occur evenly throughout a society. Indeed, some problems may be more effectively dealt with by diffuse rather than specific relationships. Socialisation and education are two processes which fall into this category.[15]

Cohesion

Cohesion in general refers to the degree to which the elements of a system are interdependent. The degree to which change in one element produces change in the rest of the system is an index of its degree of cohesion. Again systems can be placed on a continuum from 'ideal cohesion' to 'ideal incohesion'. No known system is ideally cohesive but some approach this state.

The term 'social cohesion' refers to the degree to which actions in a system are constrained by the existing patterns of affiliation and norms so that the activities of its members can continue. The extent to which people are interdependent within their affiliations for the provision and receipt of services can be referred to as the degree to which their interaction patterns are 'integrated'.[16] The extent to which they share common norms, and, hence, have similar views of what form these ties should take, can be referred to as the degree to which their interaction patterns are 'solidary'. Thus, just as social structure is comprised of both interaction and normative patterns, so social cohesion consists of both integration and solidarity. This distinction is useful for comparing social systems. Two systems may be equally cohesive, but in one case this may be mainly due to integration of the interaction networks, whereas in the other it may depend mainly on the solidarity of the normative networks. For example, the cohesion of a business enterprise depends mainly on the integration of its interaction networks, whereas that of a large group depends on the solidarity of its normative networks.

Closure

Closure refers to the degree to which an element in a system is influenced by any elements in the system's environment. No known system is totally closed but some approach this state. By definition, no system can be totally open. If a social form is believed to approach this state, the concept 'system' cannot be applied to it. Its boundaries must be redefined to include the relevant aspects of what was previously considered to be its environment. Societies are perhaps among the most open of all known systems, but even they are fairly closed.

Just as all systems have environments, so any system is itself an environment with respect to its constituent elements. When considering any one element in a system or its relationships with other elements, it is therefore crucial to keep in mind the effects of all the remaining elements in the system. This can be seen as a problem in controlling the environment of the constituent elements. It may also be useful to specify the type of environment in question. Although often somewhat arbitrary, a distinction should be made between the natural, social and psychological environments. Some social systems may be relatively closed with respect to one but relatively open with respect to another.

Dynamism

Dynamism refers to the amount and rate of interactions within the relationships which comprise the constituent elements of social systems, among these elements and between them and the environment. If no interactions occur within the system, it is 'ideally static'. No known social system is ideally static but some approach this state.[17] Interaction processes may manifest various kinds of pattern, e.g., cyclical, and the amount and rate usually vary in accordance with particular events, such as a breaking of rules by a member of a large group or the departure of a member of a small group. It is important to recognise that interactions can range from slight gestures to hitting someone. High levels of dynamism need not always involve an increased amount of verbal communication.

Stability

Stability refers to the degree to which the social structure of a system does not change. Few systems are ideally stable, and few can maintain high levels of instability without changing in such important ways as to involve redefinition of their boundaries. The location of a system in a continuum of 'stability-instability' may be partly independent of its location on a continuum of 'dynamism-staticism'. For example, a system may be characterised by a repetitive change cycle in which the structure of the system fluctuates between two states at given time intervals. Such a system would be highly dynamic, but may still be characterised by a stable equilibrium. Indeed, it is possible that a pattern of cyclical change of this kind may function to maintain a system's stability.[18] The stability of any system's equilibrium is, however, problematic, on account of influences which emanate both from the environment and from within the system itself, e.g., the discovery and utilisation of new sources of energy, or such internal phenomena as rapid changes in the amount of goods available for distribution, or changes in people's perceptions of what is socially just.

Some sets of dimensions

The position of a social system on any one of the above five dimensions tends to be related to its position on any other. Although these relationships are sufficiently imperfect to permit each dimension to be conceptualised as independent of the others, they tend to constitute a syndrome. With reference to society, two syndromes are particularly interesting. They have been called 'simple' and 'complex'.[19] We will now examine the way in which some of the dimensions of these syndromes interrelate.

Complexity and social cohesion

The social cohesion of 'simple' societies (those with a relatively low degree of differentiation and specialisation) tends to be based to a large extent on normative solidarity. The norms in such societies are likely to have an altruistic content, largely because relations among their members are characterised by diffuseness and emotional involvement. The simple structure of their interaction systems provides a basis only for relatively low degrees of interdependence, and there are relatively few opportunities for conflict either with respect to goods and services or with respect to power and authority differentials. Where such differentials exist, for example in slightly less simple societies, they are not likely to be marked by sufficient social distance to be conducive to deep-rooted tensions and conflicts. Simple societies, therefore, have little need for differentiated agencies which specialise in coordinating activities in the society. Nor is there a great need for specialised management of conflict and tension. We do not claim that simple societies are completely tension and conflict free, but merely suggest that they contain relatively few 'axes of tension' compared with their more complex counterparts. Therefore, when morale, an index of solidarity, is high, the members do not require a high degree of direction in order for cooperation to occur.

In contrast, the social cohesion of complex societies is based on the integration of their interaction systems. As a consequence of a higher degree of differentiation, they are likely to be co-ordinated primarily through the purposive activities of specialised and bureaucratically organised central agencies. The tendency towards specialised, centralised, and bureaucratised coordination in such societies results from the size and complexity of their organisational tasks. It stems also from their highly differentiated interaction systems whose role specificity and impersonal nature tend to produce a relatively low degree of consensus on norms and values. Furthermore, when consensus exists it is usually restricted to those norms and values with an egoistic content which encourage men to be more aware of their differences than their similarities.[20] Thus, like their more simple counter-parts, complex societies may also manifest high degrees of social cohesion, but when they do, it tends to derive from the deliberate action of central agencies, both at the societal and sub-system levels, and not from the solidarity produced by their normative systems.[20]

As a society becomes more complex, there is also a greater likelihood that groups with conflicting interests and values will emerge. Tension and conflict between such groups tend to be endemic in complex societies, and constitute a pressure on the specialised agencies of central coordination to manage tension and conflict. Such agencies come increasingly to perform a regulative function with respect to norms and values; that is, they attempt to use their central position and the various re-sources at their disposal in order to maintain a reasonable balance between expectations and real possibilities. In addition, due to their greater specialisation and differentiation of parts, complex societies tend to develop large numbers of relatively autonomous nuclei which are potential loci of centrifugal pressure. Such nuclei are capable of becoming self-sufficient with respect to their own coordination and the satisfaction of all their funda-mental problems. At the same time, the high degree of inter-dependence among the various parts in such a system implies that the cost incurred through the loss of any one unit would be high. As a result, a further premium is placed upon the cen-tralisation of control in order to combat the potentially fissi-parous tendencies of such autonomous nuclei and to maintain the integrity of the system as a whole.[22]

Complexity and openness

We have already mentioned that a social system may be open or closed with respect to three environments: the natural, the social and the psychological, or, in other words, the personalities of its members. Further, the actual openness of the system at any time may be less than its potential openness, which can be discovered only when the environments change, especially if they change suddenly.

Complex systems tend to be closed to their natural environments. First, they are likely to have specialised and differentiated institutions for dealing with nature. Second, they are likely to have relatively powerful technologies, although this does not derive from their level of complexity alone. However, members of complex societies are often surprised and humiliated by the powerlessness of their organisations and technology in the face of natural disasters. They are often less able to cope with such natural intrusions than members of simple societies who have never become so dependent on specialised personnel, whose simple technology is more in equilibrium with their natural environment, and whose mode of life does not insulate them from the natural world. They are more open to it and, at the same time, more adaptable.

Although complex societies are ostensibly open to their social environment because their social cohesion derives from the integration of their interaction systems, in fact they are relatively closed to it. They are able to impose their own internal patterns of specialisation, differentiation and interdependence on their relationships with the social environment. The development of such relationships can occur with relatively little effect on the system as a whole. Social intrusions may occur but their speed and depth are regulated by the existing interaction and normative patterns. In contrast, although simple societies are ostensibly closed because their cohesion derives from their normative solidarity and an essential element of this solidarity is the social definition of who is 'us' and 'them', in fact, they are relatively open, especially when they exist in relative isolation and are self-sufficient economically. Consequently, they are more vulnerable to vagaries in their social environment than complex societies are. When confronted with a social intrusion or even a threat of one, their systemic response is likely to be rejecting, especially as any accommodation will tend to require major structural change.

Complex systems tend to be closed to their psychological environment. This environment, in contrast with the social and natural environments, exists within the social and territorial boundaries of the social system. The patterns of interaction and normative regulation of societies requires only a limited participation by their members in any particular act except for those involved in certain special processes such as socialisation. Individuals are constrained both normatively and through a system of sanctions to participate in collective activities in a bounded way. Authority and power tend to be invested in certain echelons of organisations, and the conduct of both collective and personal affairs is subject to mainly impersonal regulations. Paradoxically, complex societies permit their members a great display of personal idiosyncrasies and refrain from a high degree of social regulation of much of their everyday life; as long as their members fulfil the expectations embodied in specific roles, what they do and feel elsewhere is of little consequence. However, as the fulfilment of specific roles is so totally important to the cohesion and functioning of a complex society, those in power strive to maintain highly organised sets of sanctions to ensure that these are fulfilled in a consistent and reliable manner.[23]

In contrast, simple societies are more open to their members. Although authority is apparently vested in office, it is almost impossible for members to see a person and his office as separate entities. People in such societies tend to relate to each other in terms of who they are rather than what they do. Consequently, as fulfilment of office occurs simultaneously with everyday activities and personal idiosyncrasies are dangerous, simple societies regulate the daily routine of their members to a far greater extent than complex societies do.

Complexity and instability

Change within a social system may be the result of internal or external factors. Hence, the stability or instability of a society is related to both its degree of internal dynamism and its degree of openness to its various environments.

In our discussion of cohesion and complexity, we pointed out that complex societies contain many structures which serve as axes of tension and which are potential sources of structural change. Hence, the pressure for such change within complex societies is likely to be continuous. In contrast, simple societies contain fewer axes of tension, and their potential for endogenously generated change is small. However, the actual relationship between endogenous sources of social change and change itself is problematic and complex; it is subject to many factors which are beyond the scope of this discussion. For example, complex societies usually possess highly developed technologies which enable their rulers to regulate endogenous sources of change. Nonetheless, if all sources of social change were endogenous, complex societies would tend to be relatively dynamic and unstable and simple societies static and stable.

The stability or instability of a society also depends on its degree of openness to its environments.[24] Closure to any environment is likely to be a source of stability.[25] Complex societies tend to be closed to all their environments; only a very major environmental change is likely to affect them. However, if such a change occurs, its effects may be considerable. Simple societies are more open to their environments and, hence, are more easily affected by changes in them.[26] Thus, if all sources of social change were exogenous, complex societies would be more static and stable than simple ones. The overall stability or instability of a society depends on both sources of change, and the actual mixture in any society at any time is an empirical question.

The discussion so far has been very general, and our aim has been to provide a background for the discussion of groups and their environments. We will now examine the concept 'group' from a social systems point of view, and then consider those groups which might be called 'large'. Our aim is to show what groups have in common with all social systems and what distinguishes them as a special type of social system.

Groups as social systems

In a sense, all human collectivities with more than merely logical status, such as 'people with black hair', are groups. As such they will have many properties in common, and many propositions about social organisation will apply to them. However, this is too narrow an approach. The use of the term 'group' as a substitute for 'social system' reduces the validity of the concept 'group' to denote a particular type of social system which differs from others in important respects, and hence will have certain organisation specific problems. Whereas all groups are social systems, not all social systems are groups. This is obvious if a group is compared with an industrial society. However, the difference is not just a question of size and complexity; groups differ from simple societies too. In fact, a group is a social system with definite properties of its own, which we will now consider.

A group is concerned with solving only a limited number of fundamental problems. Although its members must strive to solve all their fundamental problems, they will not necessarily do so within the context of the group. Indeed, if they try to do so, either they will fail or the structure of the group will be modified to such an extent that it will cease to be a group. As a result of its limited aims, a group must exist within the context of a larger social system on which it depends for the solution of those problems with which it is not concerned directly. Hence, a group is different from a society, however simple.

Furthermore, the limitation of its aims makes a group a relatively transitory system, no matter how long it has been established. Permanence requires institutionalisation. There are two reasons why this process does not occur in groups. First, the existence and boundaries of a group are often more important to its members than to non-members. Institutionalisation requires that non-members believe that the group's existence and boundaries should be maintained. Secondly, any one member of the group may believe that his membership will be of limited duration; the permanence of the collectivity beyond this time may be relatively unimportant to him. This is obviously true of a therapy group and, for example, it is increasingly true of industrial work groups. Thus, there is little pressure for institutionalisation either from within or from outside the group. Hence, a group differs from an organisation because it is not institutionalised.

A group is very open to the personality systems of its members. It is also part of their identity. Groups are characterised by intimate face-to-face interaction, and are fundamental to the formation and maintenance of the social nature of their individual members. As a result, a sense of being part of a whole develops; the individual becomes part of 'we'.[27] However, the potential for such internalisation is also related to stages in an individual's development. Groups which are entered into late in life may never be internalised fully by their members.

It is important to recognise that the degree to which a collectivity can be institutionalised or internalised does not depend on its size. Although many collectivities which are highly institutionalised and internalised are large, such as a church or a student body at a university, many large groups are transitory. For example, a crowd or an audience is not institutionalised and can be only superficially internalised by its members. In fact, except in unusual circumstances, these collectivities are probably not internalised at all. Similarly, some highly institutionalised collectivities are small, such as a family, and many are of moderate size, such as a university department or a surgical ward. In general, groups are highly internalised but not institutionalised. Families are the prototype of all groups, but in the sociological sense of the concept, as they are an institutionalised sub-system of the society, they are not really groups.

On the basis of a social system's perspective groups can be located on certain of the dimensions discussed above. In this way we can establish the syndrome of properties by which a social system can be denoted as a group. A social system constitutes a group to the extent that: it has a relatively simple organisational structure; it is relatively open with respect to its natural, psychological and social environments; and it is relatively unstable with respect to its boundaries.

Our treatment of groups may be contrasted with that offered by Cartwright and Zander,[28] who define groups as a set of people with the following characteristics: they have frequent interaction and are defined by themselves and by others as members of the group; they share norms concerning matters of common interest and participate in a system of interlocking roles; they identify with one another as a result of having internalised the same model-objects or ideals in their super-egos; they find participation rewarding and pursue promotively interdependent goals; they have a collective perception of their unity and act in a unitary manner towards the environment.

This definition is propositional. It states that the extent to which a set of people have these properties, they form a group. Although these properties tend to form a syndrome, the nature and determinants of their interdependence is problematic. Evidence suggests that the degree to which people are in frequent interaction is the basis of group formation. This is especially so if their interactions are demarcated in time and place in a regular and consistent manner such that the visibility of the boundaries between members and non-members is high. Shared norms arise from these patterns of interaction, and participation in a system of interlocking roles arises from frequent interaction.[29] Mutual identification, e.g., among siblings, on the basis of a commonly held model, e.g., the mother or the father or both, is probably essential to the capacity of any person to enter and participate in a group;[30] it is problematic whether all members of a group have introjected a particular object which is unique to them as members of that particular group. This may emerge in time but it is not essential for all phases of group activity. The remaining properties are also not essential, but are likely to emerge under certain conditions. Further, although it is significant that a group is the only social system which can plausibly be considered as sets of people, in fact Cartwright and Zander's approach is misleading because it implies that all social systems are groups.[31]

Groups are not all the same, and types of groups should be distinguished; propositions which apply to some may not apply to others. However, the actual classification of groups is difficult. Cartwright and Zander point out that many different classificatory schemes have been proposed. A common procedure has been to select a few properties and to define 'types' of groups on the basis of whether these properties are present or absent. Among the properties most often employed are: size (number of members), amount of physical interaction among members, degree of intimacy, level of solidarity, locus of control of group activities, extent of formalisation of rules governing relations among members and tendency of members to react to one another as individual persons or as occupants of roles. Although it would be possible to construct a large number of types of groups by combining these properties in various ways, usually only dichotomies have resulted: formal and informal, primary and secondary, small-large, *gemeinschaft-gesellschaft*,[32] autonomous-dependent, temporary-permanent, consensual-symbiotic. Sometimes a rather different procedure has been advocated in which groups are classified according to their objectives or social settings. Accordingly, they are said to be work groups, therapy groups, social groups, committees, clubs, gangs, teams, coordinating groups, religious groups, and the like.

This sort of procedure is not satisfactory. Although the typologies which result may be useful for certain purposes, they are essentially *ad hoc*, and the organisational variation within each type is so great as to equal, if not exceed, the variation between types. Such distinctions are helpful only in that they permit further specification of categories based on organisational properties. Indeed, as Cartwright and Zander use such a wide definition of groups, they include categories such as *gemeinschaft* and *gesellschaft* which apply to societies but not really to groups.

Present knowledge does not permit us to propose a classificatory schema for groups. In any case, such schema depend on the purpose to which they are to be put. However, two things are certain: although size may be important, indeed given our definition of groups, it may be more important than any other property, it may not be very useful for purposes of classification; and therapy groups should not be taken as typical of groups in general.

Large groups

In this section we will attempt to point out the special features of large groups. Although the number of people in a large group may approximate to the number of people in an organisation, the distinction between these two types of social systems is based on differences in their interaction and normative systems. Indeed, according to our approach, large groups have essentially the same kinds of interaction and normative systems as small groups and quite different interaction and normative systems from those of organisations. If there is a significant difference between large and small groups, then the problem of locating the transition point from small to large is crucial.

A growing body of literature and unpublished discussion from psychotherapy suggests that large groups are not very different from small groups. Some psychotherapists report that, to their great surprise, groups of 50 to 75 evince many of the characteristics of groups of less than 10. However, others suggest that when a group exceeds 16, members experience the group and their participation in it in a new way and begin to behave differently.[33] An alternative opinion puts this figure between 5 and 7. For example, the *panchayat* or council of an Indian village has five members, and some Englishmen say that an ideal dinner party consists of 5 to 7 people.[34] However, with such a small number of people the personalities of guests play a part, as does the food, and, as those who give dinner parties know to their cost, there is no golden rule for success. Ten people who already know each other may be a better number than 6 who do not. These examples only serve to illustrate the need for empirical research into the effects of size on group processes and, unfortunately, little exists.

In principle, many different disciplines might offer insight into the effect of size on groups, but in practice they do not. Ethology has tended to deal with behaviour which is either irrelevant to humans or too far removed from its human counterpart to be isomorphic; the fact that rats become aggressive when their population density reaches a certain point adds little to our knowledge of the effects of size on groups. Anthropologists who have studied group-like social systems, such as tribes and bands, have concentrated on the effects of variation in size on the development of new organisational forms and the disintegration of simpler collectivities, and are concerned with numbers in the thousands. Psychology and social psychology have emphasised the study of small groups. Studies of the effects of variation in size are available, but with few exceptions, the range has been from 2 to 12. Valuable exceptions are those studies of learning behaviour which show that once a group exceeds 15, the decrease in personal participation is so great that members might just as well attend lectures of 400.[35] There is an extensive sociological literature which discusses the effect of size on the interaction and normative patterns of social organisations. Although this information does not derive from studies of large groups, we will review the most relevant literature, together with findings from social psychology, and use them to examine the problem of the transition from small to large.

Any discussion of the effects of variation in size must begin with Simmel.[36] An important contribution is his analysis of dyadic and triadic relationships. Simmel saw the dyadic relationship as elemental to all forms of social organisation, and examined its effects on the two people involved. He stressed that the most extreme human feelings are experienced within a dyad; no other relationship contains the same feelings of love, hate, freedom, isolation, jealousy, understanding, devotion or betrayal. Once he established the nature of the dyad, Simmel discussed what happens to the structure of the dyad and to the two people involved when a third is introduced. He argued that these effects are disproportionately great; the addition of one person to the dyad is likely to be more important than the addition of one to any other group.[37]

Simmel extrapolated his argument to consider the effects of size in general. He pointed out that the effects of changes in size are not linear, either for one collectivity or for the relationship between clearly demarcated parts of a social system. For example, he commented that an army of 10,000 can control a population of 1 million more easily than one person can control 100, or 100 can control 10,000. Even though in each case the ratios are the same, the absolute size of the controlling force is important. Thus, size alone can be an independent factor.

Although many writers use the concept 'large' to refer to the size of membership of social organisations, it is a substitute for greater quantitative precision. Empirical evidence which focuses the problem of definition will now be considered. It is worth recalling the very early experiments of Asch on conformity.[38] They contain some information about the effects of size and illustrate the importance of the dyadic relationship. Asch showed that if a person had one close affiliate and confidant in a group, then virtually no matter how many members exert pressure on him to conform, he will be able to resist and follow his own judgement. Although in general the larger the group the greater the pressure to conform, once membership reaches 50, any further increase in size has a negligible effect. Thus, the number 50 may be the point at which a small group becomes large. However, other studies suggest different transition points; and the transition point may vary according to the type of process being observed.

On the basis of numerous experimental studies, Bales et al.[39] showed that as a group increases in size from 2 or 3 up to 15 or 20, the 'active' members tend to dominate interaction and 'passive' members inhibit their participation, and the group's discussion becomes less exploratory and adventurous, the group's atmosphere becomes less intimate and members' actions more anonymous, and generally members feel less satisfied. Unresolved differences amongst members become more acceptable. For most of these tendencies the transition occurred in the membership range 5–7.[40]

The experiments also showed that in general as the group gets larger, members show less tension, but its release is more obvious. Feelings of solidarity are expressed more openly and readily, but agreement decreases. Although opinions are less sought after and given, more ideas and information are forthcoming.

Many of these trends were interpreted as the result of two interrelated factors. As size increases, the time available for talking to each member decreases; and each person is confronted with an absolutely larger number of persons. Each member is under pressure to maintain a more or less adequate relationship with each other member. Thus, as size increases, each member has more relationships to maintain and less time to do so.

A central issue in sociological studies has been the relationship between size and the complexity of social organisation. With respect to groups, Bales et al.[41] found that a slight increase in complexity was associated with an increase in size from 2 or 3 to 15 or 20. For example, greater demands are made on the leader; the leader becomes more differentiated from the rest of the group; the group becomes more tolerant of direction by the leader; proceedings become more centralised; the group takes longer to make value judgements; sub-groups tend to form and the rules and procedures of the group become more formalised. Once again, the most obvious transition occurred when the group reached a membership of between 5 and 7.

Some sociologists have argued that within an industrial economy, the efficient use of resources in large-scale industrial organisations requires specialisation and differentiation of work. As a result, problems of communication and coordination arise, and create a tendency towards complexity, formalisation, hierarchy, and other elements of bureaucracy. This proposition is, however, the subject of debate. Most sociologists accept that increase in size leads to greater complexity and its consequences, but the more important issue is the range of sizes within which this relationship operates, and the various other internal and external conditions which might regulate it.[42] Another finding is that the larger the organisation, the more likely it is that an informal organisation will emerge which may conflict with the formal one.

The material that derives from organisations is in principle applicable to groups, and it is reasonable to assume that as groups get larger they will exhibit some tendency towards complexity. We have commented above that some people who work with large therapy groups suggest that as groups increase from 10 to 100 they do not show such tendencies. This inconsistency requires resolution. There are several possible explanations. These groups may not exhibit such changes because their members are primarily concerned with conformity to the unspoken expectations of those who have power and authority over the members and on whom the members depend. Alternatively, as these groups exist within a more formal organisation, such as a hospital, there are no organisational positions or labels which can be applied to such changes; without concepts to describe informal complexity, it may go unnoticed.[43]

As groups have little formal structure, it is easy to overlook the development of an informal structure, and to assume that groups tend to be the same no matter how big they are. Simmel postulated that dyads are the elemental structures of all groups. We would supplement this view by suggesting that dyads and triads form the elemental structures of small groups and, at a certain size, small groups form the elemental structures of large groups.[44] The size at which this differentiation occurs must be established empirically; it may vary from group to group according to their purposes. Equally, it may vary for different processes within the same group. Within large groups, small groups may be less stable than their own component dyads or triads, but again this is an empirical question. Interactions in large groups will be among individuals who represent not only themselves but their sub-groups as well. It follows that the upper limit of a large group may be equal to the square of the upper limit of a small group. However, as the upper limit of a small group still eludes us, this proposition is of limited value.

If we accept that an increase in the size of a group creates the conditions for increased complexity, it must be recognised that increased complexity presents its own problems. For example, it is harder to balance individual and collective needs and, hence, there is pressure towards formalisation. Many people prefer the relatively more impersonal and anonymous relationships of large groups. In large therapy groups, such people may be able to defend themselves against the types of feelings they might experience in a small group, in which case their preference for a large therapy group might be a 'resistance'.

It is consistent with our earlier analysis of complex and simple societies to postulate that increased complexity is likely to favour the development of egoistic normative patterns at the expense of altruistic ones. Consequently, large groups are often pre-occupied with the time-consuming task of maintaining their solidarity. Participation in the collective pursuit of this aim may provide an experience which enables members to realise that their own identities are intertwined with that of the group. In maintaining the boundaries of a large group, the members are able to maintain their own personal boundaries, and at the same time the realisation that much of the self is intertwined with significant collectivities provides a greater awareness of that part of the self which is unique. Of course, participation in small groups also provides opportunities for this experience. However, large groups may be better sources of it because of their greater chaos and potential for schism.

Groups and their environments

We stated previously that the sociological perspective is con-textual. A fuller understanding of the structure and process of any group, and especially large groups, requires that their environments be taken into account.[45] An understanding and knowledge of the societal and institutional context of large groups is one of the most important contributions which sociology has to offer. This can be illustrated by some examples.

Israel is a country in which systematic efforts to use large groups for psychotherapy have been made. Springmann uses a technique which derives from Bion and Ezriel's work on small groups;[46] interpretations are made in terms of the group's collective transference to the conductor. His evidence suggests that this is more effective than most psychotherapists would have thought possible. This may be explained sociologically in terms of certain features of Israeli society. In Israel, the popu-lation is very young. Age cohorts are not only a demographic category, but are an important structural form. They mediate between individuals and national institutions, and are the basis of peer group culture, which is an important source of social control and continued socialisation throughout the life cycle; they create and maintain standards concerning what constitutes an Israeli citizen. Israeli culture defines its citizens as members of a large group, the paradigm of which is an extended family or tribe in which geographical and political boundaries coincide with religious boundaries. It has been a matter of policy that peer groups should assist in the assimilation of the children of immigrants. Even the army takes account of this social fact. Although it is highly disciplined, relationships between officers and ranks are informal. Such informality is possible because of the high degree of mutual identification throughout the hierarchy.

This kind of societal context creates a special type of personality structure. Selves are not rigorously distinguished from others. 'Individuality' is less highly valued. It is interesting that the most common Christian name in Israel is 'Israel', which indicates the extent to which individuals are likely to identify with the collectivity. We do not suggest that Israel is without egoistic norms and is one happy family, but it does provide a situation in which participation in large groups is less likely to be experienced as a threat to personal identity or as a deprivation of an intimate relationship with another person. Consequently, interpretation of collective transference in terms of the group as a whole will inevitably have an impact on each participant.

All communications within groups should be understood in the light of the authority structures of the surrounding society. The authority of senior psychotherapists in large therapeutic groups within English hospitals and the bases of their power to control patients' lives derives primarily from the authority and power structure of the hospital and the stratification of English society. The performance and contribution of these psychotherapists within a group may be a secondary influence. Interpretations of transference phenomena which ignore this reality can be misleading; e.g., the suppression by patients of aggressive feelings may derive from their correct assessment of the consequences of expressing them.

It has been shown that in industry the degree to which subordinates in the work group are overtly aggressive to their supervisors as a result of close and punitive supervision depends on the power which supervisors have to control their jobs. The degree to which subordinates are able to displace their aggressive feelings from the supervisor by reducing their productivity depends on the structure of the system of payment. When subordinates receive a fixed salary, productivity varies inversely with aggressive feelings; when a piece work system is in operation, productivity tends to be maintained in spite of aggressive feelings. Indeed, the degree to which subordinates experienced close and punitive supervision as frustrating depended on their attitudes towards authority; manual workers were generally more receptive and found it less frustrating than did clerical workers.[47]

Similarly, symptoms that might be classified as 'neurotic' may be normative for a particular social class or ethnic group. For example, the degree to which patients openly complain and express their feelings about those who are responsible for their treatment is a cultural variable. Some ethnic groups whose members often fight with knives may interpret any facial wounds, however slight, as a sign of defeat. Intense concern about minor facial scars may be a source of misunderstanding; a member of such a group may see them as signifying a loss of status, and seek plastic surgery to restore his former status, whereas the hospital might see him as neurotic and in need of psychotherapy.[48]

So far, we have stressed the ways in which the environment of large groups influences structures and processes within the group. However, large groups may also affect structures and processes in their environment. These effects are likely to be indirect. People from different positions in structures of authority and power usually meet in role-specific situations and consequently engage one another with narrow segments of themselves. This often generates mutual fantasies and facilitates the formation of stereotypes based on positions and functions rather than more realistic mutual understanding of the various views and interests which of necessity are contained within large organisations. In such circumstances, decisions and actions are not taken on the basis of rational assessments of the resources and constraints which characterise all positions in the organisation.

When large groups from various segments and echelons of an organisation come together regularly outside the formal context of their organisational roles to discuss matters of mutual interest, communication with the organisation is facilitated. Such sharing of views and feelings may help the organisation to run more smoothly and enable members to understand that the formal structure of the organisation is not immutable. However, if change is to occur with a minimum of tension and conflict, members must be aware of the scope and limitations of their power to initiate change and of their own irrational attachments to certain types of procedure. Discussion of goals and strategies with people from all parts of the organisation may help members to understand the systematic nature of their organisation and help them realise that all change is likely to have unanticipated consequences. The use of large groups for such purposes has been called 'sociotherapy'.[49]

Although the term 'sociotherapy' has perjorative connotations for those involved in the promotion of social change, in fact, large groups have been used in this way outside formal organisations. In Chile, for example, the revolution aimed at participatory democracy. Early reports indicated that for some tasks very few decisions were made at the top. Money and materials for rebuilding houses were allocated by central government but how these resources should have been used was left to the neighbourhood. Decisions were not made on a village basis. The endogenous informal organisation was used instead. Every morning a meeting of a large group from a neighbourhood decided how the work was to be done. The size of the group varied from day to day, and the personnel also changed. So far little is known about this experiment, but undoubtedly those concerned with large groups in formal organisations would benefit from studies of it. Equally, the use of large groups within a community would benefit from more research about large groups in organisations.

Part Two

Application

The five chapters in this section are concerned with the practical application of the large group in a variety of settings: Dr Whiteley, from a background of general psychiatry, discusses the contribution of the large group to the practice of 'sociotherapy' (the discovery, exploration and resolution of intra- and inter-group tensions) in the therapeutic community. Dr Springmann, a psychoanalyst, utilises the large group in the furtherance of 'psychotherapy' (focusing on intra-personal tensions), according to the theoretical formulations of Henry Ezriel. Dr Skynner describes the use of large groups in training situations, using the group-analytic approach in conjunction with his experience of family dynamics and therapy. Myles Hopper is an anthropologist working on a project for community development in Newfoundland, and details his experiences of the large group as part of an educational programme. Trevor Mumby describes his work in industry, and the importance of large-group dynamics in understanding conflicts that may arise in the setting of an industrial organisation.

6. The large group as a medium for sociotherapy

J. Stuart Whiteley

An understanding and modification of human behaviour can be reached through investigating intrapersonal processes, and this is called *psychotherapy*. A similar goal can be arrived at through exploring interpersonal activity and this is called *sociotherapy*. While the pathways taken and the aids applied differ in many respects the general direction and ultimate goal are the same, so that a rigid division between sociotherapy and psychotherapy seems artificial. Understanding the differences and appreciating what each approach has to offer in the large group setting, however, leads to a more profitable application of either technique.

Sociotherapy or psychotherapy

The large group of 50 or so patients which is now a common feature of the psychiatric hospital usually meets with 5 or 6 representatives of the therapeutic staff from the different professional disciplines.

The techniques of individual psychotherapy would clearly be wasteful and inappropriate in this setting. To some extent certain phenomena of the small psychotherapy group do still occur, however, and can be utilised in the therapeutic transaction.

Thus Bion's[1] original Basic Assumptions still apply and can be identified in the large group's behaviour. For instance, *pairing* and the reaction of the rest of the group to the pair is a frequent occurrence, with the group somehow feeling the necessity to nurture and preserve the pair. *Dependency* on the staff or on

G

dominant group members similarly occurs in the shape of demands for extra privileges, or alternatively misdemeanours may be committed to which the staff are often the first to (misguidedly) respond. *Fight/flight* reactions are reflected in the anger or apathy of the group, the anger often directed at staff or other group members felt to be in an authoritarian position.

Furthermore, in the analysis of large-group dynamics the Focal Conflict Theory of Whitaker and Lieberman[2] has striking application, although developed from the study of small-group situations.

Thus the group meets and after throwing up a variety of topics gradually turns its energy to one or more subjects which have some linking theme. Then through a series of stages in which the group approaches its goal only to retreat because of the reactive fears then engendered, solutions are floated one by one, which avoid or overcome these real or imagined fears until the conflict is satisfactorily resolved.

However the particular qualities of the large group make it possible for an entirely new dimension of social behaviour to be explored. Its very size leads to sub-group formation and rival factions promoting the issues of conflict. Certain people demand the attention of the room or dominate the proceedings while others, made anxious by the very number present, retreat (literally) into the dark corners.

The examination of the social dynamics of such a group to the exclusion of any exploration of intra-personal life has been advocated by Edelson[3] who views sociotherapy of this kind as quite distinct from psychotherapy and a process to be kept separate.

Edelson follows on the teachings of Talcott Parsons and adopts a rather Functionalist approach to social behaviour. He has identified four processes in the large groups and sees the large-group community-meeting as coming together primarily for one of the following sociotherapeutic purposes:

1. adaptation – to existing external circumstances,
2. consummation – of currently held needs,

3. integration – of those who are new to or deviant from group norms,

or

4. motivation – the drive toward institutional norms and values.

The emphasis may shift during the group from one objective to another.

Whilst Edelson's work sheds welcome light on the dynamics of the large group his distinction between sociotherapy and psychotherapy is not shared by everyone. In Edelson's particular approach the psychotherapy is conducted in individual and group sessions separate from the large group which is seen as a task group from which psychotherapy should be excluded.

The intrusion of psychotherapy into the large group is viewed by Edelson as detrimental.

Certainly this is often the case when the completion of a group task is interrupted by an individual bringing in topics for intra-personal reasons and demanding immediate attention by psychotherapeutic interpretation. Thus after a particularly difficult and disorganised week in the Henderson Community we got round to the monthly elections for the committee. The initial apathy and unwillingness to take part was gradually dispersed as unemotional matters such as who would be the various ward representatives were discussed. Steadily the group gathered momentum as it saw itself able to accomplish *something*, when two girls, older members of the community already a little disregarded because they were on the threshold of leaving, intervened.

'I think we should talk to Annie,' said Gina. 'She's got to go up to town today and she gets this phobia when she travels on a train.'

Annie sat silent but demure, accustomed as she was to a rather attentive parental support for she was a 'nice kid', but after a brief pause the group response was angry and dismissive. The object of taking their current task to a successful outcome was seen as the important factor and at this time 'psychotherapy' would have been *obstructive* to the main issue. There is also the point that the therapist in making an interpretation, whether to an individual or the whole group, is putting himself apart from the group, in a position of superior knowledge and denying the two-way process of sociotherapeutic interchange.

On the other hand a psychotherapeutic intervention in the large group can serve as a model or learning situation if others can be involved and thus be *facilitating*.

As an example one may cite the following incident from experience at Henderson.

Jos is brought into what is really a business meeting because he is 'up tight'. We listen to his monologue about his alternating enthusiasm or depression, how his efforts go unappreciated in life, and his parents are unmoved or indifferent. No one dares to move off the topic lest Jos feels more rejected and unwanted, but 'psychotherapy' of this kind is getting nowhere and some of the group sit in numbed silence leaving the work to staff. The fact that this is the last group on a Friday evening before the major staff figures are about to leave for the weekend and the discourse is keeping them here adds to the pertinence of the situation. Doubtless others identify with his position and feelings of deprivation and neglect but they leave Jos to voice them. At last it becomes possible to ask Jos to talk about his present job in the community and how he sees his performance therein. The same extremes are present, he agrees. He is supposed to oversee the total workshop programme and record attendances at work groups and says that either people are in and enthusiastically at work without his help or that no one is in and he is incapable of persuading them to go to work. He then feels a failure but also that the job is no good as a treatment situation and he wants to resign, for it carries no opportunities for interaction with others and has many organisational defects. Others now join in to discuss how they see him in the job.

There is at first a move to accept his resignation and relieve him of his burden out of sympathy but to do so, it is pointed out by staff, would be destructive not supporting, because he would be left then with no positive role to play in the community and have to resume the role of a rejected failure. Instead he is asked to devise new methods of recording the information required and organising the job in question and, even in considering this, he begins to experience some relief of his present depression. The ensuing days then see some practical results from his efforts and some lightening of mood.

Another discrimination between sociotherapy and psychotherapy is practised at Frazer House in Australia where A. W. Clark[4] describes separate large-group meetings on certain days for the administration of the Unit and what is called *social control*, and *therapy* on other days when the object of the group is personality change. In these latter meetings 'collective foci' are identified as dominating the proceedings. The task of the therapist, according to Clark, is to expose and promote discussion on the problems arising out of situations of (*a*) threat, (*b*) loss, (*c*) gain or (*d*) frustration.

Between the two poles of pure psychotherapy and strict sociotherapy, however, remains a sociotherapeutic approach, such as is practised at Henderson,[5] in which there is less division between sociotherapy and psychotherapy and administrative procedures and less specificity in the analysis of behaviour in the large group. Many threads can run through such a group and at times will be drawn together in one theme to which different people will react in their differing ways according to individual needs. In this method sociotherapy becomes the lead into the psychotherapeutic understanding of behaviour.

The developing concepts of large-group dynamics

A study of the historical development of the concepts utilised in large-group therapy gives us some understanding of the factors involved in the type of large-group sociotherapy which has come to be practised at Henderson where, in fact, we would see the actual large-group meetings as but a part of an on-going and continuous large-group experience throughout the 24 hours of the day.

The precursors in the therapeutic use of the large group, as far as psychiatric institutions in the English field were concerned, can conveniently be taken to be the Northfield *experiments* of Bion, Main,[6] Foulkes[7] and others, and the Mill Hill *experiences* of Maxwell Jones[8] and his colleagues.

Northfield and Mill Hill were English military psychiatric hospitals in the early years of the Second World War. They presented to the psychiatric world a unique and unprecedented situation in that here were *gathered together in community living, large groups,* of *young adults,* with *emotional disorders resulting from social disturbance* – namely the infringement of war-time military service on their lives. The situation was ripe for novel methods to be tried out and Bion attempted to apply a psychoanalytic and the (then) new group-psychotherapeutic approach to the large group which comprised his ward. The experiment ran into difficulties both internal and in relation to the hospital authorities and was terminated.

In the second Northfield experiment Main, Foulkes and others conceived of the idea of the total hospital as a large group with interdependent and interrelating parts influencing each other. The role of the therapist in this *therapeutic community* was to identify the *dysfunctional* processes in the organisation, demonstrate them and even suggest ways of overcoming them. Foulkes[9] describes his role at Northfield as 'essentially analytical' and goes on to say 'out of the experiment came the idea that the occupation of any group may be of secondary importance whereas active participation in the group setting may be the essential therapeutic agency. The results of the participation depending on the good or bad effect of the interpersonal relationships which are encountered.' Such an approach, perhaps leaning more towards the psychotherapeutic, has continued to the present day in those psychiatric hospitals dealing largely with psychoneurosis and using group-analytic methods. In this approach the patient is viewed as sick and thus in conflict with his environment and at times, via transference neuroses, with his therapist. The therapist has a fixed role as the one who leads the patient towards resolution of his (the patient's) difficulties.

While Northfield was seen as a situation where novel methods of therapy could be tried out, a unique social situation can also be viewed as one likely to throw up new and different modes of social behaviour. This, in fact, was what took precedence at Mill Hill where Maxwell Jones, through initial failure of a didactic and medically authoritarian approach, found himself involved in an interchange of ideas and opinions with his patients. A mutual learning process evolved and this was enhanced by a deliberate flattening of the inhibiting hierarchical hospital structure; professional roles were blurred to decrease dependence on medical omnipotence and facilitate the two-way communication of ideas.

This model of large-group therapy was later applied to other situations where the core disturbance could be seen more in terms of a disturbance of social functioning than a psychological illness. Thus returned (and 'displaced') prisoners of war, the industrially unsettled and finally disordered families, the delinquent and the socially deviant came to be studied and treated in this way. The emphasis in this approach was rather on the remaining *functional* qualities of the group. The therapist was involved in the group life and responding to group forces, and patient and therapist were both seen as able to shift positions in order to resolve the issues of conflict between them and what they represented in the wider society.

By the late 1950s, Rapoport[10] and colleagues with Maxwell Jones at the Social Rehabilitation Unit, Belmont (later Henderson) Hospital, in collaboration had identified the sociological processes pertinent to this more *socio*therapeutic community.

They were as follows:

Permissiveness – in which the community allowed the individual to *be* his real self.

Communalism – through which everyone shared in the exploration, experimentation with, and experience of the community life.

Democracy – by which all had the right to determine community policy and control.

Confrontation – which was the technique of constantly putting before the individual what he was doing.

With the identification of these processes came the first awareness that the approach itself had limitations in its application.

There were those who, because of low intelligence, incipient psychosis, or marked inadequacy of emotional development, were too vulnerable to be exposed to these frank and often blunt interchanges. Some, because of gross personality disorders or defects, misused or were unable to apply what the method had to offer in terms of a 'living and learning' situation. Rapoport pointed out, too, the apparent contradiction between the psychotherapeutic function of the medical team and the rehabilitatory function of the workshop team which at that time occupied different parts of the patients' day and clearly had divergent aims.

In the wider field of psychiatric treatment this was also the period when tranquillising and anti-depressant drugs came into being. This factor diverted from the sociotherapeutic community a large number of psychiatric patients of mixed diagnoses who were quickly, if temporarily, responsive to pharmacological treatments, whilst leaving behind in what D. H. Clark[11] has described as the *therapeutic community proper,* those whose disorders presented more in terms of social conflict. Thus the delinquents, deviants, addicts, and those who acted out in an aggressive or impulsive way came to be the major people under treatment by this method. The term 'patient' is then less tenable and gradually has been replaced by *resident* at Henderson, since hospitals, prisons, hostels and mutually supportive communes all shelter this same individual at various times, and 'blurring of the roles' can also serve to blur the expectations on the individual tagged with the patient label.

The increased and intensified opportunity to study this type of disordered personality in the way described has led to a better understanding of the processes involved in becoming regarded as socially deviant.

The appropriate responses for use in the treatment situation have then developed more meaningfully. Sociotherapy has become a specific treatment process rather than just a liberal and humanitarian treatment attitude. Thus the Therapeutic Community at Henderson is now more clearly seen as a large group in which *interaction* can freely occur. This interaction must be *allowed* by relaxing rigid controls and dispensing with hierarchical binds and professional boundaries. The medical intervention of drug or other physical treatments to control behaviour is totally rejected. Interaction is *promoted* by devising a programme in which there is abundant opportunity for groups to meet and re-meet over a variety of corporate tasks and problems, simply concerned with the reality of living together.

Secondly, there is a tacit agreement between all participants that they are met for the specific task of examining and amending aspects of behaviour and, therefore, there has to be some method of regular and constant *exploration* of what is happening. For this purpose a group method is adopted with no individual doctor or nurse interviews.

Thirdly, and most important, there must be ample opportunity for *experimentation* with new modes of behaviour, and the community provides these through a continuous role-playing experience. An elected committee of residents looks after day-to-day happenings. In each sector such as a ward or workshop, a sub-group elects its members into roles with a specific function, e.g., as a ward-teaboy in one month and as the representative on the committee in the next. The jobs must carry real responsibility such as that of the social-work assistant, liaising with local agencies, family or employers for those preparing to leave. The tasks undertaken must also be seen as meaningful, such as in the selection of new residents, or acting as a co-therapist with staff in a group whose task is to help new residents integrate in the community.

Performance in these roles and the examination of what transpires as the roles are played out are regarded as a main source of 'treatment'. The adoption of this ideology has seen a lessening of the psychotherapy/rehabilitatory paradox. Work groups are no longer seen as training in work disciplines, but as groups they come together to do the necessary jobs to keep the communal living situation going, but with some period set aside to look at how we all accomplished the task. The old-style workshop instructors have left and other staff members

fulfil the continuity function in these work areas. The range of
work has increased and become more flexible as needs dictate
much as in any household.

Rules, formal roles and structure in the sociotherapeutic
community are the framework around which individuals act out
their problems and through which role-playing experiences with
feedback from fellows can lead to modifications in behaviour
and in perceptions of social interaction. The 'healthy' functional
aspects of the individual's personality can be brought into play
and emphasised through dealing with real problems and crises
that may arise. For instance, when a resident becomes disturbed
in the night, the other residents in their formal roles as committee members as well as informally as friends will have to
assess, cope and make the arrangements that nurses or doctors
might otherwise be called in to perform.

In sociotherapy of this practical nature an individual can often
find, for example, the resources to chair a workshop meeting,
involving considerable understanding of and negotiation with
other parties over a dispute that may have arisen. An hour
later in another situation the same individual, emotionally disturbed by some suddenly touched-off incident, can be seen as
chaotic in his own intrapersonal life and totally resistant to the
psychotherapeutic interventions which might then be offered
by the small group gathering around him. Reminded of his
recent successful venture into the less traumatic fields of the
sociotherapeutic exercise, he perhaps begins to reflect on the
abilities he has to deal with his own deeper problems, just as he
approached the less charged interpersonal problems of others.

The large-group meeting

In the foregoing 'the large group' has been taken to refer mainly
to the total therapeutic community. The experience of Henderson
has been that a maximum of 50 residents is a reasonable number
for the community. Above this total certain individuals get lost
and miss out on the continuing interaction whilst below 30
the character of the group changes to more of a small-group
dynamic.[12] The community is continually splitting and dividing

into smaller groups only to reconstitute as the large community meeting held once and possibly more each day. Thus 'the large group' has both a formal, structured coming together, and an informal and on-going existence. Just as one may make less differentiation between sociotherapy and psychotherapy, so one makes less distinction between the events occurring in the large-group meeting and events occurring in the therapeutic community's overall interaction throughout the day. The basic characteristics of the therapeutic community group are evident in the large-group community meeting but, in addition, that particular formalised meeting has its own peculiar qualities which make possible an additional method of therapy that other groups cannot offer. It cannot be viewed psycho-dynamically in the same way as the small psychotherapy group, although as already described the small group phenomena are not excluded.

The large group is a regressive situation. The large number present leads to some competition for attention and immaturity of behaviour so that one's weaker points are exposed if one elects to take part. Sometimes it is angry, excited, or demanding, and at other times anxious, hopeless, depressed and dependent on staff leads. It is nevertheless a safe situation, and aggressive outbursts will more often occur in this group than in the small or informal groups, as if something in the large group – whether it be the presence of more or senior staff, or simply of more and stronger members of the resident community – suffices to prevent the total disintegration or destructive impact of the disturbed person. After an excited, disorderly large-group meeting, the next meeting of the day – half an hour later in a small-group setting – can be astounding in its show of self-control, sophistication and appraisal of the previous behaviour in the large group.

For instance a community meeting at Henderson took the following course.

The staff expressed concern at residents cutting themselves and the lack of group involvement in looking after these incidents. A nurse complained of the way an incident was handled when Phil, a resident, brought alcohol into the community and

Penny, the chairman of the day, simply removed the bottle and threw it away but involved no one in any enquiry. Her vice-Chairman colleague confessed to a total inability to handle the situation. There seemed no stability in the administration of reasonable controls. This aroused anxieties in the staff, which were expressed openly and deeper anxieties in some residents who reacted as follows. The meeting broke into a series of petty squabbles over trivialities about rules. Many people were demonstrating an uninvolvement in the meeting by chattering together whilst Lee, who was to be considered for discharge that day because she had missed more than the allowable number of groups, was at the same time being proposed as the new ward representative! Thus her rule-breaking and its possible serious consequences were being ignored to all intents and purposes. The whole ethos of the therapeutic community seemed threatened. Nevertheless the culture and innate strength of the community and the stability of the structure – the committee, the agenda of the day, the chairman and her elected colleagues – sufficed to keep the organism alive. Staff would intervene as things flagged and little by little the various ward representatives brought in their contributions to the on-going life of the meeting and the community.

Lee and Phil (also due to be considered for discharge for the drink incident), however, kept up an angry discourse with the chairman and her two assistants, accusing them of authoritarian and insensitive control and in this they had some support. The behaviour of these current office-holders was then examined by the group in terms of their rather controlling personality attitudes and a reasonable discussion ensued. Then Lee and Phil, as if unsatisfied, began to accuse the whole group of being unsympathetic, and such were their angry and persistent interventions as the meeting went on that gradually they alienated themselves from the group. Phil finally accused older residents of stealing and hoarding food and this brought reciprocal anger and authoritarian demands from Jake, one of the vice-chairmen, for the culprits to be named. No one dared venture to give a name, such was his wrath, and again discussion and exchange of ideas ceased.

The way that Phil and Lee seemed to need to provoke this hostility to themselves was pointed out by a staff member. A resident asked if there was something *they* were *not* getting in their stay here. This was clarified by a staff member who said that they seemed to be using infringements of the group rules and procedures to attract attention to themselves, but that the attention thus provoked had not led to any satisfaction of their needs. Further, there was the inference that better-placed fellows were getting the favours and extras whilst they were deprived. The psycho-dynamic connection between 'food' and 'treatment' was alluded to.

The following day the community meeting was again over-controlled and apathetic but at the third day's community meeting someone who, in fact, was considerably anxious about and preoccupied with his own abilities and potential found the resources to question this over-control and point out the deadening effect it was having on group interaction. His reasoned approach was accepted by the chairman of the day who for the past two days had been exercising an almost manic power. There was some reasonable discussion but then a swing to excited shouts for anarchy and the abolition of all rules. The meeting, nevertheless, ended indecisively and rather chaotically.

When the small groups reassembled half an hour or so later the excited atmosphere of the large meeting had cooled and there was a pertinent discussion in the small group (of which the writer was a member) about an individual's need for external control and the fears one may have of getting out of control. The group seemed to divide into those who were exceedingly fearful of losing control and the consequences in terms of madness or badness, and those who rather defensively maintained certain controls over what they allowed to be exposed. The sharing of experiences brought understanding of the way people behave with the apparently controlling figures in life, the provocation of authoritarian control and abdication from self-control. This was seen in terms of the recent behaviour in the community and related to personal attitudes. When events were discussed at the staff meeting it transpired that similar themes had been taken up in the other concurrently held small psychotherapy groups. The overall outcome in the community was a reappraisal of our ways of dealing with rules and rule-breakers and a more reasonable approach reached.

In this way the *large group* in a therapeutic community setting is complementary to the various small-group activities, but whilst seen by some staff as the most important meeting from the sociotherapeutic point of view, the large group is seldom viewed thus by many residents, who still prefer to see their treatment in terms of doctor/patient interchanges.

An interesting survey of attitudes to and preference for the different types of groups offered in the Henderson Therapeutic Community has been carried out by Manning.[13] He showed that between 1950 and 1960 the individual doctor/patient sessions took preference over the large community meeting for both staff and patients. In 1973 when such individual sessions had long been abandoned, their place in order of preference (for both staff and residents) was taken by the small group, still doctor dominated.

A further interesting point that emerged was that the large group was seen as valuable by new residents, but then declined in favour after two months or so, only to gain in esteem towards the end of a resident's stay. Manning's comment is that perhaps it takes time for such a complex social situation to demonstrate its real value for the participant.

The *small group* however is more supportive, less regressive and competitive. It is more controlled and the 'medical' treatment process and approach more established, and it can go to a deeper and often more vulnerable level because the intimacy of its members engenders trust. It can serve as a reflective period – almost a training session – looking back on the extreme behaviour in the large group and is usually started off by themes from the latter.

The *on-going community life*, like a therapeutic group without start or finish, puts into practice the lessons learned in the large and small groups and demonstrates the continuing patterns of social interaction and behaviour. In its turn the large group can expose these in a more dynamic and accessible therapeutic setting, which has both psychotherapeutic and sociotherapeutic aspects.

The impact on the individual

The progress of an individual through a fairly deliberately structured and emotionally stressful therapeutic situation such as this follows a typical course.

Initially the newcomer cautiously or boldly sets out to create the situation between himself and others in which he is comfortable and with which he is familiar. He tries to make the situation 'viable' to use the terminology of Whitaker and Leiberman.[2] After a brief period in which his behaviour is tolerated by others, but at the same time commented upon, he begins to see that some change is required from him if he is to stay and live in harmony with his fellows. At this stage he either withdraws, unwilling or unable to face changes, or goes deeply into treatment with all the enthusiasm of a *positive transference* for the community and what it seems to offer. Acting emotion-avoiding out, his behaviour nevertheless reasserts itself whenever the individual experiences stressful situations, but gradually, with the feeling of increasing security in the group, he allows himself to experience more emotional life and acting out diminishes. The expected new self does not suddenly emerge, however, and a period of depression and hopelessness may replace the initial enthusiasm. There is something of a *negative transference* now to the community which, as he sees it, offered everything and gave so little, but the new-found security with others and the new awareness of emotional relationships usually suffice to keep him in the treatment situation until a more realistic outlook is gradually gained and sights are set for a return to society outside. Not uncommonly there is a brief return to old ways and old haunts as if to test out the actuality of any change and even to assure himself that the old niches still exist if he has to run back to them.

After leaving treatment a period of initial set-back may follow because expectations were set too high, but the lessons learned gradually assert themselves and a new identity is found with a different place to fill in society.

At the different stages in this course, therefore, different therapeutic interventions, reinforcements or interpretations will be called for. Early in treatment the experience of allowing oneself to feel emotions rather than run from them is to be encouraged whilst later the experimentation with new roles and modes of behaviour is promoted.

What Matza[14] has described in the process of *'becoming deviant'* – the drift towards those with whom one has *affinity*, the importance of being accepted by the group and doing things in order to gain *affiliation* with them, and the *signification* by others that one's behaviour is deviant thus setting expectations of future behaviour and reactions – has been identified by Whiteley[15] as occurring, similarly, in the *sociotherapeutic treatment* process. Thus the importance of the peer-group activity, the ways in which acceptance by the group can be gained and the recognition of the individual in a role which is both non-deviant and personally satisfying are all processes which need to be emphasised by the sociotherapist at the appropriate times.

That different personalities respond differently to the experience of treatment has been shown by Whiteley[16] in follow-up studies from Henderson. Put briefly, the very immature individual, infantile in emotional response and egocentric in his demands, fixated at an early level of personality development where the conflict is about his very ability to exist as an independent being, requires a stable, structured, often controlling social milieu in which to function. A little further along the road to personality maturity the problem becomes one of coping with dependency needs when the demands for succour and support alternate with rejection of and hostility for the parental figure. Lastly, the late adolescent rebellion against the authority of established society may dominate the scene. The problem is now the need to gain recognition of oneself as a person of some account. In sociotherapy situations all of these major drives will be encountered so that variations of the approach are necessary in order to recreate an appropriate social re-learning interaction. Too much diversity of approach in any one setting, however, presents problems of therapeutic cohesiveness, so that ideally some pre-selection of individuals to a milieu most likely to facilitate personality growth and not reinforce social inadequacies or isolation is called for.

The implications for staff

In comparing the techniques of Edelson and Maxwell Jones (i.e. the basic Henderson model) in practising sociotherapy Schiff and Glassman[17] comment that in the Edelson model there is more reliance on the professional role with less exposure of the therapist's self and some restrictions on the amount and type of data for analysis. The role of the therapist nevertheless in both models is more active and to some extent more directive than in a conventional psychotherapy group. The sociotherapist exposes or runs the risk of exposing his own self and feelings by his interventions, although his main task – whether from an involved or a detached position – is to identify the issues of conflict in the group, make them explicit and then facilitate their resolution. Thus it would seem that Edelson's idea of the sociotherapist is also as someone relatively distanced from the group and less personally involved, much as the psychotherapist may be. The Maxwell Jones model is seen by Schiff as more emotionally demanding on staff and the Edelson model as more demanding of specialised professional skills.

The *role of all the staff* in the Henderson, whatever their professional discipline, is to work in collaboration with the residents to ensure that information from all the areas is brought to common knowledge; to feed back at the time an incident occurs how they as individuals and/or as individuals with a staff role feel about the incident; to identify the issues of conflict in any particular group setting, clarify them and facilitate the resolution of these issues. The large-group meeting will have most of the staff present every day. No one staff member is the 'therapist' or leader of the group but certainly the doctors or those staff with forceful personalities or long experienced in the large group tend to be prominent.

Through example and, indeed, by passing on their learning experiences informally staff can enable residents to fulfil these same functions, carrying on the sociotherapeutic culture. Because of their membership of the staff group they are seen by the resident group as representative of another point of view. They are the outside body which reflects back the behaviour of the resident – either individually or as the group. This can be seen both in terms of a psychotherapeutic transference body or in sociological terms as a mechanism which makes it possible for one to gain an awareness of how one is seen from another perspective. The staff-resident 'difference' is essential to the therapeutic interchange. Attempts to destroy the difference negate the treatment potential.

The experiences which the staff go through on joining the therapeutic community are no different from those through which the residents go. Similar emotional arousal takes place with pressure to examine one's own intra-personal functioning, and enthusiasm for or retreat from the experience occurs. Acting-out takes the form of over-identification with the residents' point of view, lateness or non-communication of movements and absences. Participation in staff meetings or sensitivity groups can be superficial or avoided entirely by some who feel uncomfortable in such a setting despite their initial interest on joining. Unlike the residents they cannot easily drop out but have to think of employment and career factors. Paradoxically therefore one can be handicapped by the presence of resistant or reluctant team members whilst more committed staff members more readily progress to other fields. In this latter respect a survey at Henderson by Cook[18] showed for instance that a large proportion of nurses left to take up social-work training, although a minority did report upsets in their personal lives which they attributed to experiences at Henderson.

It is the nursing group which remains the problem group, however. On the one hand it is the largest staff group and the mainstay of the day's programme, but on the other hand Manning's[19] research also showed that this was the group with the widest scatter of ideological commitment to the therapeutic community ideology. However, Manning has demonstrated an increased allegiance to therapeutic community principles in 1973 when he compared a values questionnaire given to staff with a similar survey made in 1955.

Finally, whatever the overall commitment to the therapeutic community ideology, Zlatic and Whiteley[20] showed that the different staff members tended to regard themselves as of most value to the community when working in their particular professional role rather than indiscriminately about the community despite the professed allegiance to 'blurring of the roles' and the importance of one's own personality in the interaction with residents. Certainly under stress the tendency is to retreat into one's own professional area – the nurse to the surgery and administrative procedures, the doctor into medical opinion and terminology which distance him from other staff and residents alike.

Henderson is like real life speeded-up, commented one resident, referring to the rich variety of interpersonal experiences and intense emotional life of the large group in the therapeutic community setting. It is these often raw and primitive forces which are at the disposal of the sociotherapist if he is sensitive to them and prepared to move out of the protection and omnipotence of a strictly psychotherapeutic standpoint.

7. Psychotherapy in the large group

Rafael Springmann

In this chapter[1] I will try to describe the weekly meetings of patients and staff held at the psychiatric department of Tel-Hashomer Hospital, Israel; the development of these meetings, which occurred hand-in-hand with the maturation of the staff, some of the dynamics of these meetings from the point of view of the patients as individuals and as a group; and some of the aspects in which they are comparable to regular therapeutic groups.

Tel-Hashomer is a general hospital of about 1,000 beds. The psychiatric department was founded about ten years ago as an integral part of the hospital. It consists of two adjacent, mixed, open wards of 23 beds each, and is designed for the assessment and short-term treatment of acute psychiatric patients of all diagnostic categories, the only exceptions being homicidal patients and those whose suicidal drives are too intense to be controlled without physical restraint. Individual patients stay in the hospital for an average of about two months.

From the very beginning, it was clear that one of the cornerstones of such an open department, which relied mainly on cooperation with the patients, had to be a therapeutic atmosphere. However, most of the members of the medical staff were young and inexperienced and could not define such an atmosphere, let alone maintain it. Their attitude toward patients tended to be too permissive on some occasions, too harsh on others, with both extremes leading to a great deal of friction and mutual acting out. It was decided to try to regulate the atmosphere by weekly general meetings of patients and staff. These would provide both sides with an opportunity for controlled ventilation and the therapeutic atmosphere was later defined as an atmosphere continuously controlled by such mutual feedback.

In time the staff matured, and friction and conflicts almost disappeared. The meetings, however, were not discontinued. It was discovered that they provided a useful stage for the elaboration of various problems, and, later, characteristics could be attributed to them which exceeded the original expectations.

The meetings were held in a large occupational therapy room. They consisted of about 40 to 50 patients, their doctors, and nonmedical staff. After a while, sporadic visitors started to attend; later they were invited by us, and finally they came as a result of external initiative.

The character of the meetings underwent many changes, some initiated by the patients, others by us through their inspiration. The first of these innovations concerned visitors. Two apparently contradictory phenomena were conspicuous at that period: on the one hand, the patients felt isolated and discriminated against by the world at large in general, and, in particular, by the medical staff of the non-psychiatric departments. On the other hand, they were reluctant to allow relatives or other visitors to attend and participate in their meetings. We tended to regard both phenomena as two sides of the same coin and, after having discussed the problem with the patients from this point of view, decided to break the ice by encouraging visitors to come to see psychiatry undistorted by their projected fantasy; preference was given to those non-psychiatric personnel who were the most rejecting. Doctors and chief nurses of various medical departments were systematically invited to attend the meetings, and the problem of isolation and alienation was solved to a large degree on both sides, at least within the microcosm of the hospital. This hospitality was subsequently enlarged and developed. Medical students, students of psychology and psychiatric social work who did their clerkships in the department, as well as students from a nearby school of communication, were invited to participate; later even interested laymen were encouraged to come. The result of this innovation was a gradual but definitely perceptible decrease in the intensity of rejection of the psychiatric department and its patients by the hospital community.

The patients themselves were the first to demonstrate that this large and mixed forum could be utilised for approaching personal dynamics. The first time this occurred it was a rather painful experience for a man who had been hospitalised because of various hypochondriacal fears. He was preyed upon by the other patients who, in a matter of minutes and before we realised what was happening and could intervene, ripped apart most of his defences, exposing his hypochondriacal fears to be at least in part an expression of his fear of his dominating wife. The traumatic nature of the experience for the patient was compounded by the fact that the event took place in the presence of this feared and dominating wife. The patient, not unexpectedly, left the department on the following day, cured, not of his fears, but at least of his hospitalisation.

Despite the strongly traumatic effect on this patient, we as therapists became aware that, handled in a gentler and more judicious way, the forum could be used for the achievement of insight. A young soldier, hospitalised for assessment of a behaviour disorder, complained at the first meeting in which he participated that he had seen another patient, a disorganised elderly woman who had wandered out, being seized by staff members and brutally beaten before being given a sedative injection. Other patients confirmed the general trend of his story but denied its violent part. Thereupon, the young man confessed that he might have imagined that aspect, and a discussion was initiated about his attitude toward violence in general. He said that ever since he could remember he had been 'allergic' to violence. Encouraged to further reflection, he remembered that his abhorrence of violence had had its origin when he had been seized by a fit of uncontrollable anger and had felled his drunken father by striking him over the head with a chair, thus avenging his abused mother. This insight was acquired in a single therapeutic hour in the presence and with the help of over fifty people.

Another patient who benefited from this new, dynamic

approach was an excited, schizophrenic young mother who opened one of the meetings with a bitter complaint about her being neglected in the ward. In her long angry monologue she mentioned among other things that she had always been neglected in her home, frequently beaten and called 'the foundling'. It was then pointed out to her by one of the doctors that she had probably felt superfluous at home, that she had been carrying this feeling within her ever since, applying it wherever she went, including here, in the department. The effect of this intervention was immediate and dramatic. She replied, 'Doctor, now I know that you have understood me', calmed down, stopped shouting, and her expression changed completely.

We attributed importance to this episode for two principal reasons: one, it happened in the presence of, among others, medical students, who had been told the previous day in a seminar about the corrective emotional value of the feeling of being understood. The Q.E.D. we had here was but one example of the way the meetings could be utilised as a didactic tool to demonstrate vividly, *in vivo*, many aspects both of traditional and dynamic psychopathology and of therapeutic intervention without having to resort to artificial teaching devices or compromising the genuineness of dramatic events. Some deeper dynamic aspects of the group being thus used for teaching will be discussed below.

The second reason we attributed importance to this episode was the fact that this same patient had refused to participate in any other form of personal or group psychotherapeutic activity. It was only in the large forum that she felt safe to express herself freely. Other patients often behave in a similar way and can be first reached in this large forum. A further example of this occurred with a severely compulsive patient, a borderline case, who was completely rigid in his defences. The first time he dared to criticise his parents openly was within the framework of free associations fluttering in the large group. Subsequently he could change his attitude in the regular therapeutic group too. Here he had initially played the role of the super-ego always eager to conform, later he dared to join a discussion centring on the question: 'Whom did I love more, father or mother?' and claimed with warmth and conviction that he had never suffered any conflict in this regard, for he had always equally hated them both.

Another example of the way in which material discussed in the large convention reverberates in the regular therapeutic groups occurred with a patient who, in the small group, criticised his fellows severely for having attacked figures of authority in the large group, thus exposing his flank to an interpretative approach to his failure to recognise and express his own feelings of deprivation and furious envy.

Being a large and anonymous audience, not unlike the one addressed by artists who publicly express their feelings, the mass seems to provide enough of an exhibitionistic challenge, on the one hand, and of anonymity, on the other, to enable other reticent patients to reveal themselves, not necessarily the psychotic or pre-psychotic ones, but the 'strong', tough, taciturn characters who had never before felt the need or the inclination to express themselves. Thus a rich building contractor, hospitalised after a serious and apparently inexplicable suicide attempt, stood up in one of the meetings and, *ex abrupto*, made a long and detailed speech about his loneliness, the emptiness, superficiality, and two-facedness of his social life, a speech which he later confessed he would have made in no other circumstances and which came as a surprise even to himself. This speech had a strong cathartic value, not unlike a public confession.

On one occasion, both the head of the department and I, usually the leader of the assembly, were unexpectedly unable to attend. At the next meeting we were met by an angry silence which subsided only after the appropriate interpretations had been given. It was then that we realised that this large, heavy, cumbersome, and constantly changing mass had acquired many of the dynamic characteristics of a regular group: group transference, history, maturation, and even what, for lack of a better term, we referred to as group memory, exceeding by far the longest stay of any single patient in the department.

The two terms, 'group maturation' and 'group memory', are mainly illustrative. We postulated 'group maturation' when several years after the absence of both leading figures described above had occurred, it was inadvertently repeated. This time it resulted not in impotent rage (angry silence) but in a spontaneous and highly sophisticated discussion about ambivalent feelings caused by dependency needs and their frustration, which could easily be attributed to the temporary bereavement.

The term 'group memory' can, of course, be avoided by assuming the existence of covert channels of communication through which therapeutically valuable information is verbally or non-verbally transmitted to successive generations of patients. In any case pathologic patterns of behaviour, once successfully interpreted, were relinquished for long periods and often never repeated, even when circumstances might have warranted them.

So much about the history of this particular large group. The feasibility of achieving psychotherapy, i.e., consistent intra-psychic change in such settings, has repeatedly been contested, and it is my wish in this chapter to meet this challenge.

In order to do this I find it useful to start by going back to fundamentals and restate the basic features of psychotherapy. In my opinion these consist of enabling patients – be they individuals or in groups – to relinquish non-adaptive, destructive defensive positions, replacing them with the help of interpretations by more adaptive ones, which hitherto had to be avoided because of irrational fears.

Ezriel,[2] who developed Strachey's ideas about mutative interpretations,[3] named the imaginary reasons for avoiding certain object-relations 'calamities', fearful events such as castration which patients are afraid will materialise as direct results of certain behaviours or fantasies. These behaviours or fantasies which have to be avoided he naturally called 'avoided relationships'. In order for these avoided relationships not to cause continuous pressure, which, for fear of calamities, would lead to constant, unbearable anxieties, a further set of relationships is required, the so-called 'required relationships'.

These are defensive relationships, sometimes derived from the avoided relationships they are intended to ward off by various defence mechanisms such as opposition, dilution and

displacement. Mental health is in direct proportion to the adapta-
tive value of the required relationships any given person or
group of persons has at its disposal at any given moment in
time.

I have found Ezriel's formulations most useful in understanding psychodynamic phenomena, and the basic formulation
of his theoretical concepts is as follows:

By enabling patients, individually or in the group, with the
help of interpretations, to dispel, by reality-testing in the 'here
and now' of the transference situation the feared causal relationship between the avoided relationship and the calamity, patients
can be helped to give up non-adaptive, pathological required
relationships, whose main purpose had been to hold the feared
avoided relationship in check, replacing them with more adaptive
(less pathological) required relationships and/or venturing into
the open with the avoided relationships themselves, which have
by now been rendered harmless.

The achievement of this therapeutic task depends on the com-
pleteness (and correctness) of the interpretation which should
include all three relationships: a description of the (by no means
always conscious, or – in a group – even coherent) required
relationship, a full description of the avoided relationship and
calamity (neither of which are primarily conscious) and especially
a complete spelling out of the imaginary causal relationship
between the last two. It is only this last bit of interpretative work
which severs this causal relationship and enables the patients
to dare and reality-test the avoided relationship openly – first in the
'here and now' of the transference and later with real-life objects
as well.

This point has repeatedly been demonstrated,[4] among others,
in a small group of mine[5] in which, because of technical reasons,
two sets of interpretations were given in a single session. These
differed in that the first one contained the required and avoided
relationship only, whereas the second one, given a few minutes
later, after a small fraction of further associative material had
been gathered, contained the calamity as well. There was a
marked difference in the response each of these interpretations

evoked: the one following the second interpretation contained the overt admission of the previously avoided relationship (in that particular case, rage about having been abandoned). In the pre-interpretative material this had merely been hinted at and defended against by a variety of required defensive manoeuvres.

The possibility of the existence and interpretability of the same dynamics in the context of the large group became clear to me after the following experience:

I had been invited to witness a ward meeting of about 30 patients and 6 staff members in another mental hospital. I was briefly introduced to the group by its leader as a visiting psychiatrist and then not referred to openly any more.

There was a prolonged silence, which was eventually broken by three patients who spoke of ostensibly unrelated subjects. One patient spoke about the neglected doors and windows in the ward, then associated and complained about her father, who had never allowed anybody to lock bathroom doors, thus exposing the user (herself) to unexpected intrusion and to the danger of being discovered during her most intimate activities.

This topic was dropped and another patient spoke about her landlord, who was constantly antagonising her and her roommate, and about their inability to protest for fear of being evicted by the landlord and becoming roofless.

A further patient associated to this, saying that he had similar problems with his bank manager who had done several things which he, the patient, disliked, but could not protest about because he felt dependent on the bank manager for various reasons.

As I was a guest at this group meeting, I did not feel entitled to interpret the situation. Theoretically, the following interpretation would have been justified:

Required relationship: We either keep silent or complain only about our difficulties elsewhere.

Avoided relationship: We resent the father-doctor, who does not consult us on inviting this intruder (myself, as visitor), and thus exposes us and forces us to perform our most intimate activities (group work) in front of a stranger, not allowing us any privacy.

However, we dare not complain openly about this because we fear (calamity) that if we antagonise him (landlord, bank manager, i.e., father-doctor) he will turn us out of this group, upon which we depend and which is where we feel at home.

The theoretical prediction would be that, if such an interpretation were given, the group would have felt more at liberty to express its real (repressed) feelings of hostility against its leader and myself, and as a result, perhaps also against other objects outside.

As mentioned above, this event and its elaboration finally convinced me that Ezriel's type of dynamics were applicable to the large group too.

The first obstacle meets the eye immediately, namely the ostensible incoherence of the presented overt material. Only the fact that I had knowledge of what the situation was about enabled me to realise the internal dynamics, and this has been my experience in large groups many times since. Even if we assume that material presented by different patients as incoherent associations is really quite often (in the large group, however, by no means always), covertly coherent, it is often extremely difficult to divine the 'story behind the stories'.

As will be shown subsequently, such incoherence can sometimes itself be regarded as a required relationship and as in the last example, and a previous one, silence can be seen in the same light, i.e., attempts to express rage and suppress it at the same time. On one occasion, when a patient was overheard to remark that he would not speak this time, it was discovered that this was an expression of his feeling that he would not be understood by us anyhow, just as he had never been understood by his parents as a child. Another common form of required relationship is the periodically raised demand that the meetings be used by the doctors to provide formal lectures about the specific effect of various therapeutic measures: E.C.T., tranquillisers, etc. The frustration of these dependency demands and their interpretation as efforts to avoid painful and embarrassing issues by resorting to neutral subjects and trying to assume a passive role as listeners frequently resulted in the emergence of dynamically interesting material.

Some of Eric Berne's games, as well as Bion's Basic Assumptions can be seen as more or less sophisticated and elaborated required relationships. Bion himself describes Basic Assumption behaviour in groups as defensive manoeuvres, intended to keep at bay ('avoid') painful subjects.[6] Inconsistency and incoherence, some of the major obstacles in understanding the dynamics of large groups need not automatically be regarded in themselves as required relationships and interpreted as such. Such large changing masses cannot always be expected to find even a covert common denominator in the allotted time. External events, particularly when of special significance to the group, such as patients being transferred, therapists going on or coming back from vacation, tend to catalyse – not necessarily overt – unity and knowledge of these occurrences and, especially, acknowledgement of their importance to the group, can help the therapist to disentangle apparent incoherence and inconsistencies.

The following example would fit in here: Patients were, in this particular large group, discussing the release and rehospitalisation of some of them, lamenting their inability to weather external stress situations. Somehow associations then veered to surgical procedures and one patient said she would loathe to examine at close range the instruments with which she would later have to be operated upon.

I, as leader of the group, was at that time in some personal difficulties, a fact of which the patients were quite aware.

The calamity which I suggested to be hindering them from speaking about me directly was that if my problems were to be discussed, it might perhaps transpire that I was also vulnerable, and then the group would lose its confidence in me and would feel helplessly forlorn in coping with its problems. I interpreted the lament as being displaced from 'the tools used to operate on us' – myself, who has to be perceived in the groups' fantasy as being above and beyond the need to weather his personal difficulties, otherwise he might perhaps be seen as tempted to flee into the ward himself.

This interpretation resulted in several associations about my 'poker face', a first, feeble admission to the fact that important authority objects one feels dependent on (group leaders) might be conceived as having personal problems after all.

This session was followed by quite a few in which the problem of the group's need for the leader's immunity, omnipotence and omniscience were discussed. All these qualities can, of course, be regarded as variations on the same theme, namely the attribution of super-human qualities to the leader.

This attribution was made repeatedly, e.g., by individual patients posing questions such as 'Why is it that I'm afraid to go home?', or 'What are you going to do about my depression?' or even outspokenly: 'Why don't you give us a lecture on how to behave in order not to have to come here any more?' These demands were once even rationalised by a patient who said: 'You want us to bring up problems, all right, we did it. So now it's up to you to solve them.' With no further information supplied, such demands implied among other things my omniscience and omnipotence, and were interpreted as parts of required relationships which demanded objects to have these super-human qualities (omniscience, omnipotence, and total immunity), because a normal, human leader would not be able to hold envy and rivalry in check and would perhaps succumb under their vehemence, or never be able to face endless demands for sympathy or love.

As might be expected, this kind of interpretation frequently unleashed very strong, leader-oriented envious attacks, voiced sometimes in the most direct language and not infrequently aimed below the belt (literally and figuratively).

The leader's emerging from these attacks unhurt on one hand, non-retaliating on the other and mainly still in charge of the situation seems to me to be in line with Ezriel's notion of the curative value of reality-testing, which dispels the irrational fear of calamities.

Two points are worth mentioning here. One would be the very vehemence of these verbal attacks ('Your group is worthless', 'I'll never come here again' [a threat which is hardly ever realised], 'You are nothing but a boastful egocentric', 'X runs a much better group than you do – he asks us questions', etc.). It seems to me that the presence of such a large mass of people gives the individual, latently aggressive patient security that whatever happens, there would be enough people around to restrain him should his aggression, usually based on frustration, get out of hand. Interpretations enable the verbal expression of this anger. The presence of the crowd enables the patients to express it much more intensively than in individual or small-group sessions, with the fear of being tempted to act upon it neutralised by the crowd. The case of the aggressive young mother, mentioned above, who would participate in no other psychotherapeutic activity but the large group is relevant here. The speed with which such deep-seated anger can be psychotherapeutically reached, seems to me, for the above reasons, to be unique to the large group, and the intensity of interaction this evokes might well account in part for the feeling of exhaustion it leaves the leader in. The second point worth mentioning here is that such envious, all-out attacks are frequently followed by marked relief of tension in the group and later by real, deeply felt reparatory acts as opposed to magic undoing. These may happen in subsequent sessions, in which the previously most attacking patients set out in my defence against attacks by others, or on ward rounds, when they cheerfully discuss with me their previous seriously attacking remarks ('Did I give it to you yesterday!') or comment with undisguised reparatory intention on my beautiful shirt or new shoes. This, from previously quite withdrawn, sometimes suicidal or schizophrenic patients, who, having tested out some extent of their inner rage and destructiveness, and found it safe from both paranoid and depressive calamities, can now afford to venture into a friendly give-and-take relationship.

Another type of external event which can be utilised in understanding the undercurrent dynamics is the periodic appearance of medical students who now participate routinely in the group, during their 6 weeks' clerkship in the ward.

When they first participate, the meetings frequently become either sullenly silent, or else completely split up and chaotic. This has sometimes been interpreted in terms of students constituting my preferred objects, with silence or chaos intended to deprive me of valuable material, in order to avoid the fantasy of me using it in a mutually satisfying orgy of intellectual intercourse with the students later, a fantasy which would cause a lot of jealousy, leading, perhaps again, to calamitous results such as attacks, feeling of depression etc. These interpretations were based, among other things, on the open secret that the group meetings are later discussed with the students. They were quite often followed by open admission of jealousy, 'Why, all you have to do is look and compare the amount of time you spend with them to the amount of time you spend with any one of us'.

It is perhaps not easy to assess at first glance the therapeutic value of such open admissions of jealousy or such vicious attacks as described above. At any rate chaos and silence often give way to more open discussion of jealousy and envy of important objects, and lessening of tension and genuine reparatory attempts described above are also points in favour.

My last few examples will be of cases in which therapeutic results could be more directly observed and unequivocally assessed.

It sometimes happens that the group becomes totally dominated by a single patient. In the next case but one this happened voluntarily, the group shaping itself into a kind of chorus, acting like an enlarging, affirmatory reflecting mirror. In cases like the next one, the group simply succumbs and lets itself be manipulated into a passive position. In such cases, especially when the reason for the group's passivity cannot be fathomed, the leader is left with little other choice than to refer to the group's behaviour and concentrate his main interpretative effort on the dominating patient.

The first case is that of a young neurotic male who complained that he had never been able to tell his personal therapists (there had been several of these in succession) all his aggressive thoughts about them. Other associations of his, including some about his father's death and further interactions in the group led me to interpret that he really was speaking about his aggressive thoughts about me, envying my leading position especially in the eyes of the present females, afraid to be open about this envy for fear of me abdicating, leaving him in leading position, exposed to the same kind of envy from other patients. This led to more open confrontation with me, and eventually, to an open confrontation with his mother, towards whom he had always been passively submissive, with latent rebellion held in check.

This is among other things an example of the emergence and subsequent generalisation of a hitherto avoided object relationship.

Two further examples will be given for the substitution of more adaptive required (defensive) relationships for maladaptive destructive ones.

The first among these is still on the individual level. A young, acutely paranoid soldier who was on the verge of being transferred to a closed institution because he felt so severely persecuted by ward staff that he had alternately to flee or threaten with (defensive) violence. He was persuaded by other patients to bring his grievances to be discussed in the large group. When his fear of my retaliating to his criticisms was dispelled by interpretations, his behaviour changed overnight: He did not give up most of his paranoid ideas, nor would he commence taking medication, which he felt was undermining his health. He could however give us his overtly aggressive defence, became quite friendly and cooperative and felt no further need to flee. He openly attributed this change to his therapeutic experience in that particular group, which had abated some of his fears.

My last example is on the group level.

The group had become persecutory against the more disturbed patients among it and demanded that they be transferred 'out of sight'. It soon transpired that the ring-leader of these demands were mainly patients who had just recently emerged from such disturbed, regressed states, or those who felt themselves to be on the verge of them.

The situation was then interpreted in the following way: 'We want the more disturbed patients to be put out of sight, because they set a living, constantly tempting example which we sometimes feel the need to follow and might not be able to resist – and then we might be in danger of being transferred "out of sight" ourselves.'

Following this interpretation tolerance has increased quite considerably and has been sustained for several years.

This example seems to me to be of particular importance, because the defences used by the group (denial and projection) are very akin to those leading to minority discrimination and persecution in general. The above is perhaps an example of how such discrimination can theoretically be manipulated constructively, when irrational fears are correctly interpreted and dispelled instead of being exploited in a demagogic way. The implications for handling persecuting, discriminating mobs seem to me to be most important.

This very situation has incidentally repeated itself recently, several years later, with similar results.

To conclude: I have tried to demonstrate the feasibility of achieving stable, therapeutic intrapsychic changes in the setting of a large group, both on the level of the group as a whole and on that of the individual living in it.

This was done by applying Ezriel's type of interpretation based on his concept of object relations.

8. The large group in training

A. C. Robin Skynner[1]

There is already a well-developed use of small groups, usually comprising 6 to 12 but occasionally up to 16 members, for sensitising mental-health professionals to psychological factors. Three main British approaches may be distinguished. The first, associated particularly with the Department of Children and Parents at the Tavistock Clinic,[2] avoids interpretation of the participants' counter-transference or group interaction, focusing instead on case discussion and relying on identification processes to provide insight for those who can accept it, in the manner of Caplan.[3] The second, associated particularly with the Adult Department at the Tavistock Clinic,[4] also begins from case discussion but utilises the group interaction to illuminate counter-transference involvement and it aims, in the words of its main originator, Balint,[5] at a 'limited, though considerable change in personality'.

Both the above techniques lean more heavily on the psycho-analytic model and on the group theories of Bion[6] and Ezriel.[7] The third method, derived from the group-analytic principles of S. H. Foulkes,[8] operates closer to the depth of a therapy group: while avoiding more personal interpretation than is absolutely necessary, the developing themes and interaction in the group-as-a-whole are interpreted, with the aim of facilitating a matura-tional process in the participants. In my own application of this method[9] there is a particular focus on the shared motivation of the participants in choosing and performing their professional work. This usually proves to be rooted in pathology similar to that typical of their chosen patients or clients, and because of this the insight gained not only replaces this pathological interest by more mature and realistic motivation, but also enables the participants to become especially sensitive to the area in which their typical clients or patients find personal difficulties.

All three techniques are appropriate to different situations. The first is more suited to professionals with little previous sensitisation to psychological issues in themselves or others; the second to an intermediate group such as some general practitioners; and the third to some more sophisticated mental-health professionals who are able to tolerate the temporary disturbance brought about by increased personal insight and questioning of their basic professional motives.

The use of large groups for training is by contrast relatively new. The yearly Tavistock/Leicester Group Relations Conferences have included a large group exercise for some years,[10] and Rioch[11] has described the introduction of a similar method into the USA through collaboration between the Tavistock and the Washington School of Psychiatry.[12] Rioch's clear and interesting account indicates that their large groups, like the Tavistock small-group training situations, are usually structured around a clear aim or task (at present the study of leadership), with particular valuation of intellect and rationality in the tradition of Bion. It is to be hoped that more detailed accounts of this approach, which would be especially appropriate to situations requiring a greater degree of structure, will become available in due course.

In what follows, I shall present some examples of large groups conducted in the group-analytic tradition. In this neither intellect nor emotion is seen as paramount, both being viewed as possessing creative potentials which, if harnessed through reciprocal exchange of thought and feeling, initiate a developmental process in the group-as-a-whole from which new forms of understanding and new ways of relating emerge without prior imposition of a doctrine. Two large groups, each different in many respects, will be presented. Both are composed mainly of psychiatrists, psychologists, nurses, social workers and other professions involved in mental health. The first was much larger, was 'artificial' in the sense that the participants did not normally work together, and it met for only seven weekly sessions with multiple leadership. The second was much smaller, comprising the staff of an institution which was meeting and working together between the weekly sessions described, and it is reported over eighteen months, with a single group conductor.

A larger, unstructured group

For several years, the Institute of Group Analysis has run an introductory course in group work for psychiatric staff of different disciplines and levels of experience, in which the membership is deliberately widened through including professionals from related fields, such as sociologists, priests, etc. This course runs for an academic year, taking up one afternoon a week, of which the first $1\frac{1}{2}$ hours is devoted to a lecture/discussion concerned with theory, the second $1\frac{1}{2}$ hours being used for sensitivity groups of 12 members each led by a group analyst. It had been the practice in the past to hold plenary sessions at the end of each term mainly to provide some possibility of communication between the course members and the staff as a whole. In 1970/71 there were 72 students and 7 staff members.

Because the staff had become increasingly aware both of the need for more understanding of large-group dynamics among the students, especially those working in therapeutic communities, day hospitals, etc., as well as of the limitations of their own knowledge in this field (even though half the staff in fact work in therapeutic community situations), it was decided in planning the course for 1970/71 to have no lectures during the third term, but to meet as a large unstructured group comprising all students and staff, as in the plenaries, for the first half of the afternoon. It was clearly explained to the students that this would be a learning experience for the staff as well as for them. A series of 7 meetings of this kind were then held in the third term, there being no programme or structure other than a seating plan of 3 concentric circles (as in the previous lectures), and a time limit of $1\frac{1}{2}$ hours. The experience which followed made a profound impression on many of us, and demonstrated a potential in the large group that seemed to surprise even those with much experience of such situations.

The first session was fairly tense and uncomfortable throughout. The inner ring was almost empty, and members seemed to be crowding towards the back away from the experience. The discussion was mostly concerned with structure – seating, timing, lateness and so on, and it demonstrated anxieties over losing control for fear of chaos and destructive conflict. Interventions by the leaders were welcomed since they structured and polarised the group temporarily, like a magnet giving a pattern to scattered iron filings.

At the second session, the inner ring was full, and this time the group seemed to be crowding to the front rather than trying to escape. Splitting and projection in the Kleinian sense were prominent – a tape-recorder introduced by staff without prior discussion was the object of hostile feelings, while a pop group playing loudly in the room below received projections of primitive violence and orgiastic sexual fantasies. A crucial interchange took place between two group leaders; one, a follower of classical psychoanalytic ideas and techniques, appearing to represent reason, intellectual control, and a necessity for verbal, personal communication to allay the anxiety stimulated by the large group; the other, interested in family therapy, encounter techniques, and mystical and religious experience, advocating by contrast an abandoning of previous expectations and self-exposure to the uncertainties of the new situation. The latter expressed enjoyment at a sense of non-verbal contact and communion with the group as a whole, which was enjoyable and fulfilling, but which fear of envy by others made him reluctant to acknowledge. Following this, other members, staff and students alike, began to report similar enjoyment and the 'space in the centre' of the circles became increasingly significant in the contributions. One member said, 'That space is like God – everything is there, yet nothing is there!'

At the third session a new polarisation and splitting appeared between the outer rings (representing reason, ideas, the large group, and perhaps paternal authority), led by one staff member who repeatedly expressed preference for large groups in an aggressive way, and the inner ring (representing feeling, experience, the small groups, and maternal intimacy), led by another staff member fiercely defending the small-group experience. A violent altercation between these leaders, which continued for some time, was finally interpreted by the staff member interested in family therapy as both a manifestation of depression in 'father' and 'mother' because the 'children' were becoming independent and leaving home, leading to the defence of splitting and projection between the parents, and also as parental intercourse (there were many associations suggesting this as well.) This staff member was in turn dethroned by the course members who discussed his role in the family and decided, amid laughter, that he was the 'lodger'. Another staff member who had chaired the lectures, and was until this point regarded as the main leader, was next addressed without his medical title, while a non-medical course member was addressed as 'Doctor'. The irritation of the former at his loss of status caused much amusement, but he was able to point out how the group was using the leaders in a new way, as experts and advisers rather than as parental figures.

By the fourth session this maturation of the group was already striking. Many members had become aware of the formation of the group through periods of deeply meaningful silence, and there was increasing acceptance of being, existing, living in the moment, and finding this complete in itself, with a lessening need to do, to achieve, or know and 'understand' intellectually. The staff member who had previously seemed to support reason and verbal communication at the second session this time took the lead in reporting his experience and challenging the escapes of his colleagues into activity. Following this, a course member, referring back to the staff member who had endorsed uncertainty and abandonment to the group experience two sessions before, declared himself as 'enjoying being lost', arousing mingled admiration and envious attacks from others by his evident enjoyment of his experience, which was expressed in terms of the fantasy of being on a picnic. Another course member attempted to join him, but playing, as someone later expressed it, 'Cain' to his 'Abel'. Eventually, fantasies of sexual orgies appeared in the associations, and disappointment was expressed that although the staff member/parents had had exciting intercourse the week before, and the student/children were able to indulge themselves on this occasion, there could be no total orgiastic fulfilment in the group as a whole, because of the incest taboo. Themes of the crucifixion, the resurrection, and hopes for a saviour appeared several times during this interchange.

At the fifth session, after expectations of a corpse on the floor in the open space, and an inquest regarding its significance, the first group dream was reported where the large group, in colour, was conducted by a long-haired stranger (Foulkes? Freud?), while the small groups were all supervised in the same room by the speaker's own small-group leader. Anxiety over the leaders' quarrel two sessions before, repressed in the previous session, reappeared and the leaders were asked if the quarrel was subsequently resolved in their staff meeting. Suspicions were voiced that the leaders used the large group to resolve conflicts they could not deal with in ordinary ways. The leaders evaded this latter question repeatedly, as if deaf, but finally one confirmed that the leaders did in fact use the large group to resolve staff conflicts and were indeed usually provoked to do so by the students. Several staff members continued to make bids to retain their role and status, the champion of the large group still trying to force everyone to discuss 'ideas'. (His colleagues left him to the group who dealt with him effectively.) Two other leaders, champions of the small group, who set themselves apart by making interpretations from 'outside' or 'above' (i.e., 'You are anxious', or 'The group is anxious', rather than 'I feel anxious'), were also put in their place and it was suggested that their need to continue this interpretive function was an expression of their own anxiety. There was increasing association to anal material; words like 'shit' and 'crap' being repeatedly used in contexts suggesting a regressive defence against genital sexuality. The latter was expanded by the previous lecture chairman to the idea of loss of ego-boundaries generally, including mystical experience and the oceanic feeling. Members commented on the absence of splitting and the remarkable cohesiveness of the group, one remarking that he arrived feeling 'in pieces' after many mishaps during the day, and that he felt he had been put together and made 'whole' by the session.

In the sixth session which began with lively, relaxed talk until silence eventually fell, the sense of maturity and responsibility in the group as a whole continued to increase; some students spontaneously dealt with noises and interruptions outside, tasks normally performed by the staff. The main themes were of crypts, coffins, death, of eating the group as in the communion service, and of the course as a seed pod bursting and scattering its seed/members broadcast to reproduce their own groups. Those who had tended to remain silent before began to contribute, and some splitting and conflict over the issues of talking or remaining silent occurred. Towards the end, restlessness and a desire to smash the group, to 'get it over', appeared and concern was expressed whether the experience could be preserved despite the imminent ending.

At the last session, a knocking overhead (where repair work was in progress in the room above) gave rise to associations of Shakespeare's *Macbeth,* of murder, of guilt, and of being 'untimely ripped'. Two course members established a bid for dominance which also demonstrated new-found though still uncertain independence, polarising the course into conflict which was used temporarily to escape the pain of separation. However, splitting was once again averted, and the painful affect was contained and shared. Increasing individuation was demonstrated despite loss of ego-boundaries and the obstacle to this combination of a simultaneous sense of personal identity yet communion with others was seen as the fear of freedom and responsibility for living one's own life. Themes of violence once again intruded, followed by the balanced dual image of ambivalence, leading on to the recognition that the integrity of the group had been preserved to the end. Valuation of the experience was expressed and the staff member who chaired the lectures finally remarked, 'We survived!' The leadership struggle continued to the end and would clearly continue after the end, yet this seemed more a measure of the leaders' own growth than a disruptive power struggle.

A smaller, task-oriented group

The second example is taken from a staff group at the Day Hospital at the Maudsley which increased in numbers during the first 9 months in which I met with it from 16 to over 25 members, demonstrating in the process some of the main issues which become more prominent in the large as compared with the small group. This Day Hospital, which is part of the postgraduate training complex of the Bethlem Royal and Maudsley Hospitals and the Institute of Psychiatry, plays a singificant part in the treatment and rehabilitation of psychiatric patients, many of them long-term and seriously disabled, from the local district for which these hospitals have assumed a responsibility; it admits patients who can manage without full-time admission, but are too incapacitated for out-patient treatment alone. The daily life of the unit is structured around paid industrial work, supervised by occupational therapists, which simulates the expectations and rewards of everyday life. In this context, the head of the unit has encouraged the use of a form of social therapy combining the so-called 'therapeutic community' techniques which help patients to cope with their emotional difficulties, with those principles of 'milieu therapy' which increase patients' ability to hold their own in everyday life. The staff is divided into 3 therapeutic teams, each of which meets 4 mornings a week with its own 'small group' of patients; the whole community comes together once a week in a large staff/patient group of about 55 people altogether. In addition there are behaviour therapy programmes supervised by the psychologists, social work provision for patients and their families, and the usual range of physical and other medical treatments.

Three years earlier, a consultant from the Psychotherapy Department had been invited to meet weekly with the staff group. The original purpose had been to provide some supervision of the group and individual psychotherapy, but this

session with an outsider present had often permitted the beneficial ventilation of staff tensions. These seminars became highly
valued, and when this consultant retired I was asked by the
Psychotherapy Department to continue in his place. I think the
pleasure and interest I have found in doing so will show through
in my account, but it is only fair to add that the situation is
exceptional and it is difficult to know to what extent the group
development described could be repeated elsewhere. The trainees
rotating through the Day Hospital and other units in this main
postgraduate teaching institution are particularly lively, well-
informed, and open to new ideas, while the whole staff has
come to possess over the years high confidence, morale, and
willingness to leave the security of familiar methods. I have
felt particularly fortunate in collaborating with a consultant (I
have called him below the 'Senior Psychiatrist', to avoid confusion with the Tavistock tendency to use the word 'Consultant'
for something closer to my own function here), who has always
believed that the Day Hospital needed an organisation which
would allow any member of the staff to act rapidly, confidently,
and independently, and who considered that his staff could
adjust and reorganise their work effectively only if they had
opportunities in a group situation to master their accompanying
anxiety and stress. Thus, the group interactions reported here
are a culmination of a long sequence of previous developments,
and my own contribution has merely facilitated a flexible and
responsible mode of staff functioning envisaged many years
before.[13] I have been lucky also to work with a Sister (Senior
Nurse) whose memory of, and kindness to, me in my own days as
a trainee could never be guessed from the support and respect
she has shown towards my present role. It should be added that
the Senior Psychiatrist had not attended the meetings with the
previous visiting psychotherapist for fear of inhibiting the
discussion, but after much argument among the staff it was
generally agreed that the seminars could be far more fruitful
if he joined them, which he did from the beginning of my own
attendance.

What follows, then, is a description of these weekly meetings with the staff since I began to visit, and of the changes accompanying its development into the 'large-group' category. As the account seemed to fall fairly naturally into a number of phases, which perhaps simplify the complex interaction a little, I shall follow this method of description.

Phase I

The first 2 sessions and the beginning of the third were concerned with the structure of the meetings themselves. The first session was lively and spontaneous, but the main issue discussed: 'Should patients be allowed to read their notes?' (a patient had requested this) revealed an underlying preoccupation with our own boundaries and limits. Though this issue was settled for us by a hospital rule forbidding such disclosure, the ensuing discussion revealed one sub-group favouring, and another opposing, the need for hierarchy, structure and clear boundaries generally. This polarisation was even more intense at the second meeting, the psychiatrists-in-training pressing for totally unstructured meetings and Maxwell Jones[14] type 'role-blurring' and 'flattening of the authority pyramid'; while others, particularly some of the more permanent staff, demonstrated increasing anxiety about such proposals and protected themselves by setting up their own boundaries, withdrawing into silence, or showing only guarded and limited participation. I perceived, by the end of this session, that more structure was temporarily necessary if the situation was to feel safe enough for all participants, and I opened the third session myself by expressing this view and imposing a rule that we would begin each time with a work problem though there would be no restriction on the discussion which might arise from this. This proposal was strenuously opposed in principle but followed at once in practice by the young doctors, and my action appeared justified by the increased trust, spontaneity, and general participation that followed. (In fact, the rule about beginning with a work problem soon became unnecessary and was dropped.)

Phase II

The remainder of the third session, and the 4 sessions following it, took us quickly through the developmental phases we were to work out later in more detail, revealing in broad outline the unresolved family transferences normally operating in such professional groups. The case discussed at this session was a female patient whom all feared to criticise for fear of her self-destructive and perhaps suicidal tendencies, so that she was often allowed to dominate situations. Gradually it emerged that this patient was viewed as a favourite of the Sister (who was absent from this session), the Sister's disapproval being the real danger. Next it became apparent that the ambivalent feelings towards this patient were displaced from the Sister herself and that these in turn were not realistic but were the result of transference of ambivalent, infantile attitudes towards mothers generally. 'Don't attack mother or she will die and there will be no one to care for us' was the eventual interpretation, leading to recognition that the Sister was unfairly burdened by these transference feelings and that such maternal, nurturing functions should be shared by all the staff.

Next the Senior Psychiatrist came under disguised criticism, feelings being expressed that he should be more authoritative and firm, especially towards patients who were fit to be discharged but resisted leaving. These attitudes were in turn perceived as transference from early attitudes towards fathers, and such controlling, executive functions were also seen as responsibilities to be shared rather than left to the Senior Psychiatrist alone. At the following session a staff member asked to be excused attendance at the small groups with which each day began (in which everyone normally participated) because her personal psychoanalytic sessions obliged her to be late. No one actively rejected this request from a popular colleague, but there was obvious ambivalence about the 'special attention' she was receiving. I pointed out the feelings of envy and indulgence she was arousing, emotions normally experienced by elder siblings towards the baby in the family.

As might be expected, this progressive uncovering of

unconscious, infantile components in the professional relationships aroused increasing resistance, and also a focusing of ambivalent transference elements in relationship to me. At the sixth session almost everyone was late, the atmosphere was tense and ambivalent and there was a good deal of teasing and banter towards me and towards psychoanalytic ideas generally. Analysis could not really be condemned, said one of the younger doctors, because it 'took place between consenting adults in private'; it might therefore be justified as enjoyable, even if of no practical use! Sexual themes, already coming near the surface in such comments as this, emerged clearly in session 7. Indeed, on entering the coffee room where I normally joined the staff for refreshments before we proceeded upstairs for the seminar, the subjects of conversation proved to be the stage show *Oh! Calcutta* and newspaper reports that day of nude girls helping to advertise cars at the motor show. The subsequent discussion revealed a high level of anxiety but feelings were open and amenable to examination and understanding. The staff had clearly been able to tolerate the emergence of sexual themes at the large staff/patient group the previous week, where one patient had spoken of wishing to marry another, and a third had affectionately stroked the hair of a psychiatric social worker (the staff had complained previously of difficulty in helping patients to talk of sexual matters).

Phase III
What had been learned through interaction between the staff, and with me, now began more obviously to affect the management of patients. Session 9 was taken up not only with discussion of professionals who clung to the partial viewpoint of their own speciality, failing to consider the needs of the total situation, but also with patients who sought special privileges in a similar way, particularly by playing off staff members who clung to attitudes characteristic of their specialty. The latter were seen increasingly as 'quarrelling parents' who could be manipulated by the 'children' because they valued their personal needs more than the welfare of the family as a whole.

By session 10, the more determined, challenging attitude developing in the staff was clearly evident. The large group that week had been stormy, a fight had broken out, and there had been much argument not only among the patients but between the staff as well. When I pointed out that this might be an inevitable, healthy phase, I was attacked too: it was easy for me to talk, they said: I didn't have to do the work!

Session 11 brought a temporary regression following on the successful suicide of a chronic patient. There were heavy silences and a depressive preoccupation with the dangers of aggression and sexuality. At times a further regression occurred to paranoid-schizoid mechanisms, as a scapegoat was sought in the male patient who had been seeking this woman's favours. The reassurance of the Senior Psychiatrist, who had supported this woman through 6 years of suicidal threats and attempts, helped to relieve the guilt, but my use of the experience to illustrate depressive and paranoid group mechanisms stimulated a mixed reaction of anger at my 'callous' disruption of their mourning together with relief at being called to resume a professional role. Practical measures were then planned to support those patients likely to be most affected when the news was broken.

By session 12 the staff had recovered, but the session was quiet, thoughtful and relaxed. They had been through a lot, had had enough for the moment, they said; they needed a rest, were looking forward to Christmas. Looking back, we were surprised to see how much had changed over the 3 months of our meetings. A withdrawal by the staff of projections of dependent and aggressive feelings was taking place, leading to more confident, reality-based therapeutic interventions. There had been a further row as an occupational therapist had challenged the most manipulative patient over his cheating at work and the hospital was reported almost empty, an unprecedented number of chronic patients having been discharged.

Phase IV

There was one further session (13) before Christmas, and in this a new theme (or re-emergence of an old theme at a deeper level) commenced. The psychologist announced the integration of his students into the therapeutic teams and pressed for the inclusion of all students working in the Day Hospital into our seminar. Others accepted this in principle, but there was considerable resistance and a general feeling that change should be more gradual. During the next two sessions, this argument over the enlargement of the seminar to include the students was accompanied by a series of confrontations. At this session the confrontation was kept safely externalised between the Day Hospital and the Rehabilitation Unit next door, the staff demanding that the senior psychiatrist, who was medically responsible for both units, should have a show-down and impose the Day Hospital's new philosophy on its neighbour. Interpretation of all this in terms of a displacement of an emerging internal conflict was confirmed at session 14 by a report that the doctors (the most powerful specialty) had been confronted by the patients in that week's large group and told they were untrustworthy, likely to experiment on people, etc. This was followed in our seminar by a confrontation of the Senior Psychiatrist by the trainee psychiatrists, both developments being regarded by him as signs of healthy independence and ability at last to cope with negative attitudes towards authority. By session 15, the confrontation had moved towards me. People were slow to arrive at the seminar, there was a long silence and an impression, voiced by some members, of unusual tension and resistance. The issue of enlarging the seminar to include the students, always near the surface, took a central place again. Some supported their joining, especially the psychologist (as the only specialty with only one member he was perhaps more in need than others of an ally) but many resisted fiercely, claiming the seminar was much too large already. As in Menzies'[15] description of defence mechanisms in a nursing population, which I described to the seminar, the students were being used as receptacles for projection of the more irresponsible, childish, rebellious 'id' aspects of the members, just as the Senior Psychiatrist and I had been used to contain the more controlling super-ego aspects before. The students had in fact criticised the staff in that week's large group (which the students were already invited to attend) and the fact that one had done so from a position of lofty superiority, reversing the projection in an infuriating way, only made these fantasies about the students more transparent.

At session 16, I arrived to find the students present. As expected, they proved less satisfactory receptacles for unacceptable projections when present than when absent, especially as they were models of good behaviour (one was a priest!). The staff's difficulty in accepting these projections back was illustrated by even greater lateness (the students were on time while even the Sister and the Senior Psychiatrist were late) and a long initial silence. The remainder of the session was taken up with confrontations and defining of boundaries between specialities and other sub-divisions – nurses versus psychologists, full-timers versus part-timers, maternal versus paternal role stereotypes. Such discussion led in this and the following session (17) to the increasing questioning of existing boundaries, with excitement at the prospect of blurring roles and sharing more functions together with fears that such crossing of role boundaries and mutual examination would reveal formerly hidden inadequacies. In session 18, my boundaries were crossed and my skills examined as well. 'Why do you always sit in the same chair?' queried a nurse, usually silent and overtly submissive. 'So you can take it from me,' I answered. 'And what do you think you have got that anyone would want to take?' she replied. This opening was followed by increasing criticism of me. I was accused of being unwilling to discuss the small groups (I had been longing to do so); of not knowing where I was going and instilling uncertainty, yet also of making them dependent and coercing them. They claimed I made them self-conscious and fearful of revealing themselves by the way in which I interpreted their behaviour in family terms, causing them to feel like children. Would they go on behaving like children then, and allowing me to do it? I asked. No! they cried.

Phase V

There followed 5 sessions in which the seminar worked through a depression occasioned mainly by the loss of the previous situation, which though a 'large small-group' of 16 now seemed in retrospect intimate and cosy, and by the difficulties of relationship and communication in the present situation, which had now become a 'small large-group' of around 25. How could one hope to coordinate so many people? said the Senior Psychiatrist, a view echoed by the Sister, the Senior Registrar and a student. There was laughter, and some lightening of the atmosphere when I pointed out that, despite their evident fears of chaos, the despair was at least being expressed in hierarchical order. The increase in size also heightened the other source of anxiety and depression which had been expressed before and which indeed had influenced the decision to include the students: namely, an increasing awareness that the existing sharp definition of professional roles was largely defensive; that we needed to develop towards a greater sharing of skills and responsibilities; and that this process would be painful since a weakening of professional identities would inevitably place greater stress on personal resources and social skills. This period brought the main crisis in the group's development, with resurgence of previous defences and new ones in addition. Splitting and projection occurred more intensely, with attempts to make scapegoats of the students and, when that failed, the psychologist (the newest, least firmly established discipline in the team). The Senior Psychiatrist and I were both attacked more strongly and increasing demands were made on us to impose arbitrary solutions. A psychology student opted out altogether at this point and the psychologist himself said he might have to come less often though in fact he remained and was, throughout, a vital member. Escapes into intellectualisation, including demands for more structured discussions; rallying around a common task or premature definition of aims, as if round a flag; or retreat into more strictly defined professional roles: all were utilised one after another. But by the twenty-second session the corner was turned. The Senior Psychiatrist said that he had realised that he could never coordinate and control the situation himself – it was just too big – and that he would have to trust others in a way he had never needed to do before. He was the first (except for myself) to come through the depression but his healthy 'loss of false hope', like the despair, was clearly being passed down the line.

Phase VI

A further enlargement of the group was now proposed, the Sister and nurses suggesting the inclusion of a male senior nursing officer, actually a member of the central administrative nursing staff but responsible for liaison with the Day Hospital and often called upon in crises, especially when the doctors were off duty. Conflicting views were expressed, many resisting a further expansion of the group so soon after the students had arrived, while the senior nurse was also clearly used as a receptacle for projection of super-ego components just as the students had been used for projection of id components earlier. The 'Young Turks' among the trainee psychiatrists, in particular, foresaw all their good work being undone and there were sexual associations to a fantasied 'undressing' which would no longer be possible. A 'unilateral declaration of independence' from the parent hospital was proposed by some, while others saw the value such a link could have in securing administrative sanction and support for the changes occurring in the Day Hospital's functioning and indeed in enabling successful aspects to receive, in time, a wider application. By the end of the session everyone saw the need to seek changes in the part only in the context of the greater whole and at the succeeding session (23) the decision to invite the senior nursing officer had been taken.

The next session (24), is headed in my notes 'Psychiatric social workers' lib'. It was reported that the psychiatric social workers had been attacked by some patients in the large group that week for not being sufficiently indulgent (their colleagues at a neighbouring hospital, who were said to give 2-hour interviews, to find people houses and to give them money, were held up as paragons) and for demanding, instead, that patients make an effort and learn to help themselves. The Senior Psychiatrist expressed concern over this ordeal the psychiatric social workers had suffered, but was attacked by them for his pains and told they did not need his protection, as well as for demonstrating that he was not as familiar with the details of their specialty as they would have liked. Others watched with ambivalent interest this 'blooding' of the psychiatric social workers, now strong enough to be attacked and to attack in turn.

The staff had for some time been studying and planning the use of conjoint family techniques for diagnosis and treatment (I had been appointed specifically to teach conjoint family and marital approaches in the hospitals) but until this point little systematic use had been made of them in the Day Hospital. However, in session 25 a visit from an American family therapist (Dr Salvador Minuchin) acted as a catalyst (a turnover of staff at this time, also an important factor throughout, was also relevant). I returned from two weeks' holiday following it not only to find the senior nursing officer present at the seminar (his attendance proved as valuable as many of us hoped) but a lively, cheerful, and welcoming group. The Senior Psychiatrist confirmed the impression of high morale by saying that they were 'over the hump' and the others informed me that the whole admission procedure was changed: initial interviews were now routinely being carried out with whole families rather than the referred patient alone, and this was being done not by the doctor as formerly, but by a team of three staff disciplines which might include a doctor, or might not!

Over the next 6 sessions (27–32) I was used more as a resource person to supervise the new family work than as a group analyst facilitating the seminar. The usual swings of attitude occurred and needed clarifying, of course – after the very positive session described above, for example, there was the usual 'backlash' and I sat alone for 5 minutes waiting for anyone to arrive at the next session: the session continued with an aggressive attack on the neighbouring unit and then the successful provocation of the Senior Psychiatrist to become more active and 'take over' again. However, these regressions were soon seen by the seminar as due to fears of increasing shared responsibility and loss of the former safe professional boundaries. Subsequent progress in the new conjoint techniques was in fact striking and swift.

Later phases

The record will not be pursued further in detail, since this period of nine months covered the main difficulties presented by conversion of the seminar from a 'large small' to a 'small large' group as well as the general principles along which these problems were resolved. A further six months has elapsed at the time of writing this account, and while the sessions have been even more interesting they have mainly been concerned with working out the issues already outlined at deeper levels and in more subtle, detailed ways. In addition to further withdrawal from patients of projected aspects of the staff's psychology, the central theme has continued to be the search for new forms of interdisciplinary cooperation, real sharing of responsibility, and group communication, to replace the traditional hierarchical, one-way communication and control – changes which brought increasing demands for mutual adaptation (often painful and at first resisted) but which have also led to greater opportunities to develop and employ personal and professional skills and to engage in more real and satisfying team work. The earlier attempt to escape from safe but stereotyped professional roles has led on naturally to a similar questioning of sexual stereotypes, with some evidence already that benefits can accrue by greater sharing of so-called 'masculine' and 'feminine' roles without any loss of what is most valuable in real differences of sexual identity. The 'territorial' concept of gender, like that of specialty ('I am what you are not, I exist where you do not') is giving way to one of the mutual exchange and responsibility ('I am increased because we share and exchange with one another, yet are different').

Perhaps it is not too much to hope that experiments such as this may lead, in time, to a true marriage of skills and disciplines in which the parts relate harmoniously through their perception of the need to serve the whole, rather than through an externally imposed order alone. Like the Senior Psychiatrist,

I have become aware that a group of this size is beyond my ability to control it, consciously or unconsciously; so that, like the others, I am constantly exposed to new attitudes and concepts that contradict or extend those I brought to the situation.

Discussion

Other contributors to this volume will be providing more detailed accounts of the development and present state of theories regarding large group functioning, particularly those aspects which are illuminated most clearly by Kleinian theory. To avoid repetition, I shall therefore do no more than summarise the main principles briefly, particularly as they apply to training, with some emphasis, however, on those concepts about which my own experience may have led me to different conclusions from those expressed by other investigators.

1. In common with most students of large-group phenomena, I am impressed with their power, for good or ill. Though as yet we do not have even the rudiments of a truly scientific explanation, it is *as if* some form of energy is generated when a number of people interact, proportional in some way to the numbers involved and available, like any other form of energy, for constructive or destructive purposes.

2. If uncontrolled, the forces concerned tend towards primitive, disintegrative types of interaction with break-up of the group itself into warring fragments, leading to scapegoating and exclusion of parts; or to the creation of an external enemy or 'bad object' in order to avoid this internal conflict and maintain unity. On the level we are concerned with here this results in patients or staff members being scapegoated and leaving, only to be followed by others, or there is a running battle with the Hospital Management Committee or other external authority. While this often happens in spite of the best intentions of the leadership we are only too familiar, in larger, more chaotic social situations, with the way in which unscrupulous leaders can encourage and actively exploit such splitting and projective processes. One has only to experience an experimental large-

group situation to understand all too easily the phenomenon of a lynch mob, or of the Nazi persecutions.

3. However, if something more akin to Klein's 'depressive position' functioning can be maintained, with containment of painful affect, acceptance of ambivalence and sharing of experience between similar but unique and separate individuals (rather than the splitting and projection of the 'paranoid/schizoid position' already described) it is *as if* energy becomes harnessed to other purposes, with increased consciousness of self and others, awareness of relatedness and interdependence, a sense of wholeness both in the individual and of the group – indeed also of what is beyond the immediate situation as well – and a remarkable creativity in the group as a whole not emanating from a leader or sub-group alone. One can see a connection here with the religious use of groups for constructive ends.

4. This achievement of constructive functioning seems to depend particularly on a certain form of involvement in a sufficient part of the membership. The following aspects seem to be important:

(a) A capacity to tolerate silence. Even more than in the small group the most important events of the large group seem to occur in the long periods of profound silence. These are often experienced initially as uncomfortable and indeed painful, almost unendurable, but if survived without escape into defensive manoeuvres, particularly intellectualisation, they can become extremely pleasurable periods in which members experience direct connection and communion with each other, deeper and more sustaining than anything achieved through words. However, this requires a capacity of the individual to lose his ordinary boundaries without losing himself; or to put it another way, a willingness to abandon feelings of identity based on professional and social roles, on 'doing things' or 'getting somewhere', and to trust to a deeper identity based on 'being' what one essentially 'is'. This 'oceanic' feeling is indeed like floating in the sea, which also requires a cessation of activity as well as a trust in one's own essential buoyancy and in the support that will be provided by one's surroundings. Many cannot bear this letting go, this loss of familiar ego-boundaries, but cling to their familiar roles and distance themselves from the experience by intellectualising, by making interpretations, by making light of what is happening, or protesting that 'nothing can be going on', instead of letting it go on.

(b) It also requires the willingness of the individual to maintain his separate identity and personal values despite the destructive envy that this arouses in others, which is experienced as greater and more terrifying as the size of the group increases. (The fact that the envy seems to diminish, once the danger is faced, indicates that this must be to some extent a projection of the individual's own envy, multiplied by the number of people into whom it is projected. The difficulty most people experience in speaking for the first time in a large group, and the crucial change, often generalised to other situations, they often report when they succeed in doing so, is clearly related to this phenomenon.)

(c) Whoever can demonstrate to the group that it is possible and desirable both to lower defences and become one with the group, while at the same time maintaining individuality and standing against it (or rather for oneself despite it), is a true leader who enables the group to 'bind' its ambivalence and move towards more creative functioning. If the designated leaders fail in this, then at best there is defensive functioning where they lead an orderly retreat into limited problem-solving within restricted boundaries, usually intellectually focused; at worst they abdicate and allow 'mad leaders' in the group to push it towards more destructive ends. Harrington, Stauble and Christ[16] have pointed out the dangers of confused, fearful or indecisive leadership. It seems essential, therefore, that those who will be concerned with large groups professionally should themselves receive some experience of a large training group, in order that they may develop confidence in facing such situations and in their management.

5. One special aspect of the projective processes characteristic of large groups is the manner in which positive qualities of the participants become projected into the leaders at certain

stages, just as negative qualities may be projected into scapegoats (or into the leaders also, of course, at other times). For this reason the leaders seem to be, and indeed are made by the group, immensely powerful at certain points, while the participants appear to lose their capacity for independent thought and criticism. The ability to contain and utilise these ego functions despite the influence of the group develops with experience in a large-group training situation, and is one of its main objectives.

6. Several authors have commented on the tendency for large-group interaction to take place between sub-groups, repre-sented by 'spokesmen', rather than between individuals as in the small analytic group. Though this is sometimes seen as a handicap limiting its therapeutic value, others perceive it as one basis of the large group's often astonishing effectiveness. Curry[17] has provided an excellent review of the literature on this topic, and I will only add my own view that the greater feeling of anonymity in the large group, with the possibility this gives of developing insight and gaining confidence by vicarious means, does enable the leader to make interpretations at far deeper levels and to facilitate potentially disturbing insights at a far quicker pace than would be appropriate if the less insightful and more vulnerable participants were in a small-group situation. The main burden of self-revelation is borne at first by those most able to tolerate it, who become spokesmen for sub-groups, but the other members are able to follow at their own pace, both by identifying with the spokesmen and often by subsequent increased participation; at the start they can retain their defences or hide silently in the 'crowd' until they are ready. The small group, on the other hand, involves more personal confrontation and a greater demand that all members shall 'keep together' in the therapeutic movement. In training, this feature of the large group is an enormous advantage when staff of widely differing status, skills, insight and ego-strength need to be seen together, as in the examples described above.

7. However, for this advantage to be secured, the leader(s) must recognise the need for more active, directive and controlling

interventions than are usually necessary in small groups, especially in the early stages and when individuals threaten to become
scapegoats, or at any time when anxiety rises beyond an optimal
level. This crucial requirement is discussed particularly well by
Schiff and Glassman,[18] and also by Christ[19] in his critique of the
position taken by Maxwell Jones (1965)[20] which contains serious
inner contradictions regarding issues of authority. Though
these authors are speaking of staff/patient groups, staff training
situations also require a similar feeling of safety and control if
participation is to be wide and 'drop out' problems avoided.

Though leadership needs on average to be more active than
with small groups, it should ideally be 'phase-specific', with a
fairly high degree of structure, support, and acceptance of dependency and idealisation of the leadership in the early 'paranoid/
schizoid' and 'dependent' phases, followed by more active,
provocative intervention in the anal-resistant, passively rebellious phase that follows and then firm 'standing of ground'
and acceptance of challenge in the later, more actively-attacking
anal sub-phase. Eventually, as genital level functioning develops
with increasing individuation and sharing of leadership, an
analytic model becomes appropriate and the leaders can take a
more neutral, passive role.

The amount of structure and degree of intervention required
at each stage will also depend on the overall level of ego-strength,
insight and professional confidence in the group as a whole.
I have described elsewhere[21] the utilisation of a large group in
sensitising the staff of a comprehensive school to psychological
issues, where a much greater degree of control and focus on
case discussion was needed than with professionals experienced
in the psychiatric and social-work fields.

8. As with all large groups, the situation is so complex for one
person to grasp, and the emotional pressures so great, that
multiple leadership is an advantage; this is especially valuable
if it is truly multiple, with room for normal expression of disagreement among the leaders rather than avoidance of conflict
by formation of a 'monolithic block' around a particular theoretical model. As illustrated in the first example above, honest and

open disagreement between the leaders provides the most powerful stimulus of all towards individuation of other participants. The conflicts can be fierce and it seems that immediate or clear resolution of them is not necessary, provided the staff group as a whole, or different parts of it at different times, can contain and 'hold' the conflict sufficiently to maintain adequate structure and sense of safety, as well as to keep the discussion open. This naturally requires a good basic relationship between the leaders, with a willingness to put the training task before personal preferences or rivalries, a state of affairs that probably develops only over a sufficiently long period of collaboration to permit the development of mutual trust.

9. The impossibility of containing and controlling fully the large group's interaction is perhaps one of its greatest assets. Anxious leaders can certainly block or restrict its creativeness but in my experience one cannot avoid being exposed to new and challenging ideas which put one's whole outlook in question. I have suggested elsewhere[22] that small groups tend to become like neurotic families, preserving a cosy security by colluding with the leader and reinforcing his defences. So far, the large groups I have taken part in leading have opened up new and exciting perspectives, throwing seemingly secure conclusions back into the melting-pot. In the smaller group reported here, an entirely new approach to marital and professional relationships appears to be developing; in the larger one we seem each year to be brought to face the most fundamental questions of man's existence, and find emerging themes which illuminate the great myths, legends and religious symbols in new and unexpected ways.

9. Large groups in natural settings
An anthropological view

Myles Hopper

This paper summarises our work to date in an experimental community development project in Newfoundland using large groups in natural settings.[1] These groups were initiated as one desirable means to organise and encourage wider community involvement in efforts towards social change, although there is no doubt that people participated in them for personal therapeutic reasons as well.

As director of the project, the author came to this experiment as an anthropologist with professional experience in applied work in both urban and rural areas. What is presented below are observations regarding large groups which have emerged during the course of this work and which have been broadened by the Newfoundland experiment. Because the entire subject matter under discussion in this paper, and indeed in the other papers presented in this volume, is relatively new it should be pointed out that the issues raised reflect some of the major interests and predilections of the author and not necessarily those of anthropology as a field of study.

There is much in anthropological literature which indicates the existence and importance of numerous types of large groups in society. However, little formal attention has been directed to the specific study of large groups used deliberately as vehicles for therapeutic experiences. At the same time, it can be stated that the general approach of anthropology is well suited for the subject matter under consideration in this volume.

Many features of the discipline might, but for considerations of space, be discussed at length. Instead, several might be mentioned which seem to be most relevant to the considerations of other types of professionals, and can therefore be most usefully presented in the present context.

For the most part, anthropologists have been properly preoccupied with enquiries into the manner by which peoples solve the multitude of problems confronting them and thereby organise their daily lives into what has usually, though not always usefully, been called 'culture'. All of this is to suggest that, as a discipline, anthropology has consistently been concerned with the natural setting of human groupings and the ways in which *Homo sapiens* attempts to order his life in relation to his constantly changing physical and social environment.

Thus, of central concern to the discipline are the conscious and unconscious mechanisms for individual and group problem-solving or adaptation. To some, the focus on issues of bio-social adaptation represents a more coherent attempt to deal with the various phenomena often considered under the general term 'sociocultural change', either planned or unplanned. For example, an anthropologist might wish to partially view the emergence of large groups as an adaptation process involving relationships between some community problem, the group, and the 'individual'. One might wish to enquire into the means by which the individual ultimately adjusts or reacts to emerging group norms. One advantage of this type of thinking within the discipline is that the focus is placed upon the idea that, while man is invariably shaped to a considerable extent by his cultural milieu, he is also the very agent of its change.

It is imperative, when considering large-group phenomena in natural settings, that we also consider the other processes occurring in that setting. That is, we must examine the relationships existing between the large-group process and the other means by which people are coping. In so doing, careful attention must be paid to how the group members in the natural settings view their involvement and what potential they ascribe to the group for solving critical issues of daily life. This relationship between large-group process and solving community problems is a theme which is predominant in the natural setting and one which is being explored in our project in Newfoundland.

The project and its natural setting

In this section, a brief description will be offered of an experiment involving large groups which is taking place in the Province of Newfoundland and Labrador, Canada, under the direction of the author. The project, known in Canada as the 'Family Life Project of Memorial University', is funded by the Vanier Institute of the Family (a private institute committed to research and action via projects such as ours). It is administered through the Extension Service of Memorial University of Newfoundland. As of July, 1973, the pilot phase of the project has been completed.

Space does not permit a full elaboration of the current political climate of Newfoundland, but it is important to place our programme in a somewhat broader social context. The population of Newfoundland is approximately 522,000, scattered in slightly over 900 communities spread over more than 6,000 miles of coastline and linked by poor transportation systems. Of the approximately 900 communities, 831 have populations of less than one thousand and average about 238 people per setting. Some inhabited areas are presently reached only by air or sea, and during the winter freeze, by air alone. Nevertheless, throughout the province, there is a heightened political awareness, most often expressed through labour strikes, student unrest, and widespread pressures for improved essential services in rural communities and the older sections of urban areas. There are also, however, widespread feelings of apathy, which seem to result generally from isolation problems and a heritage of British colonial domination, poverty, and generations of rule from the outside, as well as by a small group of economically powerful local families.

In such a milieu, with its communication difficulties and recent heavy demands for information and consultation services, widespread dissemination of adult education and community development information can be facilitated through the use of sophisticated electronic aids. The Extension Service operates a system of video stations throughout the province and, in many areas, has field staff trained in the use of video equipment. These staff members participate as general consultants in community development efforts. In addition to these activities and its adult education courses, the Extension Service is involved in assisting communities in making known their problems before regional and provincial officials, primarily through public community conferences. These conferences afford local people the opportunity to present briefs regarding various matters of concern and, by inviting government officials to participate, assure at least a hearing for complaints and suggestions.

Because of these types of involvement, the author approached the Extension Service to sponsor a community-based programme dealing generally with family life and social change. It was decided to utilise the period of September, 1972, to September, 1973, as a pilot phase wherein the utility of the programme content and concepts would be tested. Depending upon the results, tentative plans were laid to seek larger grants for the expansion of media content, research activities, and evaluation materials.

A combination of adult education and community development, the Family Life Project constitutes an attempt to encourage communities to articulate clearly and act upon various problematic issues of importance to the local population. Using specially prepared audio-visual materials, the following sequence of events was envisioned: (1) viewing of the material by the community; (2) discussion of the material and related issues; (3) identification of community-based problems related to the material and/or discussions; (4) brainstorming regarding the community's priorities vis-à-vis the above; (5) possible organisation into action – or task-oriented groups to effect change within the community.

The basic content of the material used was directly related to family and kinship matters with emphasis upon the examination of the individual in the context of his family and the family in the context of the community. The material dealt with the following issues in order of their presentation: (1) Strengths and stresses of a three-generation extended family; (2) ageing and the growing use of homes for the aged; (3) birth control and family planning; (4) 'illegitimate' children; (5) common law marriage; (6) sex-based division of labour within the family unit, and (7) sex education within the family and schools. All of the material consisted of studio interviews and in the case of the sessions on three-generation families and ageing, footage shot in the interviewees' setting (i.e. in the household and the institution).

The decision to concentrate on the above topics was the author's and was made for several reasons. Because the initial stages of the project were exploratory and because the material might ultimately be used in a variety of urban and rural settings, the topics had to be of general interest rather than geared to the specific conditions of any one community. Secondly, it was assumed that topics of wide interest (i.e. of relevance in virtually any North American setting) would provoke less resistance to discussion than topics which could be interpreted by a community as prepared specifically for use in their 'problem situation'. Thirdly, and somewhat arbitrarily, certain topics were omitted. Issues such as divorce, family finances, adoption, and others, were not treated separately, although they were touched upon periodically in the other tapes. One of our aims was to put the material, general as it was, into the field situation and refine and revise it at a later date, depending upon the evaluations and suggestions of our audiences.

The subjects who appeared in the material were all residing in or near the capital and university city of St John's. In the case of the three-generation family, the community setting and occupations of the father (fishing and Department of Highways road-crew supervisor) reflect a transitional condition of many once rural communities now under the socio-economic influence of the nearby capital. This setting was chosen partly because it reflected many of the changes occurring in many Newfoundland communities and partly because of practical considerations of cost and time related to programme production. All subjects in the remaining material (except for the session on birth control) were born in and/or had lived for considerable periods of time in small rural communities. Again, these people were chosen as subjects for more than one reason. To begin with, they were all articulate and showed evidence of being able to organise their thoughts well during interview situations. Secondly, they had a good understanding of rural life, the primary target of the programme. Thirdly, they were conveniently located, enabling production to be completed more simply. Fourthly, and perhaps most important, they were not presently residing in small communities. This last factor is a critical one and open to debate. It was assumed by the author, after careful thought and consultation, that an appropriate 'distance' should be maintained between the interviewees and the audiences. Because of the sensitive nature of the material, we were concerned with the negative effects of presenting issues in such a way as to force people to construct immediate defences, especially a hasty denial of the relevance of a given problem to themselves, their families or their communities. Thus, a somewhat neutral studio setting was used (except in the three-generation and ageing material), along with individuals who were clearly no longer residents of communities such as those of the audiences but who had, in every case but one, been so at one time and could easily discuss their own lives in such settings. While this entire issue needs more careful testing, the idea was to present material in a way that would allow audiences to identify enough with the interviewees to feel that the programme was relevant to their own lives, but not so much that the material could not be discussed with a degree of comfort and objectivity at the outset.

Four communities were selected as sites for the pilot effort. They were chosen because they represented different geographical regions of the province and because among them they exhibited a range of sociocultural factors which needs careful scrutiny.[2] A brief description of the communities follows.

Community A
Community A is composed of a main town with satellite settlements and subdivisions nearby. The town's population is 7,770

I

and the total area population is 12,417. Unlike many smaller out-port communities, Community A does not appear to be ordered by an egalitaria nset of values. Rather, it is a rapidly expanding town undergoing the process of urbanisation, complete with the development of corresponding occupational and social hierarchies. There is also a distinct geographical division in the town with the more affluent families living in a newer section, which is not even governed by the same municipal council. Significantly, many of the people living in this subdivision are outsiders who have moved to the community to fill the top jobs in government agencies and in the expanding local industries.

Community B
Community B (population 752) was selected to represent coastal Labrador. This is critical as this area is geographically distinct and distant from the island of Newfoundland, and is also culturally distinct, containing as it does the remaining Indian and Eskimo settlements. While being politically under the jurisdiction of the same provincial government, coastal Labrador is popularly regarded as being less important socially and politically than the main island or inland Labrador. This attitude helps to reinforce the very real feelings of physical and social isolation and deprivation of the coastal communities which can be reached only by boat or aeroplane. Naturally, there is little communication among these communities, not to mention between the coast and the island population.

Of equal importance, however, are the current talk of political separation from the island part of the province and the upsurge of local and government interest in improving the lot of coastal communities. This has stimulated the formation of a Provincial Royal Commission to study the quality of life of the entire area.

Community C
Community C (population 666) is the smallest of the four project communities. Located on a small island ten miles from the main island, the town can be reached by short runs by either ferry or plane, which to some extent makes the island isolated.

Community C's feelings of physical isolation are not so severe as those experienced on coastal Labrador; however, in recent years, older residents have felt increasingly isolated since their children now almost invariably leave the island when they are grown. One of the major reasons for the selection of this community for the pilot project was the fact that the Extension Service, through the regular visits of one of its field workers, had already had much contact with the island's 'development committee' and 'community school'. The development committee is an indigenous group formed to promote community development, and the community school (which is unique in Newfoundland) is organised and operated by the residents to facilitate the exchange of information and skills among the residents of the community. One frequently used resource in the community school is the university's video-tape equipment. Thus, the residents were familiar with both group involvements and the use of video tape. It was hoped that this familiarity, plus the sponsoring of the series by the Extension Service, might enable the project to capitalise on the residue of interest generated during the earlier animation of the residents.

Community D

Community D (population 2,593) is perhaps the most interesting of the project communities. Regarded as one settlement, it is spread along two geographically distinct sides of a harbour which exhibit some sense of separate identities and between which there is little communication or community spirit. Community D is also larger than most outport towns, and its population is growing. In recent years, being the largest community in the area, it has tended to attract people from smaller outlying settlements.

One unique social feature not found elsewhere in the province is that Community D is the operational base of an international philanthropic organisation involved in the delivery of provincially-funded health services to northern Newfoundland and coastal Labrador. This organisation has developed a powerful political empire and a paternalistic attitude which tend to keep local residents in a state of dependency. Doctors and nurses are usually recruited from other parts of Canada and from Britain, a factor which intensifies the organisation's social and emotional distance from the people and which also causes a sizeable number of outsiders to pass through the town on a one-to-two-year cycle.

Community D is characterised, in part, by a traditional absence of active citizen groups and could be regarded, with some justification, as a politically oppressed community. While this judgement might be passed on many Newfoundland communities, the presence of such a powerful outside force lends a special character to the area which cannot be ignored.

Following the selection process, we attempted to locate one or two people in each community who would serve as group leaders for the project and who would be the primary liaison between the communities and the project staff. In all cases, except Community D, we were able to recruit local residents. Community A was represented by a physician in general practice, Community B by a housewife interested in community affairs, and Community C by another housewife assisted by the local priest. No doubt indicative of the socio-political climate in Community D, we had to rely on the services of a British public health nurse employed by the medical organisation discussed above. She, in turn, recruited an able assistant who lived in the town and was also employed by the same organisation but was from another part of Canada. For their services, the discussion leaders were paid a small honorarium of 300 dollars Canadian (approximately £125).

The leaders were convened for a three-day training workshop run by the project director and staff. During this time, training was administered in the use of video-tape equipment and some of the procedures for leading group discussions and encouraging a free exchange of ideas. The video tapes themselves were previewed and the training group engaged in a series of discussions about them led by the project director. As much as was possible we hoped to simulate a process which would soon be repeated in the various communities. We recognised the limitations of our training, but time considerations hampered us in this respect.

It should be mentioned that one of the items which we wished to explore during the pilot phase of the programme was whether, in fact, relatively untrained but eager members of a community could successfully encourage an active and productive large-group process in their communities. Throughout the actual operation of the project in the communities, there were project field staff available to the group leaders in case of any difficulties and the project director was in constant contact with them.

The leaders were asked to manage local publicity in their own communities and, ideally, to schedule one tape and discussion per week on a night suitable to the participants. The opening evening, during which prepared excerpts of the tapes would be shown, was to be spent discussing schedules and any other details peculiar to each setting. The leaders were encouraged to use the utmost flexibility in scheduling and, if necessary, to use a workshop concept in which, for example, several weekends would be spent with all of the material. Including several delays caused by inclement weather which interfered with shipment of materials and discouraged people from leaving their homes, the tapes were shown and discussed in all four settings in approximately three months.

Following each evening's session the audience was asked to fill out an evaluation sheet. This was handled in a delicate fashion, the leader merely indicating the availability of the forms and our desire to have them completed by as many people as possible. Since many of the audience members could not read or write very well, and since others were expected to be reluctant to fill out forms, we hesitated to place anyone in a potentially uncomfortable situation – one which no doubt would have interfered with the relaxed atmosphere the leaders were attempting to create. The group leaders were also requested to tape-record, periodically, their own comments regarding the programme and its progress and to send them to the director for transcribing.

Our commitment was that the ultimate goals of the project

I*

and the precise processes by which they might be achieved should be decisions arrived at by a community with our consultative advice. In short, we provided a framework within which interested people might begin to discuss a number of issues important to them. The group leaders were asked to allow their groups to move in whatever direction they wished, using the video tapes as a stimulus to thought and discussion.

Briefly, our reasons for operating in this manner were dictated by two considerations. First, the pilot project itself was exploratory and sought to determine what type of responses could be expected and what level of interest the communities might exhibit. Secondly, we believed that the long-range success of community development efforts is associated with the articulation of needs and organisation of resources *by the community*. Thus, even if outside consultants and community groups develop different priorities and operate on different definitions of the local situation, ultimately the communities must be allowed to make the final decisions regarding action. This is, of course, very important in initial stages when the group is forming, ideas are being exchanged, and people are beginning to explore with each other the ways in which they define the problems of their community. A local perception of reality must be allowed to emerge, be discussed, and with the help of consultants at proper moments, be refined and translated into locally meaningful action.

Before discussing some of the results of the pilot project and its implication, it would be helpful to summarise succinctly the major goals from our viewpoint:

1. The development and constant refinement of a set of video-tape materials which would deal with a variety of topics pertaining to family life and social change and could be used in numerous communities and professional training situations;

2. The use of this material in developing ongoing consultative relationships with four Newfoundland and Labrador communities which would concentrate on interests and activities generated by the communities and based on the video tapes, but reaching beyond them in ways unique to each community;

3. The development of long- and short-range planning and action goals of the communities and the determination of our own appropriate professional service-oriented responses in context of community requests;

4. The emergence, out of the large-group process, of organisations of community residents who, having elaborated specific goals, would work together to achieve them and use our professional assistance when needed.

Results and implications of the pilot project

The pilot project was successful insofar as it generated, for the most part, a great deal of interest and activity in the communities and significant information regarding group process in natural settings. Although examination of the entire project experience to date is beyond the scope of this paper, what will be discussed are selected features of the large-group process of which those working in natural settings must be keenly aware. Understandably, the observations offered here are based not only on the Newfoundland experience, but also on community work involving large and small groups in a variety of urban and rural settings. To a considerable extent, however, the current project has helped crystallise the author's perspective.

The pilot project has tended to confirm an impression that in the natural settings two distinct styles of behaviour apropos of the large group tend to emerge. On the one hand, some people seem to wish to use the large group very briefly, if at all, and to pass almost immediately into an organisational phase with defined tasks and hierarchies of responsibility. On the other hand, there are those who initially wish to use the large group for more extended periods of time to refine its goals and the members' working relationships further. There is of course nothing inherently wrong with either posture, yet in practice there are certain strengths and weaknesses in both.

It is useful, therefore, to consider that at some relatively early point in its existence, a large group must attain what might be called a 'take-off point' at which members have developed the necessary interest and momentum to withstand what is otherwise likely to be a critical problem, a decision must be made whether to prolong the large group as a further learning experience and for an indefinite period, or to begin organising for action more immediately. Three communities in the pilot project appear to have reached this take-off point while the fourth, Community D, does not. Examination of all four cases should give a tentative indication of some of the factors which can help or hinder a group's progress toward a take-off point and influence the decisions it then makes. What follows is a brief analysis of some of the factors which contributed to the group process in each community.

Community A

An average of 47 of Community A's 12,417 residents attended the series weekly, with the group varying from 23 to 70 persons. The leader was drawn from the upper stratum of the local society and he, in turn, requested assistance in organising local efforts from his peers. As a result, members of the local upper class tended to dominate the group.

A didactic approach was taken to the issues considered in the project and, in discussions, the group was encouraged to arrive at a statement with which all could agree. This approach tended to reduce the possibility for group discussion and was contrary to the suggestions offered during the training sessions. Overall, many people became sceptical of the group's worth and failed to develop a commitment to it. The group ended the project agreeing that the town needs a family-life education programme, but only a few people possessed any inclination to continue their involvement until the needed programme was developed. This attitude of resignation largely reflects the group's attitude that they had solved their own personal problems and that the programme was aimed really at 'other' (or welfare) families. This impression was not effectively counterbalanced by the group leader, who, it seems, was also caught up in local class prejudices. Any future group involvement is likely to centre in those few people whose interest has been sufficiently stimulated towards action. However, there is every indication that these members persist in regarding the programme as their own opportunity to help others who cannot, for some reason, help themselves.

Community B

In Community B, the project drew an average of 20 persons per night (varying from 13 to 32 persons) from the town's 752 residents. Group members seem to have been impressed by the depth of the thoughts expressed during the project and most members indicated discussions would have been even better had they had the opportunity to divide into smaller discussion groups.

When considering some issues possibly offensive to individual members, however, the group tended to reduce anxiety by avoiding discussion. This avoidance is partly a result of life in a small community where everyone is familiar with and socially dependent upon one another and where isolation makes it especially problematic to engage in encounters which might produce conflict. Reflecting a desire to organise for action immediately, the group is currently considering conducting a cooperative study of family problems existing in their town.

Community C

Nightly attendance in Community C varied between 22 and 43 people, with an average of 34 of the town's 666 residents attending weekly. Primarily, the series attracted those people who normally attend all functions on the island regardless of their purpose. This group was relatively large for a community of 666 people and represents a cross-section, except for the portion of the community which is usually not socially active.

Perhaps reflecting their concern about the out-migration of their children from the island, the community tended to consider the topics to be relevant to, and informative about, their children's lives away from home but often ignored the relevance to their own way of life on the island. There was considerable reluctance to confront local issues and the project at one point began to develop the character of an interesting television series. One topic did, however, generate great interest in Community

C – developing a better sex education programme for their children. In discussion, the parents blamed their own lack of information for their inability to instruct their children about sex and expressed a desire to break this cycle. Thus, the tape and discussion helped crystallise concern about a topic of immediate and widespread interest in the community, and it is very likely that there will soon be further group action on this problem.

The extensive interest in this problem is important organisationally. By focusing on a topic of immediate concern the group will more likely be able to be attentive to both its internal dynamics and its ultimate organisational problems, all of which must be dealt with in order that maximum efficiency might be reached. In future, a stronger, more active and successful group will probably move on to new issues and, ultimately, to cohesive social action efforts.

Community D

Community D is the only one of the four communities which failed totally in generating the necessary interest to continue in any fashion. Additionally, there was very little information on the community's reaction to the project offered spontaneously through evaluation forms and discussion leader's comments. Until a special framework for a follow-up study of this community is devised and implemented, we will have little information other than our own general knowledge of Community D upon which to base a discussion of why this group did not reach a take-off point.

As was noted above, Community D has some unique problems which tended to affect the success of the project. In addition to these factors, Community D (like Community A, the next least successful in the pilot project) is larger than most outports. Residents tend to be even less closely involved with one another or dependent upon one another than in the other settings of the project. For example, unlike instances in the two smaller towns, the leader in Community D reported that she did not know some of the participants. As a result of these and other combined conditions, the series drew an average attendance of 16 persons (varying from 14 to 19) of the community's 2,593 people. This group usually consisted of some people connected with the hospital, one to three local adults, and about a dozen high school students.

What little discussion did occur was carried mainly by local project organisers. The experiment failed to tap into any binding forces or relevant topics which could have drawn people to the group and strengthened it.

Analysis and conclusions

From the above discussion it seems clear that in large groups in natural settings the state which we have conceptualised as a 'take-off point' is a very critical one. There is no guarantee that the decision to prolong the group *qua* group or to organise for action will be the proper one at any particular moment in time.

In Communities A, B, and C, the factor that is most likely to maintain the group process is an urge to 'do something' about a specific issue. In none of these communities have we found any evidence of a desire for (or even consideration of) prolonging the large group simply for the value of experiencing this process and learning from it (even though in each case there would be at least some value in the group following this course).

In small communities in Newfoundland the potential connection of the large-group process to ultimate organisation for action must, it seems, be made clear fairly early in the group's history if a relatively high level of participation is to be expected. Accordingly, local group leaders are likely to encounter a very strong pressure towards developing a more formal organisation quite early and must be prepared to encourage or resist it, whichever is appropriate, while at the same time helping to structure the group's experience in such a way as to allow them to examine their own motivations very carefully.

What complicates matters considerably is that the communities with which we are working (and others as well) sometimes manifest the tendency to early organisation as a defensive reaction against some of the more uncomfortable personal and interpersonal confrontations which can result in a group process

of any duration. This is especially understandable in small
communities dominated by face-to-face relations. And to com
plicate matters still further, it is often exceptionally difficult to
assess whether periodic or permanent loss of interest in the group
process (sometimes to the point of severely diminished attendance and/or cancellation) is a result of a legitimate reaction to
boredom and programme irrelevance or again a defensive
reaction to stress. In any event, what the leader must be especially sensitive to is the tendency to 'flee' from the group process.
What we have found repeatedly is that community workers and
group leaders have failed to identify and respond to this phenomenon properly.

The necessity for sensitivity to this particular aspect of group
process is apparent for leaders of groups in general. However, the
demands are even more complex in the natural setting. This
appears to be especially so when that setting is a small community
(or a geographically distinct segment of a large community)
in which significant face-to-face interaction among members
constantly occurs outside the group. At such times, members
and non-members will discuss issues ostensibly internal to the
group, but naturally of importance to the community at large.
When the group does meet, the members' behaviour will tend
to reflect their sense of place in a community as well as in the
group. Group process will therefore be directly influenced by
larger community processes. Thus, leaders must constantly
remember that what they are observing is a complex reality
wherein members are struggling to reconcile what is best for
them as group members with what they, or others, consider
best for their community.

Let us assume, for example, that a group is in the process of
discussing the nature and quality of sex education in the community's school system (as did occur in Community C). Our
experiences indicate that the discussions are likely to be wide-
ranging and will include everything from individuals' overt
concerns about their own sexual identities to very generalised
remarks about the quality of the school system and its relationship to Provincial education planning. From this, a leader

must help to coordinate the process over a period of time by sensing the members' most real concerns and allowing a pattern to emerge and become a focus or theme. The group will constantly struggle with maintaining a balance between the tendency to concentrate steadily on very personal or idiosyncratic problems and the tendency to concentrate instead on general social problems of the community. It is imperative that both these movements be capitalised upon since they are not, of course, mutually exclusive. Put simply, the problem is one of proportion and timing. Keeping in mind that the ultimate concern of our project was the well-timed transition from large-group process to informed action-oriented organisation, a productive mixture of personal psychotherapeutic benefits and identification of community-based social problems must be maintained. This is made even more difficult because of the variety of views in a group as to what should be considered community problems and how they might be solved once defined. Naturally, this variety will be conditioned by *idiosyncratic* needs which are often superimposed by the individual upon the broader social scene and considered by him to be *community* needs. Through the group process, however, an individual can come to realise this projection and alter it accordingly.

Sorting out this confusion is, to a great extent, the function of the leader. Like everyone else, though, he must strive ultimately to balance his own needs with those of the group and the community in which it exists. While attempting to do this the leader is usually caught in what could be labelled a 'push-pull' phenomenon which increases his difficulty in interacting with group members. Leaders in our experiment, because of certain communication skills and a generally more cosmopolitan orientation to social problems, often tend to identify strongly with high status outside professionals and begin to separate themselves intellectually and emotionally from other members of the group. This attraction can prompt a rejection of the leader by the group if the movement appears to be too great. The pressures on the leader can sometimes be intense (as they seem to have been in Community A) and are exacerbated by the demands placed upon him by those outside the community. The leader must function as a constant liaison between the group and the project staff and very often function in a planning capacity with that staff. He is thus encouraged to maintain a dual role which structures his involvement in such a way as to separate him, immediately and further, from the other members of the group. To a great extent, this separation is inevitable. It might also be desirable. We can foresee the possibility, in at least one of the communities, of the group rejecting the present leader (made easier by his somewhat removed stance) and selecting another – an act which could serve as a powerful binding force in the group's existence.

One can readily see that an effective leader must be an extremely secure individual to deal with this rejection and, perhaps, to encourage it in certain circumstances. One of the most pronounced sources of stress for the leader in this type of situation is the fact that events in the group will carry over into the daily life of the community so that rejection in the group context will undoubtedly affect one's general acceptance, as well.

Clearly, then, the problems of leadership have, from the outset, been a central theme in the entire Family Life Project. Of the many things we have learned, perhaps the most important is the need for increased training of group leaders. While this need may seem obvious, and we did indeed anticipate it, we were unclear as to what mixture of skills would be most appropriate. Group leaders in the natural setting will have to develop greater expertise in community-work methods related to animation and social action, basic group-work skills related to running meetings and leading discussions, and the infinitely more demanding requirements of group psychotherapy, at least at a basic level of competence.

By indicating the need for group psychotherapy skills, it is not being suggested that therapy *per se* should be emphasised in the type of project discussed above. However, it is impossible to avoid the repeated evidence of the need in such groups for personnel skilled in assisting the members to come to terms with personal and group problems which are sometimes very complex. The depth at which these problems are explored will probably be less than would be the case in other types of group settings, but they must nevertheless be examined since they are clearly related to ultimate group effectiveness.

As our work continues and as we expand the number and variety of natural settings in which we operate, one of our central interests will certainly continue to be the problems of leadership and leader training. Developing a training programme, for indigenous or outside leaders, needed for the type of community work we are engaged in is no simple task. As professionals move increasingly into working relationships with communities of people in their natural settings appropriate modifications of present group psychotherapy methods must emerge. Blending the proper mixture of psychotherapy and social science will demand considerable effort but the needs exist and the results to date appear to warrant further experimentation.

10. Large groups in industry

Trevor Mumby

'. . . When you walk through our factory gate you have your initiative amputated . . .' (Foreman in large group.)

Understanding the complex barrage of psychological influences under which that foreman exists is synonymous, in my opinion, with understanding industrial large groups. For the purpose of this chapter therefore, and within the context of a book which covers the structure and dynamics of large group behaviour in detail, I shall focus attention on only three areas. The first is the extent to which the technological aura of an organisation affects behaviour; secondly, how large-group phenomena relate to that behaviour and, finally, a discussion of the application of large-group methods to organisation change objectives.

Organisation life
Large groups were conducted for employees from part of an international petroleum company, which, at this location, employed 4,000 people, 1,000 of whom were managerial staff. There are a number of ways in which this particular location could be described. In industrial terms it is a capital intensive, highly technological chemicals plant. From an employee's point of view, it is a gigantic chemistry set, impossibly sensitive to every conceivable breakdown and forever needing to be tampered with in order to maintain a balanced production process. The most lucid description from a socio-psychological point of view came from a visiting colleague who walked around for two hours and described it as a soulless jungle of cold winds

and hissing steam pipes, where humans, if seen at all, were merely pawns controlled by gigantic vessels, columns and pipes.

This description may sound somewhat Orwellian but, nevertheless, it describes the stage upon which many human beings act out a large proportion of their lives. There is a very powerful technological aura on the site and it is because of this that many of the behaviour patterns are different from those found in other organisations. My first impression when I joined this company was the extent to which employees identified with the technology or the company as though, in some way, they were 'married' to it. Of course, there is nothing new about this and, in fact, it is a human variable that has been deliberately used to create company loyalty by many firms: Port Sunlight, Lord Leverhulme's village for Unilever workers in Cheshire, England, being the visible reality of this.

The consequences of the tension within this technical or company 'marriage' are symptomatised by innumerable activities. Returning to the chemical plant, we witness a gigantic, throbbing complex of enormous power, extreme temperatures, high explosive conditions and delicately controlled chemical processes which can, by a slight drop in temperature, produce tons of rubbish. What effect does this have on everyday relationships?

I think that the reason why managerial theory is very often neglected and behavioural science applications in industry are consistently only short-term palliatives, is that they are not based on essential realities. 'Most behavioural science is focused on human motivation and group behaviour without fully accounting for the technical environment which *circumscribes, even determines,* the roles the actors will play.'[1] It is as though, to use object relations concepts, we focus on the symptoms of marriage (to the company) and ignore the primary relationships established in infancy.

The man/technology interaction
The area in which man's relationship with technology is most clearly demonstrated is in the behaviour surrounding industrial safety. I am sure that any industrial safety manager could list

dozens of incredibly unsafe actions which occur frequently and have potentially disastrous consequences.

The first significant psychological man/technology interaction can be described in sado-masochistic terms. Domination versus submission; freedom versus slavery; absolute power versus absolute helplessness.[2] It seems that workers in this environment will 'punish' the technology or be punished by it after neglecting it. In human terms, this is very often acted out between operations people and technologists or engineers.

For example: A particular plant which has been in operation for ten years and manned by the same people was assessed as being ready for closure because of its poor performance. As a last-ditch effort, it was decided to invest intensive technological investigation, which in managerial terms means that the technologists were given a free reign to sort the 'old thing' out. A thorough survey was made into all the operating conditions and steps were taken to implement recommendations. A fierce battle developed between the operating and technological groups which had to be resolved by high status managers commanding the operating men to do as they were told. Action was implemented without significant improvements. It was therefore considered that the plant should be closed and an official date was announced. From then, when the plant operators knew their plant was doomed and, in fact, their interaction with the technologists had sabotaged its future, the plant began to achieve record production results, and to my knowledge is still operating.

Despite all management theory about democratic versus autocratic organisation structures, this very powerful over-identification with the technology by operating personnel is by far the most fundamental cause of friction on complex technological sites.

The man/manager interaction

I would suspect that many people outside large industry assume that there is a dialogue, or at least a continual flow of communication from shop-floor to higher management. All the discontent publicised in newspapers is a symptom of poor relationships and misunderstanding. If this were the case, I doubt that we would ever have a strike, and that British industry would be thriving.

Not only is there no real dialogue between shop-floor and higher management, there is more often than not extreme friction and animosity *between* functions. The relationship between operational, engineering, and technological personnel needs much more careful attention than the worker/management relationship. The conflict between these three core groups is intense enough in many cases to generate displacement on to the white-collar functions and, despite this, they still ostensibly work together and produce results.

I discovered a similar dynamic amongst shift foremen. Sitting with them during the silent 'twilight' hours in smoke-filled tea-rooms, scattered with cups and copies of the *Daily Mirror*, it was then that the so-called trivia emerged and the 'momentous' man/manager daytime obsession disappeared.

What were the important issues?

The least important issue was the management. Many of the men could not name the manager two rungs up the hierarchy unless he was an 'interfering bugger who would not leave us alone'.

The important issues were:

'Engineers leave their mess all over our plant and never clear up after them.'

'Everything gets bodged during the day and we are expected to make do.'

'You can't get on with your work during the day because the managers or technologists are always fussing around.'

At the end of this survey I had collected a large amount of 'trivial' data about the foreman's job and what he considered to be important to him. Ninety per cent was about practical issues which to the naive would appear to have been completely unnecessary, e.g., 'I am always having tools and equipment stolen – can't we have a system which works to stop this?'

I can almost hear the collective reactions to these complaints from the managers and training officers. When synthesised they amount to the following statement. . . . 'That's all very well but we cannot afford the time to meet such trivial complaints and anyway you will never satisfy people, they will always create new complaints.' In both of these situations and in fact for a significant amount of the time men in this highly technological environment are being more influenced by, and are relating to, the technology than to the human system.

My hypothesis therefore is that any form of group experience is likely to generate incongruent emotions which, if channelled into the technology, would create more understanding than when channelled into the human system. By directing it into the human system it is likely that the group member will experience confusion, hostility and de-skilling.

The groups

The large groups were a part of a five-day managerial skills development programme described by Ken Harrison[3] within the same company and were conducted for 850 managerial grade employees. Any one course would have a mixture of seniority from top-level management, down to first-line foremen who were fresh from their promotion from the shop-floor. Altogether, there were forty courses in each of which there were at least three large-group sessions. Each course contained 18 to 28 members. Harrison highlights the themes of the large group in the following manner:

- individuality and identity in a large organisation
- identification and use of resources
- risk-taking and the use of initiative
- authority and control
- decision-making in large groups
- fight/flight; pairing, dependency
- growth of fantasy and mythology
- managing differences in the amount of participation
- aspiration of power élites and sub-groups
- attempts to cope with stress by changing layout of chairs.

This remains an accurate professional observation of the groups and certainly worth 'scientific' acknowledgement. The questions which still remain, however, are: Do the participants experience these phenomena? If so, how do they articulate them? And finally, does the organisation have the faintest idea what all that language is about in straight perceived experiental terms and in a way which they can extrapolate and initiate organisation change? One, amongst many vivid memories, occurs to me.

This was the second large group on Day 3 of the course. It quickly generated a very high level of anger and, within minutes, a leader emerged who told the staff to get the hell out of it and 'we would re-arrange things the way we wanted them'. It is interesting to note that this leader was a middle manager with the reputation of being a 'company man' and therefore expected to toe the company line as manifested through the trainers. This incident stayed in my mind after conducting at least 75 sessions. The leader of the 'revolt' described the experience weeks later and with equal venom as 'complete bloody rubbish, an utter waste of time and company's money' and the trainers as 'charlatans'. What is the large group doing when it evokes this intensity of feeling which goes deep into our life for weeks afterwards? The explanations can come from innumerable sources, from literature, politics, sociology, etc. Tofler would describe the man as 'the unprepared visitor who suddenly finds himself in a strange situation where yes may mean no, where a "fixed price" is negotiable, where to be kept waiting in an outer office is no cause for insult, where laughter may signify anger. It is what happens when the familiar psychological cues that help an individual to function in society are suddenly withdrawn and replaced by new ones that are strange and incomprehensible.'[4]

In explaining the reaction in future shock terms, one could say that this man was faced with the naked reality of future organisation structures. As a second description: being a 'company man' he had internalised the company's values which, on the whole, as Roger Harrison[5] points out, operate in most large organisations, from a 'power' and 'role' oriented position.

From the power sense, he was proud of his company's wealth, size, prestige and power, and was concerned to maintain the hierarchical distinctions. From the role sense, he placed maximum value on rational and orderly thinking. He was preoccupied with legality and legitimacy and judged everyone on their sense of responsibility, dependability and correctness.

The large group was complete anathema for him as the organisation man. It represented all his worst fears about chaos, anarchy and eventual loss of personal status.

These are two explanations. There are scores of books and authors who would address this isolated behavioural reaction from their own position and the reader would find a sense of truth and insight from any one of them. We are truly in the age of 'over choice'. And so what is this one reaction within the large group which epitomises so much the individual's behaviour within large groups and, in fact, within society as a whole?

The group's environment

The men come to the large group from an environment which I described earlier as a gigantic, throbbing complex of enormous power, extreme temperatures, highly explosive conditions and delicately controlled chemical processes.

They come to a luxurious training centre, located in the heart of an exclusive residential area and with a delightful view across the Cheshire countryside. This environment is completely and utterly opposite to the works. What effect does this have on the group member? The dynamic of radical adjustment is created the moment the member drives his car along the tree-lined wide avenues of this incomprehensible situation.

To what extent are classrooms, couches or cloisters ever designed to do no more than seduce the man to make the adjustment necessary before his teacher, analyst or priest will communicate with him?

The only people who are comfortable in this setting are the trainers. It is their territory and they are perceived along with the environment as being strange and incomprehensible. It is not surprising therefore that the participant's behaviour is exaggerated and so easily dismissed by them afterwards as unreal. Within their normal working context the large group *is unreal*. Irrespective of trainer styles, personalities, course objectives and organisational pressures to attend, he would still experience unreality. Does all this indicate some direction large-group activities should take, particularly for industrial employees? We see in the large group the man who, for whatever reason you wish to ascribe, withdraws from what he sees. That is his reaction. Visit that man at work supervising an equal number of people and he is full of authority, fun and the *normal* feelings by which his subordinates identify him and relate to him. They would say, 'He is a bit shy, but he can be a bastard when he wants.' His reflection of the large group would be typically, with genuine curiosity, 'Tell me, what was that large group all about?'

The same could be said of the rational, intelligent speaker in the group. Other members relate to him as the 'saviour' of the situation. 'As long as you can keep up the patter we are all right, mate.' See him shortly after the course and he would be exhausted and express considerable annoyance at his sense of being exploited. His working identity formulated by his subordinates is one of being somewhat stupid, arrogant and insensitive with the occasional moment of concern and rational thinking.

Not wishing to bore readers with further case studies, I will simply state that in my perception *the large group in this setting seemed to promote behavioural incongruence. Organisation behaviour was not the same as most large-group performances*.

What critics will now say, of course, is that large groups are not meant to offer members congruent experience. They are designed to exaggerate the underlying drives and emotions within the member and by experiencing himself in relation to others expressing these underlying emotions in the open, he will gain insight into his organisational self.

This reminds me of the delightful old wives' tale which was formulated at the end of the last century about masturbation. It seems that observers visiting what were then known as lunatic asylums, after collecting a significant amount of data, concluded that masturbation made you mad. Their data was gained through seeing many 'lunatics' masturbating in the wards.

Organisations *are* large groups and the context into which you place their employees in order to promote more effective managerial skills is *in* the organisation, not on the euphemistic 'cultural island' described by Schein and Bennis.[6]

The question however remains, that if you don't take them to the 'cultural island' how do you approach this task? In order to answer that question we need to go back into the work place and analyse what may be the essential issues which emerged for the member. What, first of all, does he do and how does he explain it to himself?

> *He panics:* 'I just didn't know what to do. There seemed to be no rhyme nor reason in it all. I just wanted to get up and walk out.'
> *The writer:* 'Tell me what would you have done if you had been faced with that situation at work?
> *Member:* 'I never am, am I? It was just bloody silly!'
> *The writer:* 'What about when you are faced with a breakdown on the plant which you cannot understand?
> *Member:* 'Well that is different isn't it? That's not people . . . that's machinery!'
> *The writer:* 'Yes, but do you feel the same way?'
> *Member,* pausing with a gleam of recognition: 'Yes . . . I think you are right. I do . . . bloody machine . . . It's just the same . . . just like that silly group . . . you can't get it to work!'

I found this same reaction with many people, all of whom experienced different emotions during the groups. They could not relate their experience to *people* at work.

Many statements made after the group indicated that the member was in some primary comfort giving relationship with familiar *objects*. 'Thank God I can get back to my drawing board', 'Roll on Monday, let's get the bloody pump sorted out', etc.

In fact, however striking it may seem, industrial man's interest in management or unions only surfaces as a consequence of having his attention drawn away from his relationship with his work, in the same way as 'T' groups create absurd vacuums in which the members' identity suddenly disappears.[7] Large-group leaders therefore *become* the projected authority figure under two circumstances. The first when the man is *not* at his work and the second when the leader *attracts* his attention with a sufficiently significant 'noise'. Namely, I am the leader and I control the answer to your current emotional confusion, etc.

In group-analytic terms, it would seem that the background against which the member has his primary significant relationships is most often not people at all, but the technology: and therefore the essential conceptual assumptions about groups, whether they are based on training 'by the group, of the group or in the group'[8] can no longer be the sole reason for supporting the rationale for conducting them.

Positive and negative consequences

One thing is quite convincing about the large group within the one-week course. It generated feelings and drives! The feelings ranged from depression through to exhilaration and the drives from destructiveness to creativity.

I would like to attempt in this section to relate these consequences to two types of people who participated and, particularly, their role in the organisation. The theme so far has attempted to focus on man/technology organisation interactions and dilute the significance of human interaction because, in psychological terms, it seems impossible to extrapolate with sufficient accuracy to make the diagnosis operationally relevant (except for psychologists and sociologists). Until very recently, man in industry has been primarily preoccupied with interpersonal issues and organisations preoccupied with intereconomic issues, e.g., growth and expansion in relation to finance or market 'cornering'.

The irritant for the first is the apparent depersonalised nature of the organisation and for the second the personal nature of employees. Why can't employers understand our needs? and, why can't people stay collaborative while we grow and achieve high quality technology? There is no doubt that, over the last ten years, the behavioural sciences have drawn attention to the

K

human as the most neglected natural resource, and by publicity and shrewd courtships many organisations have been seduced into launching large-scale human relations type organisation change programmes such as Blake and Mouton's Managerial Grid programmes.[9] Motivation and releasing human potential are the buzz words inside progressive organisations. The end result of this massive behavioural science organisation courtship appears woefully sterile in terms of organisation effectiveness. The technologist and engineer are still, by far, the organisation's 'blue-eyed boys' and behavioural scientists retain low credibility. The polarisation between growth and economic growth is gradually changing and, in terms of the effectiveness of behavioural science, perhaps what it has done is to 'soften' or humanise the management structures of organisations, thus making them more willing to look at people as the vital ingredient of organisations whether inside or outside them.

What is equally significant is that behavioural science has done something for itself. It has focused down much more on individuality and self-development not simply on growth from interaction with others.

A number of organisations have introduced self-development programmes where employees during the course of a three-day workshop, having identified their personal problem areas, set out on a self-directed course of exploration and problem-solving. The results of these more creative, 'responsible for self' techniques so far seem to be highly favourable both for the individual and his organisation.[10]

In terms of organisations acting in their corporate role, this human emphasis is being demonstrated by the increasing levels of self-consciousness about wastage and pollution. It seems that organisation/society interaction is at last being considered as a significant element in corporate life. John Humble's recent 'management tool for survival' entitled *Social Responsibility Audit*[11] clearly points towards a change in attitude about human values.

I feel there is in these two movements both the explanation for historical frigidity and future fertility in relation to humans in organisations.

For the purpose of this chapter I can say that the large group emphasised two human conditions, one intrapersonal and the other inter-personal.

The first was due to a felt pressure to come to terms with personal conflicts, and the second, a pressure to come to terms with role conflicts.

Let us now go back to the large group and our individual with his personal-versus-role conflict. Which people were stimulated by the group in constructive mode and which destructive? Which people were depressed by the group and attacked it or withdrew from it?

The first striking observation was that the assertive person always responded powerfully either positively or negatively, but he was the person with organisational power, either as a militant foreman or assertive senior manager. In following up this person, it was very apparent that his primary relationship was with his organisational task. He was 'married' to it, either through technical competence or company loyalty, the latter, in many cases, accompanied perceived *technical incompetence*.

The aggressive company man was usually destructive and seemed to operate on displaced hostility where the technically competent man would attack constructively, both usually giving up in the end, after having been de-skilled by the group.

These observations are best articulated by the mid-career manager who generates a whole new spectrum of alternative life goals and seriously considers resigning in order to pursue them.

The second comes from the organisational 'marriage' manager who suddenly understands his place in the organisation and rapidly discards the energy-sapping activity of trying to understand group behaviour on a global level. In this case he starts to attend to the trivia of his small group on the assumption that it is much easier to comprehend and grow than the political maelstrom of incomprehensible total organisations.

The personal alternative

This first man in the large group has experienced depression and expressed vehemently the futility he sees in the gyrations of the large group.

> 'God . . . if this is what large organisations are all about why the hell do I stay?'
> 'There is no difference here. The militant will always be militant. The politicians will always manipulate and stay sitting on the fence. The isolates are made more isolated. The rational thinkers continue to plead for common sense and reason.'

He locates himself on a long continuum. The amorphous, dinosaurian organisation at one end, and he, with his uniqueness and integrity at the other. To him the task of changing the organisation is a task for Don Quixote.

The role alternative

This same insight creates totally different responses in the organisationally/technologically married manager.

> 'Now I can see what being a small cog in a big wheel really means. I can make choices about whom I confront in the organisation and how I do it.
> 'It is I who avoid conceptualising the total department because of my catastrophic expectations. In order to change the organisation I need to attend to my department, it will then impact other departments.'

Here are the beginnings of organisation development based on intra-departmental change. The 'trivia' is given attention. He is not pleading for someone 'out there' to do something fo rhim. Both of these illustrations are real but represent polarities.

The large group, without doubt, makes external realities blatantly obvious. No one can hide. The bluffing, pompous autocrat is quickly identified and confronted. The inarticulate confuser is forced to be quiet or make sense. The quiet isolate is forced into deeper isolation and, hopefully, eventually attracted into the group.

The political or behavioural façade cannot stand this withering exposure for long. 'In this situation group dynamics become extremely clearly defined and atmospheres, attitudes, ideas, and ideologies make themselves evident not as cloudy, idealistic non-sequiturs but as definite climates which can be seen as either impeding, coercing or promoting communication.'[12]

This level of authenticity is what exists at the grass roots of organisations in great abundance, to such an extent that the men usually have given up playing 'silly buggers' with the pseudo-managerial behaviours of their seniors and, in more recent times, even with their union leaders. 'Let us get on with the job and hope they leave us alone.'

Allegiances to the technology are much stronger and will remain so until managers and unions relate to the 'definitive climates' exemplified in the large group.

Returning therefore to some of the questions I have raised in this chapter: What is it that the large group evokes in the individual? To what extent does the industrial employee place significant emphasis on the human system as against his technological system? What alternatives are there to 'cultural island' training programmes? Is there any way of integrating the undisputed value of large-group dynamics with organisation-change objectives?

The challenge for organisations

The only mass meetings that occur in organisations arise when the unions call the men out. It is astounding that these methods have not been developed by organisations for their own purposes.

What would happen if an organisation decided to implement large-group meetings and every department held one each week? The same thing as in a 'cultural island' large group? Exposure to frustration, anger, incompetence, chaos, and gradually a sense of corporate perspective. 'Is this what we are really like as a department!' It would expose weaknesses which have perhaps for too long been compensated for by counter-productive autocratic behaviour. It would expose strengths in people who until then had been buried in the bureaucracy. It would localise authority figures and powerful subgroups – very often they are located in the informal system, despite the manager's illusion that he carries the real authority for promoting effective task achievement. It would surface stress which, instead of being hidden in accident and medical statistics, or taken home, could be counselled in the work situation.

What is perhaps the most revolutionary consequence is that it would create a very powerful departmental identity which would challenge both the larger, anonymous organisation and union structures. If a series of departments really voiced their opinions and also produced highly effective results in their work they would be the authentic reality-based pressure groups. At the moment we have union/management players on a politically ideological stage losing credibility because of their distance from the 'trivia' which is so important to people trying to retain integrity within the natural absurdity of large organisations.

The practical issues

'It is, in fact, nothing short of a miracle that the modern methods of instructions have not yet entirely strangled the holy curiosity of inquiry: for this delicate little plant, aside from stimulation, stands mainly in need of freedom: without this it goes to wrack and ruin without fail.'[13]

I find myself increasingly convinced by the value of using large groups for organisation and individual growth. The basis upon which I place this confidence is that multitude of symptoms in our society which signal the human's need for freedom. Freedom to grow, choose, control, express.

These symptoms are being exploded into our society from industry: they are too innumerable to name and yet in our dialogue with this basic need for freedom, we are incredibly clumsy, incoherent and unsophisticated. There are still the pressures for more pay, more holidays, more production, more autonomy, more profit-sharing *ad infinitum*.

How does an industrial organisation address this issue? Again we can look at the large group and see its processes. It exacerbates the sense of imprisonment, of restricted freedom and creates exaggerated symptomatic behaviour. As it progresses, individuals begin to perceive the realities of a large organisation which until then were invisible, intangible chains, exercising some form of pernicious control. They see that under the façade of power, there is little power and very often a little man with skills which cannot match his organisational role demands. They see subgroups which are obstinate, insightless, unwilling to collaborate, and which are restricting his freedom by their behaviour. No longer it seems is the 'management' all to blame. Perhaps, most of all, they experience an inner sense of powerlessness and emerge out of it with a new sense of personal freedom and behavioural qualities which had been submerged in the amputating industrial culture.

If organisations wish to subscribe to the development of individual freedom perhaps they need to stop departmental production for one and a half hours per week and give managers a sound conceptual and experiential grounding in large-group dynamics. I wonder if they ever will? Perhaps the proud ideological pomp that exists between unions and management is more important in our current society? After all, no one is taught in his educational process to perceive and conceptualise the group dynamics of everyday life: and yet the task is much simpler than many of the established educational objectives we currently set for ourselves. Perhaps it is their very simplicity that eludes us in this age of 'knowledge over choice'?

Summary

I have tried to integrate the dynamics of a large technologically based chemicals plant with the dynamics of a large group. This is based on two and a half years inside the organisation and after conducting over 75 large-group sessions. It seems clear to me that, so far, scientific 'observer' data has not captured the essence of either of these situations and tended to be reported for scientific rather than client populations.

Man's relationship to technology is far more influential than we have assumed and human interaction is usually based on attraction or stimulation 'noises'. These 'noises' are being felt to be less meaningful than Man's powerful responses to the technology. The 'cultural island' large group evoked equally powerful responses which were felt to be unreal in relation to most human relationships. I considered that these powerful responses were based upon the deeper threat through exposure to felt rigid control (imprisonment) and the emergence of a new sense of perspective about personal freedom and organisational roles.

Large groups on 'cultural islands' provoke a level of unreality which cannot be easily extrapolated into organisational effectiveness. There is evidence to support the contrary effect, that is, that managers remain totally confused about their experience for weeks afterwards. In terms of using the large-group dynamic inside organisations it seems essential for the management structures to learn about large-group dynamics and operate from a belief that the pursuit of freedom of choice, expression, control and growth are creative aspirations. The dynamic conflicts of large groups are closer to 'grass roots' authenticity than the current industrial symptoms of wage, holiday, fringe-benefit demands, stealing and absenteeism. If organisations chose to relate to these more authentic symptoms through large departmental meetings, it is likely that the sense of freedom gained through the experience would place a more realistic emphasis on employer/employee relations, thus diluting the drama of industrial relations scenarios based on the crude and perhaps outdated definition of collective freedom.

Part Three

Conclusion

Overview

Malcolm Pines

'Psychiatry must be continuous in theory with neurophysiology on the one side and sociology on the other' (Stanley Cobb)

Mulling over the chapters of this book as they have been completed has been a heady, exciting experience. Like the reader, I have been exposed to the thoughts of psychotherapists and psychoanalysts, to the approaches of sociology and anthropology. The collaboration of these disciplines in this volume is noteworthy above its inevitable partial success or failure. Like most readers, I have not been trained in all of these disciplines though, perhaps unlike many, I believe that the training of the modern psychiatrist and psychotherapist should include them all. The facts of the prevalence of emotional disorder and the limited resources available to meet treatment needs must turn our attention to new approaches to treatment and to training; the *large group* is coming into focus as a possible location of treatment. Between neurophysiology and sociology there is room to study many types of groups, small and large, as well as the individual.

Observations of crowds, of 'collective behaviour which takes place outside the pale of social institutions', are not part of this study though large-group psychology had its origin in Lebon's work in this field and the fruits of this research have influenced much later work.[1] Nor is this the study of a total institution, such as the psychiatric hospital, though again work in this area is relevant to our volume.[2] Here we are concerned with an intermediate field overlapped by both these other areas. This is the structured large group, the group meeting, the assembly of comparatively large numbers of persons for the purposes of training (Turquet, Skynner), communication (M. Hopper, Mumby) or therapy (Springmann, Whiteley, Main).

Community and communication, these are two foci of this work; to understand and to make use of these concepts we need the tools of many branches of psychology (here I include psycho-analysis, communication theory and child development studies, particularly Piaget) and of sociology. Few psychotherapists have been trained in all of these disciplines and many would regard them as not relevant to their work. Their orientation is the in-dividual as the unit or treatment. Others place much more emphasis on the individual as a member of a group, be it the family, the work group, the therapy group or the community group.

The earlier phases of Freud's work exemplify the study of the single individual (Turquet's 'singleton') almost to the exclusion of his social environment. In his studies Freud revealed the massive forces of the irrational unconscious and thereby moved man's concept of himself on from an overemphasis on rationality, the heritage of eighteenth-century enlightenment. Working at the same time, the sociologist Durkheim made claims to the priority of community for the essence of man's psychology.[3] These two disciplines, of psychoanalysis and of sociology, converge in the depth psychological study of large groups, particularly in the realm of community.

The medieval concept of hospital as offering asylum and care for the sick individual, who was a brother under God, gave way to the later concept of the individual as an atom of society to be studied and to be treated with the technology of a modern society. The concept of community was disregarded when the large psychiatric hospitals were established in the nineteenth century, the century during which sociology had rediscovered the concept of community. 'The rediscovery of community is unquestionably the most distinctive development in nineteenth century social thought . . . . Community is founded on man conceived in his wholeness rather than in one or another of the roles taken separately, that he may hold in a social order.'[4]

This regard for the whole person and, therefore, not viewing the person solely as the encumbent of the sick role, led slowly and inevitably to the concept of the 'therapeutic' community. A central figure in these innovations is S. H. Foulkes, a contributor to this volume. Foulkes is a representative of the Frankfurt Institute of Psychoanalysis, the first to be tied, even indirectly, to a German University and which also maintained a loose connection with the Institute of Social Research of Frankfurt where the integration of psychoanalysis and sociology was first seriously attempted.[5] Psychoanalysis, sociology and Gestalt psychology all contributed to the particular blend of theory that led Foulkes to evolve his concepts of the individual as a nodal point in a network of relationships and to conceive of illness as a disturbance in this network that manifests itself in and through the predisposed particular individual. The logical extension from this is treatment of the network rather than treatment of the individual.[6]

In many ways Foulkes gave impetus to the work recorded in this volume, in which it appears that we are seeing the emergence of a new idea system, the psychology of the large group.

General comments[7]

In the unstructured large-group situation the 'normal' expectations that the person has as to his social and psychological environment are no longer met, and the difficult task of adaptation to this new state takes place only after considerable anxiety and experiences of disorientation. These experiences are of great interest psychopathologically and can usefully be linked with:

1. The study of how normal persons adapt to a new environment (coping mechanisms).[8]
2. The difficulties that the 'sick' person has in coping with his ordinary environment; e.g., persons suffering from disturbances of the self-system or certain aspects of ego distortions, i.e., the border-line personality (de Maré).
3. The study of communication and thinking in groups.[9]

The authors who concern themselves with the psychological experience of people in the group seem to reach a considerable degree of consensus as to the nature of their experiences. There is, however, less agreement as to how the person can adapt to the environment of the large group, and as to the creative, constructive possibilities available both to the individual as a member of the large group, and to the collectivity of the large group.

Consensus as to the subjective experience – both conscious and pre-conscious

The individual feels lost, frightened, out of touch with aspects of the self and of others; fears domination by the large group (Turquet, Main) by the leaders or by the technological environment (Mumby); the individual feels immature, reacts to this by becoming competitive, or may be reduced to a state of helplessness (Whiteley). He is unable to find a familiar or useful role, becomes deskilled, disorientated (Turquet). He is, nevertheless, caught up in a sense of change that threatens alteration and therefore loss of his sense of individuality.

By definition to 'belong' to the group means to involve, hence to 'give up', part of the self to the group.[10] Scheidlinger suggests that the individual group member's perceptions and attitudes towards the group as a whole can be seen as a process of identification involving two related elements. 1. Ascribing to the group an emotional meaning. 2. The giving up of an element of 'self' to the group.[11]

It is an inevitable part of a person's experience of the unstructured large group that he feels that the part of the self that has been involved or given up to the large group is ignored, unappreciated and only incompletely responded to (Turquet, Main). This experience represents a narcissistic blow and to understand the person's reactions to this entails study of the vicissitudes of narcissistic development and the part that narcissism plays in normal personality functioning, an area of which our knowledge is increasing rapidly.[12]

Kohut emphasises that the forces of narcissism should be

studied in their own right, as a 'third force' on a par with the sexual and aggressive drives. Narcissistic impulses do not simply transform into object-directed tendencies; in normal development the change is more from primitive 'archaic' narcissistic structures to a more mature narcissistic economy, syntonic with the higher values of the ego-ideal and super-ego, themselves representing internalised values of the individual's society. Part of the individual's narcissistic economy is vested in the values, attitudes and status of his group. 'Group cohesion is brought about and maintained not only by an ego-ideal held in common by the members of the group, but also by their subject-bound grandiosity, i.e. by a shared grandiose self . . . the psychic life of groups, like that of individuals, shows regressive transformations in the narcissistic realm. When the deployment of higher forms of narcissism is interfered with . . . then the narcissism of the group regresses, with deleterious consequences in the realm of group behaviour.'[13] The consequence is narcissistic hurt and rage. Kohut accepts that the group 'exists', that we have legitimate hopes and claims for satisfaction from the social milieu. This view contrasts with those who hold that the group is more of a fictive object, used in states of defensive narcissism as a container of unwanted parts of the self (Main).

Mechanisms involved in adaptation to the large group
'It is impossible to be skilful in a truly novel situation'.[14] There is agreement amongst our authors that changes in ego-boundaries are inevitable. Primitive defences, especially projective identification and splitting, are mobilised. 'Psychotic thinking' (de Maré) emerges from the large-group situation. De Maré also points out that the 'self-system' is far more directly involved in the large-group, as opposed to the small-group situation, and because of this there is a diminishing contact with the time-bound basis of the self. This observation can usefully be brought into relationship with Spiegel's[15] notions of the differentiation of the cognitive and the perceptual selves and to the task of the ego in integrating these two functions. Many authors also

point to the obstructions in thinking that emerge in the large group.

What then do we know of the basis and origins of the self-system and of the integration of perception, cognition and affect in the emerging self. Leo Speigel[16] has given us a novel and important guide to this. First, we recognise that the self is a construct, just as are the notions of the id, ego and super-ego.[17] The ego and the self must be distinguished: the polarity is of self to object as ego is to other psychic structures. Speigel brings together a physiological-perceptual and a psycho-analytic model. The physiological-perceptual is based on evidence from experiments of adaptation of the sense of weight and of normal visual experience under abnormal perceptual conditions, such as the use of prismatic spectacles. He adduces evidence and points to hypotheses as to the manner in which the self integrates perceptions and creates for itself a sense of normality. The perception of internal states requires a frame of references that possess continuity in time; 'self' is such a frame of reference, or zero point, to which representations of specific mental and physical states are referred, and against which they are perceived and judged. The operational significance of the concept of self is in its function as a framework. The relationship of perception to self-feeling is through the ego-function of relating single or small numbers of self-representations to the self considered as a framework. The origins of this framework are in the 'pooling' of traces of mental representations of tension and relief leading to an average representation of these states, now possessing permanence and continuity in time. In the average person these become interconnected leading to a steady frame of reference which can, in many ways, be equated with the sense of self, which now acts as a steadying 'flywheel' to overcome disturbing discontinuity, of intermittent self-representations. The constancy of this self-feeling can be disturbed if the framework has not been properly established (borderline personality) or if there is a rapid fluctuation in 'input' stimuli that cannot be 'pooled'. Alterations of self-feeling as such are normal in adolescence, as new quantities of cathexis (energic composition) from internal sexual stimulation are not yet pooled by the ego to become part of the self and lead to rapid alterations in self-feelings. Eventually these become integrated at a new cathectic level of the self and a new steady ratio between the single self-representations and the self is re-established. Neutralised energy makes much less demand on the pooling function of the ego than do steep gradients of instinctual energy.

Conditions such as Speigel hypothesises as leading to disturbances in the self-feeling clearly obtain in the large-group situation where both the framework of self and the quality and quantity of internal and external stimuli are grossly altered and the person requires time to become readapted to the new situation. 'Novelty which is most disruptive of behaviour is background novelty.'[18] The self-system can now integrate the previously novel and threatening stimuli, both internal and external, of the large-group situation and the person is now no longer assaulted by anxiety and can begin to explore the potentialities of the situation.

Psychological isolation

It is clearly pointed out by Turquet that the individual who is unable to adapt successfully to the large-group situation passes into a state of relative psychological isolation within the group. The isolation-fusion dilemma causes him great psychological stress. From the extensive literature on the psychological effects of isolation, a contribution that appears relevant to the psychology of this large-group experience comes from the observations of Charney[19] who studied the effects of isolation in disturbed children. Charney outlines four stages:

1. Initial intense anxiety with panic and a fear of breakdown.

2. A recompensation of defences where the individual fights against yielding to the objects in his environment, attempts to turn the tables and acts now as if he were isolating himself rather than being isolated.

3. Loosening of personality organisation, where the child now begins to live a separateness from the introjected image of the mother, and it is in this process of externalising the introject

that the height of anxieties is experienced. The children hallucinate their mothers coming to destroy them, thus living out their original perception of their mothers' denied destructiveness, and the externalisation of their own suppressed fury at their mothers.

4. The fourth stage is that of the intensification of the resistance where they spring back from the depths of disorganisaton to a prolonged and tenacious resistance, which is possibly a necessary concomitant to the process of deep personality reorganisation. The person has now experienced the possibility of separating from the mother's image of him, but still does not dare to do so. Defences are organised around the projection of the original anger at the depriving mother. It is at this stage that significant therapeutic interventions can be made and show the patients the possibility of change, of owning their own impulses and separating them from those of their mothers. Concomitant to the personality reorganisation that can now take place is something akin to a rebirth experience (Skynner).

Three significant processes occur in the process of successful re-emergence from the isolation experience and the working through of the process of change:

1. There is a regressive loosening of defensive stabilisation.

2. There are alternating periods of successful re-stabilisation against the regressive impact of the isolation situation.

3. There is a significant shift in the child's sense of itself now being able to acknowledge dependent needs and making constructive use of the available adults.

The whole process acts as a lever to unblock the stalemate position and permits the child to use the anxiety-engendering experience for further growth, for redefinition of the ongoing interpersonal relationships with adults at the very point of maximal existence. 'Under certain conditions, states of deprivation not only promote regressive disorganisation, but serve to invite and facilitate a constructive use of reorganisation of deeper resources within the individual.'

Charney points out that as internalisation begins, despite resistances, re-externalisation of already present introjects begins.

This, however, can lead to rapidly oscillating ego states which in turn lead to great anxiety and to retreat from contact, or it can lead to a process of acting out to halt the depersonalising and derealising processes that accompany it. The work of Rinsley[20] and Masterson[21] also points to many features in the personality structure and reaction to the more structured treatment milieu of the disturbed adolescent that seems to resemble in many ways the experiences of the 'normal' adult in the unstructured large-group situation.

What these authors and the contributors to this book who work in the large-group situation are struggling to achieve is a conceptualisation of not only affective, regressive experience, but those of cognition in the large-group situation. This is, as yet, a relatively unexplored field; one concerned with that which the great Swiss experimental psychologist, Piaget, has termed the Cognitive Unconscious.[22] Piaget is concerned to try to show the present and possible future relations between the study of the cognitive functions and the psychoanalytic understanding of personality development. 'I am persuaded that a day will come when the psychology of cognitive functions and psychoanalysis will have to fuse in a general theory that will improve both.'

Piaget points out that affectivity is characterised by its energic composition (cathexis), whereas the cognitive aspects of conduct are characterised by structure. Both affect and cognition possess a similar dimension, in that they arise from unconscious structures and that the person is only aware of the conscious level of experience. The innermost mechanisms that produce these and results in consciousness are characterised by complete unconsciousness. The cognitive structure is the *system of connections* that the individual can and must use and can by no means be reduced to the contents of conscious thought.[23] As de Maré points out, we are only beginning to become conscious of the nature of thinking in the large-group situation, which is characterised by the development of a containing network with thinking potential that is characterised by lateral affiliative modes, and that this will not develop if a hierarchy persists in maintaining power in the large group and retaining control over informational exchange.[24]

De Maré emphasises more than any of our other authors that the problem of communication between the individual and society is related to the degree to which informational flow can be negotiated. Large-group thinking brings together different contexts – psychological, politico-economic and socio-cultural, and certain types of social insight, which he terms outsight, can only emerge in the meaningful context of the large group. Though, according to de Maré, the large-group process facilitates the emergence of primary process equivalents, it also allows for learning of secondary process equivalents which contain the primary process equivalents by a peculiar process of learning based on the negotiation of communication and developmental organisation. The problem in the large group is of how to think, as opposed to the small group's problem of how to feel.[25]

To return to Piaget; he points out that a process akin to conscious suppression, or unconscious repression, also applies to the emergence of cognitive structures, analogous to the process that involves repression or suppression of affect. Here, however, it is a question of whether certain earlier cognitive structures become conscious (regression from reflective thinking to sensory-motor schemata).[25] Whether a schema becomes conscious or not depends upon the person's adaptation to their environment. Constructs and conduct that are adaptive do not lead to conscious awareness or appraisal; for instance, we do not question ourselves as to how we go up and down stairs, and if we were to do so we might well lose the ability to do this. Foulkes and Edelson also refer to this: Foulkes describes the group that meets to study itself as facing a task like that of the centipede that is asked to study the way that it moves; Edelson's description is in terms of a group that has neglected its heteronymous adaptive function.[27]

The process of becoming conscious and aware of our cognitive processes is akin to catharsis in terms of affect, but Piaget points out that catharsis is not a simple abreaction but that all memories or feelings from the past that are produced in the present have to go through a process of reorganisation before becoming conscious. Thus, in the large group we seem to have an individual forced to become conscious of certain aspects of his experience of self and of his processes of thought of which he is normally unconscious, but of which he may become conscious again until cognitive and affective reappraisal of the situation has occurred and he is now able to cope (Turquet, Spiegel). A suggestive statement of Piaget's is to the effect that there is evidence of a correlation between the development of schemata of the existence of permanent objects, and of the whole process of establishment of permanent object relations in the early life of the infant. Other developmental schemata that may well need to be integrated with this study of the individual's experience of establishing a sense of self and becoming secure within the large group, relate to the processes of individuation and separation.[27]

The clinical use of the large group in the psychiatric hospital

The complex type of western society has allocated the task of coping with severe mental illness to the hospital. The 'fundamental problem' (Hopper) of the social system of the hospital is, therefore, to contain mental illness and to try to transform mental illness into mental health, as defined by the wider society of which it is a part. The conception of the hospital as a social system, the structure of which may aid or hinder this task, is relatively novel (Main,[28] Foulkes[29]). The clinical use of a large group in the hospital setting, one which involves both staff and patients, entails recognition by the social system of the whole hospital that such a group has a legitimate and potentially useful function and the legitimised group has, therefore, become 'institutionalised' (Hopper). Practitioners of the therapeutic milieu[31] and therapeutic community approaches will not need to be reminded how much effort is involved in maintaining the institutionalised status of the large group.[32] Often the larger society of the hospital as a whole and the social environment of the community outside the hospital will act in a manner that threatens the continued existence of the large group. This is, in part, because the very existence of the clinical large group runs counter to the forces and pressures in society that has for so long regarded the mentally disturbed patient both as irresponsible and lacking in the normal skills required for socialisation. The role of the mentally sick patient[33] was, until comparatively recently, that of a person deprived of civic rights. The role of patients is constantly undergoing renegotiation as part of the constant flux of society,[34] and the clinical use of the large group both reflects this changed status of the patient and in turn is an important factor in the continued alteration of the action pattern of the sick role. Thus, the existence of a clinical large group, in which the roles of sick and well are not clearly confined to and identified with the roles of staff and patient, threatens the fundamental process in the wider society which has resulted in the creation of the hospital as a system for isolating and containing mental illness. Both staff and patients in their 'social unconscious' (Foulkes) contain, and are to some extent controlled by, this powerful unconscious image of the proper relationship of patient and staff and the distribution of health and sickness. The staff are expected to be well and the patients to be sick (Main). The threat to the continued existence of the large group, therefore, comes not only from the society outside the group but from the 'internal saboteur' that is part of the average social self-expectations of all its members. It is essential, therefore, that some members of the large group, both staff and patients, should have a concept of mental health and mental illness that is significantly different from that of the wider culture, and who therefore can envisage and foster this constant renegotiation of roles.

Psychiatry in the twentieth century, inspired by Freud, has continually attempted to communicate with the mentally ill and to go beyond containment and symptomatic relief. The communicative effort has extended from the individual seen as a 'singleton' (Turquet) in his isolated psychic self (one-body psychology[35]) to exploring the meanings of the patient/therapist transactions, transference and counter-transference (two-body psychology) to the transactions of a group of patients and a therapist, small-group psychotherapy (multi-body psychology), and now inexorably moves to examining the transactions between larger numbers of persons, social psychiatry (large-group psychotherapy) Each step along this continuum brings closer involvement with social processes and greater detachment from the current concept of illness in western society, that of the isolated individual containing an 'illness'.

The community meeting[36] represents the creation of a new social system that accepts as its fundamental problem control, containment and treatment of mental illness. The attempt is made to foster the development of a society whose 'shared understanding and common intellectual and emotional discourse' (Earl Hopper) are based on the insights of psychotherapy which state that mental illness results in, and may arise from, faulty communication,[37] that mental illness has meaning that can be understood and that all persons, sick or well, have more in common than they can easily recognise.[38] The psychotherapeutic viewpoint emphasises that emotional disturbances have roots in failed developmental tasks which centre on the resolution of issues of dependency, autonomy, authority and sexuality.[39] The resolution of these issues is renegotiable in the transactions of psychotherapy,[40] and it is expected that they will appear in the social transactions of the group, and thereby offer opportunities for psychotherapeutic work. The psychotherapeutic effort is to raise these issues to the level of conscious understanding where they can be acted upon in more mature and adaptive ways than have been open to the individuals heretofore, and which are unlikely to be renegotiated in the unstructured large group, where as contributors to this volume have shown clearly, very considerable anxieties and confusions assail the individual (Turquet, Main, Skynner). Others (Springmann) have shown, however, that in the large-group situation matters can be handled in such a way that the individual gains from the experience in terms of greater ability to master anxiety, more insight into his own deeper psychotic processes and the acquisition of 'outsight' into his social relationships and the impact upon him of membership of a group (de Maré, Whiteley). Therefore, what is potentially harmful and disruptive can become helpful and constructive. The psychotherapeutic and sociotherapeutic effort has the function of raising the group interactions and processes from the primitive to the mature. The lowest common denominator has to be raised to the highest common factor.

Psychoanalytic development psychology[41] shows clearly how certain fundamental developmental tasks have to be achieved before the individual acquires that type of psychic structure that ensures the laying down of a foundation for healthy psychic functioning. Below this level of development psychic structure is far from being a 'given'. The higher level of psychic structure is often poorly represented in the hospital population[42] though, hopefully, it exists in the majority of the staff population. Thus, the development of a social structure may give the sicker members of the group an opportunity to acquire, by learning or by modelling, the ability to function at the more mature level represented by the healthier members of the community. Opportunities for appropriate transactions within the system have to be created.

The system created will have as its emotional 'input' the feelings that arise from the individuals in the group, patients and staff, and by virtue of the patient population will at all times be dealing with primitive, powerful emotions and attitudes which have already evoked negative, rejecting or frightened reactions from the person's social group. The emotional input will not, however, be confined to the disordered emotions of patients, but will also have to contend with the emotions evoked by the very existence of the social system of the hospital,[43] notably conflicts within the staff system and between staff and patients (Hopper).

The task of sociotherapy[44] is that of creating the structure in which large-group psychotherapy can take place. The sociotherapeutic structure is the analogue, in the group situation, of the individual's psychic structure. It has to allow for the display of such functions of reflection, thought, containment of anxiety and transformation of primitive anxiety to signal anxiety[45] for the exercise of secondary process functions and of the cognitive self-system of which many of the individuals within the group are deficient in themselves. When this level of social organisation and social functioning has been achieved, the actions and transactions of the large group will become therapeutic for some of the individuals exposed to the situation, but for others non-therapeutic, or even anti-therapeutic. We have, as yet, little data to enable us to predict and thereby to differentiate selectively between those persons who are likely to be helped and those who are unlikely to be helped in large-group therapy. We can, however, begin to understand the effects of the large-group situation upon people and thereby to understand the stresses of the situation. All our authors agree that the self-system is immediately and powerfully assailed by the psychological stresses involved in participation in the large group. From William James[46] onwards we have recognised that the concept of self is intrinsically bound up with social interaction processes. The self-experience is central to the individual's sense of identity and adoption and acceptance of the sick role inevitably involves a change in self-definition.[47] This change in self-definition may be reversible or irreversible. As in all role relationships, it is contingent upon the responses of other persons who are involved in interaction with the sick person.

Their acceptance of the person in his sick role involves legitimisation (Parsons)[48] of certain behaviour patterns and within the psychotherapeutic situation marks the beginning of interaction patterns that may confirm the patient in his sick role, or help him to redefine himself in such a way that the role is abandoned and he reverts to the non-patient role. This again marks a change in the person's self-definition. Thus, it is clear that just as self-definition from the start is based upon interaction between the person and his human environment, so changes in the self-system may come about throughout life, not just in infancy, through social interaction processes. The renegotiation of self-definition is one of the aims of psychotherapy and the large-group situation exerts a powerful effect upon this system. Redefinition may arise through a renegotiation of the person's relationship to his human environment. The opportunity for this is offered by the person's involvement in a network of relationships that are significant to him personally, through them being members of the person's family or reference group, or through the group of strangers (fellow patients) who have become sufficiently significant to him emotionally that changes within this network will effect changes in the person's self-definition.

There is ample evidence from the work of Turquet and Main that the unstructured large group becomes significant for the person not as a network of involved and significant others, but as an agglomeration of anonymous and, on the whole, threatening others and that the individual retreats from, rather than emerges into, significant involvement with the other members of the group. The impact of the large-group situation upon 'normal' people is sufficiently powerful and confusing to render the situation unpleasant and anxiety-provoking for many. It was my own experiences of this difficult and confusing aspect of the large training group (Skynner) that led me greatly to modify my attempts to use the large group as a psychotherapeutic technique in an inpatient psychiatric unit (St George's, Atkinson Morley's Hospital). It seemed to me essential to devise methods to counter the threat of anonymity, the experience of confusion and the inability to find an appropriate role for oneself in the large group (Turquet) before it could begin to become an effective tool for treatment. I begin to see the ward meeting much more as de Maré describes it, as a situation where a relevant informational network could be developed and where personally significant issues could be presented and transacted. The conditions for information flow had to be created and the relevant type of information that could then be transmitted through the network had to be determined.

Creation of the network

First, an atmosphere conducive to information flow had to be created so that people would come to the large group expecting both to hear and to provide the necessary data. Heavy, tense, brooding silence, in which people are unsure where the next word will come from or what it will be about, and not knowing whether to listen for it or to shut themselves off from the painful tension of anticipation, does not foster this atmosphere. This applies particularly to the beginning of a group meeting, whereas after the group has been together for a while the individuals in it can tolerate tensions, silence and sudden switches of topic, and often are able to integrate them into a coherent whole. Roles had, therefore, to be created for people whose function it was to start the information flow going. The roles that we have created are those of patients' chairman ('process-guardian'), whose job it is to see that the meeting begins and ends on time, to ensure that other people with defined roles should be present, and to call upon them in a predictable order, to provide their quota of information. These roles are those of:

1. *Patients' representative:* Each group of patients under the care of a particular consultant may number from 12 to 20. One person in each of these three groups is nominated patients' representative and in the large-group meeting his role is to facilitate information flow for the whole group about each person in his sub-group. His usual way of obtaining this to is make a round of all his fellow patients before the group meeting and ask if there is anything they wish to convey to the group. Facts which have come to be recognised as important to convey relate not only to the patient's feeling state, but to such matters as changes in treatment régime, alterations in drugs or physical treatments, discharge and leave dates, renegotiations of the terms and conditions of being a patient in the hospital, interaction with family members, involvement with other patients, behaviour that impinges upon the feelings and actions of other patients. The 'patients' rep' is also empowered to enquire from staff members, nurses and doctors if there are any matters which the staff wish to have communicated to the community as a whole regarding any particular patient. The aim here is to reduce the amount of confidential information held by the staff and withheld by them from the patients. Relevant items from the staff may include changes in the expectations that the staff have of a patient's behaviour in hospital, plans for leave and discharge, changes in the physical aspects of treatment and expressions of staff attitudes towards the patient. It is important to emphasise here that the report of the patients' representative is designed to

facilitate the discussion by the patient or by others, and not to replace it. The skill of the patients' representative in giving the report naturally varies very considerably according to his natural abilities and to his own state of mental health. It is interesting, and indeed remarkable, to observe how confident some patients are at involving other people and evoking from them significant contributions to the group discussion.

2. *Staff reports:* The patients' chairman calls upon a member of the nursing staff to give a ward report in which a member of the nursing staff may comment upon such items as atmosphere and mood of the ward during the previous 24 hours, significant events involving individuals or groups, and these reports often usefully include declarations of feelings and attitudes held by the nursing staff towards the community or towards particular patients.

3. *Occupational therapy report:* The occupational therapists have succeeded in finding a new role for themselves beyond their individual transactions with patients based upon traditional skills. They have taken the lead in creating small-group situations where role-playing and encounter techniques are used to explore underlying emotions and attitudes. Painting, modelling and other expressive techniques are used to evoke and express feelings that relate to such universally held and highly charged topics as trust and mistrust, sexuality, aggression, sense of identity, self-esteem, family relationships, problems of re-exit from the hospital into the community, and so on. A description of the way in which the small group has explored and coped with these deeply felt and highly charged topics is fed back to the large group and thereby deepens and intensifies the emotional current that flows through the communicational network.

This initial report to the group which acts both as a warm up and as a necessary form of information feedback usually occupies some 15 to 20 minutes of a one-hour session. One aim is that all who are patients in the unit, whether present at the meeting or not, should be mentioned by name. No one is to be forgotten or ignored. Anonymity is to be countered.

The order in which these items appear is predictable and regular. It seems to provide both patients and staff with a sense of competence and reliability in their roles both as listeners and speakers in the initial difficult stages of the large group (Main). Even though the large-group situation is not popular with many patients, it is still recognised and valued by them as the beginning of a working day. They will continue their psychotherapy in small group situations, but prefer to do so after a large group as this has got them into the mood for talking. A recent innovation has been to begin the day with the report-back stage of the large group which is then followed by breaking up into small groups and reassembling for discussion and reportage of the events of the small group. This programme occupies the whole of a morning from 9.15 until 11.45 and gives the participants a feeling of having engaged in a considerable amount of work. The atmosphere seems to become one in which participation and exchange of feelings and thoughts become much easier by the end of the morning, even within a group of as many as 60 to 70 people.

This type of structure of the large-group situation seems to counter some of its negative effects. The group does not become overwhelmingly powerful and alien. The members of it feel themselves, to some extent, to be in control of the processes and able to regulate them. The gains to some people seem to be clear. They begin to become much more articulate about their experiences both within themselves and within the framework of the ward and the community. The intrapsychic becomes the interpersonal and may even reach the level of the transpersonal.[49]

Example
Within one week of admission, Patient A, a young man in his twenties, intelligent, athletic, physically attractive, has succeeded in provoking great hostility in many male members of the community, both patients and staff, particularly older men. He is insultingly sardonic to them and seduces (and is seduced by) young girl patients into open caresses and intimate bodily contact. One of these girls mutilated her face during this week and A is blamed for his. An atmosphere of hatred and potential violence

pervades the wards and a group of older men request his discharge.

9.30 Staff report: Focuses on A's provocative and hostile behaviour. He has threatened a nurse's security by threatening to manoeuvre his discharge. Hearing this, the male patients become even angrier and demand the doctors discharge him to a 'real hospital'. Some facts are cleared up about what has actually happened. The patient's doctor points out that A has recreated here the situation he has repeatedly been in before, and that the girls involved also have interlocking pathologies. The atmosphere remains that of a witch hunt and a tribunal.

10.0–11.0 Small group meetings: A is the main focus in all. Staff try to work with the other patients on the counter-provocation they offer to A, and to show how they might better cope with him.

11.0–12 noon. Large group. Report back from groups. The hostile 'black and white' atmosphere gradually changes as A is brought into a dialogue, which he breaks off as soon as he receives the slightest provocation. We discover that he wants to be a doctor, but cannot study; that he wishes to become a surgeon, that his father was a surgeon and that there was 'agro' between them; he avers that to be a surgeon is to be a technician who does not have to concern himself with human feelings; a girl tells me that he is wrong. She has had major heart surgery and chose the surgeon who could help her most as a person. A is impressed by this, the formerly angry men abandon their paranoid leader; one asks A if he has difficulties in relating to men as he seems to spend his time with the women; another tells him how important atmosphere is and that a bad atmosphere harms everyone. The meeting ends fairly peacefully; staff and patients all seem to feel that good work has been done, that a situation that was experienced as primitive, split and violent has altered as a result of reflection, negotiation and integration. The higher level functions of mind have been attested and confirmed. The Lower Common Denominator was hate, scapegoating and expulsion: the Higher Common Factor is communication, understanding and a sense of community.

Conclusion

The personal impact of a large-group training experience is both powerful and exciting and is beginning to influence the treatment we are offering to patients. Excitement must be tempered with caution as we are dealing with powerful forces of which, at present, we have little knowledge. We are becoming aware, however, that the psychodynamic approach may be able to share with the chemotherapeutic the ability to influence many more persons than previously through procedures involving greater numbers, such as small and large groups. Research in this area is difficult and the basic theoretical models are just beginning to emerge. We are, I believe, beginning to see in 1974 the outlines of the psychotherapy of 1984, an approach that will help to conquer the loss of individuality that Orwell feared and predicted. The person who can find and retain a sense of being a full and effective person in a large group will not suffer the fate outlined by Canetti,[50] that of the person who seeks a crowd in which to lose his painful sense of individuality, who cannot bear to give up that crowd in which he finds escape, and who therefore surrenders to the crowd inside him, becoming fragmented, a lone crowd, sufficient unto himself, schizophrenic.

Nisbet has stated that 'the appearance of a new idea system is not the consequence of methodology, much less of computers, of mass data gathering and retrieval, or of problem definition however rigorous, or research design however aseptic. It will be the consequence, rather, of intellectual processes which the scientist shares with the artist; iconic imagination, aggressive intuition, each given discipline by reason and route by reality. So it has always been and so it is now in those contemporary intellectual areas of most intense creativity. Foremost is the passion for reality – reality not obstructed by the layers of conventionalisation, but reality that is direct and unmediated'.[50]

These words well describe some of the contributions to this volume.

Notes and references

Introduction – Lionel Kreeger
1. de Maré, P. B., 'Large Group Psychotherapy: A Suggested Technique', in *Group Analysis* (GAIPAC) Vol. 2 (1972), p. 106.
2. Kreeger, L. C., 'The Background and Application of Large Groups', in *Group Analysis* (GAIPAC) Vol. 2 (1972), p. 103.
3. Freud, S., *Group Psychology and the Analysis of the Ego.* (1921) Standard Edition, Vol. 18 (London, Hogarth Press, 1955), p. 69.
4. Foulkes, S. H., and Anthony, E. J., *Group Psychotherapy* (Harmondsworth, Penguin Books, 1957).
5. de Maré, P. B., and Kreeger, L. C., *Introduction to Group Treatments in Psychiatry* (London, Butterworth, 1974).
6. de Maré, P. B., *Perspectives in Group Psychotherapy* (London, Allen & Unwin, 1972).
7. Main, T. F., 'The Hospital as a Therapeutic Institution', in *Bull. Menn. Clin.* (1946), 10, 66.
8. Foulkes, S. H., *Introduction to Group-Analytic Psychotherapy* (London, Heinemann, 1948).
9. Rapoport, R., *Community as Doctor* (London, Tavistock Publications, 1960).
10. Rice, A. K., *Learning for Leadership* (London, Tavistock Publications, 1965).
11. Wax, J., 'Analysing a Therapeutic Community Meeting', in *Int. J. Group Psychotherapy*, Vol. 15, No. 1 (Jan. 1965).
12. Curry, A. E., 'Large Therapeutic Groups: A Critique and Appraisal of Selected Literature', in *Int. J. Group Psychotherapy*, Vol. 17, No. 4 (Oct. 1967), p. 536.
13. Jones, M., *Social Psychiatry* (London, Tavistock Publications, 1952).
14. Goffman, E., *Behaviour in Public Places* (Glencoe, Ill., Free Press, 1963).
15. Wilmer, H., 'The Size of the Group', Paper read at 6th International Congress of Psychotherapy, London, 1964.

16. Herbst, P. G., 'A Theory of Simple Behaviour Systems', in *Human Relations,* 14 (1961), pp. 1–11.

17. Small, I. F. and Small, J. G., 'The Significance of the Introduction in Large Group Psychotherapy', in *Int. J. Soc. Psychiat.* 9 (1963), pp. 127–34.

18. Schiff, S. B., and Glassman, S. M., 'Large and Small Group Therapy in a State Mental Health Center', in *Int. J. Group Psychotherapy,* Vol. 19, No. 2 (April 1969).

19. Jones, M., *The Therapeutic Community* (New York, Basic Books, 1953).

20. Edelson, M., *Ego Psychology, Group Dynamics and the Therapeutic Community* (New York, Grune & Stratton, 1964).

21. Edelson, M., *Sociotherapy and Psychotherapy* (University of Chicago Press, 1970).

22. Springmann, R., 'A Large Group', in *Int. J. Group Psychotherapy,* Vol. 20, No. 2 (April 1970).

23. Clark, D., and Myers, K., 'Themes in a Therapeutic Community', in *Brit. J. Psychiat.,* Vol. 117 (1970), p. 389.

24. Jacobs, Isabel, 'Report on the Large Group at the European Workshop on Group Analysis, No. 1, held in London, January 1973', in *Group Analysis* (GAIPAC), Vol. 1/3 (1973), p. 143.

25. Thurber, James, *Vintage Thurber* (London, Hamish Hamilton, 1965).

1. Problems of the large group from a group-analytic point of view – S. H. Foulkes

1. Foulkes, S. H., 'On Group Analysis', in *Int. J. Psycho-Anal.* 27 (1946).

2. Foulkes, S. H., *Therapeutic Group Analysis* (London, Allen & Unwin, 1964).

3. Foulkes, S. H., and Prince, G. S. (Eds.), *Psychiatry in a Changing Society* (London, Tavistock, 1969). Chapter 7.

4. Foulkes S. H., 'Access to Unconscious Processes in the Group-Analytic Group', in *Group Analysis,* 4 (1971).

5. Mark, R., 'Minority Verdict' (BBC Dimbleby Lecture, broadcast 6th November 1973).

6. Foulkes, S. H., and Prince, G. S. (Eds.), op. cit.

7. Anzieu, D. *et al., Le Travail psychoanalytique dans les groupes* (Paris, Dunod, 1972). Summary in *Group Analysis,* 6 (1973).

8. Whiteley, J. S., Letter in *Group Analysis,* 1 (1968).

9. Gregory, B. A. J. C., 'The Day Hospital as a Therapeutic Community', in *Group Analysis,* 1 (1968).

10. Foulkes, S. H., *Introduction to Group-Analytic Psychotherapy* (London, Heinemann, 1948).

11. Ibid., pp. 155 et seq.
12. Foulkes, S. H., *Therapeutic Group Analysis* (1964); *Group Analytic Psychotherapy: Method and Principles*. (In the press.)
13. Foulkes, S. H., ibid., and Foulkes, S. H., 'The Leader of the Group: the group-analytic view'. [Chapter in forthcoming volume in honour of Alexander Wolf. (In the press.)]
14. 'My concept "ego-training in action",' Foulkes.

2. Some psychodynamics of large groups – Tom Main

1. An earlier version of this paper was read as the Kincardine Foundation Lecture to the University of Edinburgh, March 1971.
2. Bannister, K., and Pincus, L., *Shared Phantasy in Marital Problems. Therapy in a 4-person relationship* (Hitchin, Codicote Press, 1965); and Main, T. F., 'Mutual Projection in a Marriage', in *Comp. Psych.*, Vol. 7, No. 5 (1966).
3. Freud, S., *Group Psychology and the Analysis of the Ego* (London, Int. Psycho-Anal. Press, 1972).
4. Menzies, I. E. P., *The Functioning of Social Systems as a Defence Against Anxiety* (London, Tavistock Pamphlet, 1961).
5. Jaques, E., *The Changing Culture of a Factory: a study of authority and participation in an industrial setting* (London, Tavistock, 1961).
6. Main, T. F., 'The Hospital as a Therapeutic Institution', in *Menninger Clinic Bull.*, Vol. 10, No. 3 (1946).
7. Searles, H. F., 'Psychotherapy of Schizophrenia', in *Brit. J. Med. Psych.*, Vol. XXXIV (1961), pp. 169–193.
8. P. M. Turquet has described a similar state in large unstructured groups of executives on study courses as *homogenisation*. It appears to be the same phenomenon and to have similar underlying dynamics. See 'Threats to Identity in the Large Group'. Winter Lecture of the British Psycho-Analytical Society (Unpublished, 1969).

3. Threats to identity in the large group – Pierre Turquet

1. With pleasure and gratitude I wish to make the following acknowledgements: First, to the late Dr A. K. Rice sc.d., formerly Chairman, Centre of Applied Research, Tavistock Institute of Human Relations, who first invited me to join him in taking large groups when they became part of the programme of our Group Relations Training' Conference. [For further details see Rice, A. K., *Learning for Leadership* (London, Tavistock, 1965)]. It was an adventure that we jointly shared. As ever he was particularly generous in sharing his ideas with me and in encouraging me to express mine.

Secondly, I wish to thank Drs Margaret Rioch, Roger Shapiro and Lynom Wynne for so generously providing the initial opportunities to develop many of the ideas expressed in this paper.

Thirdly, without the help of Mrs Jean Wagstaff this paper would never have seen the light of day.

Lastly, and not least, I have to thank the many large groups who have worked with me as their consultant.

2. Op. cit.

3. Currently there is further investigation of the nature and characteristics of the median group, of 20–35 members.

4. Bales, Robert F., *Interaction Process Analysis* (1950).

5. Conversion: *vide* Miller and Rice: *Systems of Organisation*. My use of this term derives from but is only approximately similar to theirs.

6. The term 'conference member' is used here to describe those people who, having signed on, as it were, for work, have attended the opening conference plenary. They might perhaps more appropriately be described as 'conference entrants' since as yet they have not taken up the role of 'conference member'. It would appear that some 'conference entrants' never take up the role of 'conference members', and in their continuing presence at the conference should be called 'conference attenders'.

7. I use the term 'I' to refer to the person who has not yet achieved a role status in the large group, or to a person who has momentarily left such a status for whatever reason, possibly in order to search within himself for a model or a skill; a member in transition.

8. The term 'singleton', in addition to its bridge connotation, is used, I understand, in Buckinghamshire, to describe the isolate duck, separate from the main 'huddle' of ducks.

9. See Sartre, J.-P., *Huis Clos*. Translated as *No Exit* (London, Hamish Hamilton).

10. I am using the term 'matrix' here in the sense of 'a place or medium in which something is bred, produced or developed' and hence in the sense of 'a place of origin and growth'. (*Oxford English Dictionary*).

11. Macneice, Louis, *Modern Poetry,* Second Edition (Oxford 1968).

12. Bion, W. R., *Experiences in Groups and Other Papers* (London, Tavistock, 1961).

13. Thoreau, H. D., *Walden* (New York, Thos. Crowell, 1966).

14. Bion, W. R., op. cit.

15. Compare this with a letter from John Keats to Richard Woodhouse, 27th October 1818:

A poet is the most unpoetical of any thing in existence; because he has no Identity – he is continually in for – and filling some other Body . . . . It is a wretched thing to confess; but it is a very fact that not one word I ever utter can be taken for granted as an opinion growing out of my identical nature – how can it, when I have no nature? When I am in a room with People if I am ever free from speculating on creations of my own brain, then not myself goes home to myself: but the identity of every one in the room begins (for so?) to press upon me that, I am in a very little time annihilated – not only among them; it would be the same in a Nursery of children . . . .

16. Marshall, S. L. A., comments on the loss of knowledge of the importance of small weapons' fire, learnt from the Second World War, in the Korean War. See *Men Against Fire* (New York, Wm Morrow).
17. *'La garde se meurt mais ne se rend pas.'* The guards die but do not surrender. . . .
18. Bergson, Henri, *Time and Free Will* (London, Allen & Unwin, 1910). Translated by F. L. Pogson Macmillan from *Essai sur les données immédiates de la conscience* (1889).
19. Bradley, A. C., *Oxford Lectures on Poetry* (London, Macmillan, 1909).
20. It is reported that at meetings of the British Cabinet names are not used, only titles.

4. The politics of large groups – Patrick de Maré

1. Jaspers, K., *General Psychopathology* (Manchester U.P., 1963).
2. Lévi-Strauss, Claude, *The Elementary Structures of Kinship* (London, Eyre & Spottiswoode, 1949).
3. Foulkes, S. H., and Stewart Prince, G., *Psychiatry in a Changing Society* (London, Tavistock Publications, 1969).
4. Caplan, Gerald, *Principle of Preventive Psychiatry* (London, Tavistock Publications, 1964).
5. Menzies, Isabel, *Social Systems as a Defence against Anxiety* (London, Tavistock Pamphlet, No. 3, 1970).
6. Watzlawick, P., Beavin, J. H., and Jackson, D. D., *Pragmatics of Human Communication* (London, Faber, 1969).
7. Bertrand, Alvin L., *Social organization* (F. A. Davis Company, 1972).
8. de Maré, Patrick, 'Large Group Psychotherapy – a Suggested Technique', in *Group Analysis* (Aug. 1972).
9. Cooley, Charles, *Human Nature and the Social Order* (New York, Scribners, 1902).
10. Marsh, Cody, *Mental Hygiene* (1933).

11. Trotter, W., *Instincts of the Herd in Peace and War* (London, Ernest Benn, 1916).

12. Foulkes, S. H., Correspondence in *Group Analysis* (November 1972), pp. 153–5.

13. Morowitz, H. J., *Energy Flow in Biology* (London, Academic Press, 1968).

14. Bion, W. R., *Experiences in Groups* (London, Tavistock Publications, 1961).

15. de Maré, Patrick, *Perspectives in Group Psychotherapy* (London, Allen & Unwin, 1972).

16. Brown, Phil, *Radical Psychology* (London, Tavistock, 1973).

17. Wilden, Anthony, *System and Structure* (London, Tavistock Publications, 1972).

18. Buckley, Walter, *Sociology and Modern System Theory* (Englewood Cliffs, Prentice-Hall, 1967).

19. de Maré, Patrick, and Kreeger, Lionel, *Introduction to Group Treatments in Psychiatry* (London, Butterworth, 1974).

5. A sociological view of large groups – Earl Hopper and Anne Weyman

1. The debate about the nature of social science is a continuing one. Science is both a body of knowledge and a way of knowing, a source of new knowledge and a method of validating what we 'know' about the world. Any particular science consists of a set of theories which form its basic paradigm. New knowledge is obtained by using the hypothetico-deductive method to test and extrapolate this paradigm. Sometimes new findings challenge the theories to such an extent that they have to be replaced or altered. The origin of the hypothesis that is being tested is not important, although it will usually be derived from the existing theories available to the scientist. In the social sciences this creates special problems because not only is the 'scientist' part of his subject matter, but also he has definite views about it; and his own views may influence his formulation of an hypothesis, and his interpretation of evidence. Ideally this should not matter as his work can be subjected to critical scrutiny by other scientists, but they may have the same values, and so the basic assumptions which underlie his work may not be challenged. We should also remember that all categories and problems are social constructs and that these form the foundation of science and affect its findings. These difficulties in no way negate the value of the scientific approach, for despite its constraints, sociologists have produced knowledge which is unsurpassed in its validity, reliability and utility.

2. It is worth remembering that the 'first men' appeared in a breeding group, some members of which were undoubtedly apes, and that some animals such as monkeys can only really be 'monkeys' if they are brought up with other monkeys. Harlow, H. F., & Harlow, M., 'Social Deprivation in Monkeys', *Scientific American*, 207, No. 5 (1962).

3. The concept of internal volition is itself problematic. If a man needs to earn and he knows that another has control of the means of his livelihood and that there is no chance of his changing this situation, is his 'acceptance' of it 'internal volition'? Some sociologists answer this question by arguing that 'what people have to do becomes what they want to do'. However, we believe this to be an open question, the answer to which requires more empirical evidence, especially concerning the conditions under which complete internalisation of the *status quo* develops.

4. The first of these two properties has been ignored by those whose training has been primarily in social sciences and the second by those who are psychologists. The first group tend to reify social phenomena and to have an over-socialised concept of man, whereas the second are usually resistant to any perspective which denies the primacy of human action and the view that action derives mainly from the organism. Curiously, it is not the most orthodox of analysts who fall into the second category. Despite the meta-psychological Kleinian assumption of the inborn nature of certain infantile fantasies, Klein herself, as well as Fairbairn, Guntrip, Winnicott and others, view the human being as essentially an internalised social system in interaction with his contemporary social system.

5. To do so is to admit helplessness with respect to control over one's immediate situation and alternatives for action. This may help to account for the resistance to sociological insight among those people who experience a lack of personal control as frightening, to be avoided and even to be judged as immoral, cowardly and childish. They used the slogan 'The individual is what counts' to counteract sociological heresy. On the other hand, some may use it as an excuse, a welcome but strenuously denied relief, for maintaining the *status quo* and avoiding the effort of isolating what can be changed in the existing situation from what cannot.

6. It is surprising that whereas intelligent people have no difficulty in accepting the existence of invisible forces and phenomena in the explanation of the physical and natural universe, even when sub-atomic particles are no longer expressed in terms other than 'energy', they refuse to accept that such phenomena as social

classes or groups exist and are real in the sense that they are more than an aggregate of their personnel.

7. Problems specific to the organism are primary since they must be solved, at least to some extent, before people can seek solutions to all other problems. Hence they are universal. Examples of such fundamental problems are socialisation, education, economic activity, social coordination, and conflict and tension management.

It can be argued that this last problem would not exist in an ideal social system, and that even though such a system has never existed, it is not a theoretical impossibility. If the socialisation process were complete, so that all could participate fully in any form of social organisation, and if the coordination of activity benefited all equally so that some groups were not excluded from achieving certain goals, many sources of tension might be removed. Thus, the need for tension management may be due mainly to the existence of exploitation and inequality, and not only to ineffective socialisation. Hence it may be more a property of particular forms of social organisation and their effect on individual characters than inherent in the human condition. As such, it may be more useful to regard the need for tension management as organisation specific.

This is not to ignore the classical debate within both sociology and psychology concerning the natural character of aggressive feelings and aggression. To some extent this has become a problem of semantics. We prefer the view that aggressive feelings are a function of frustration but that the capacity to realise this process is innate. In so far as frustration is fundamental to the human condition, so too are aggressive feelings. Nonetheless, many psychologists have not given sufficient attention to the various social conditions which regulate this process.

8. Problems specific to organisation are numerous. Ordinarily, they are not universal because no particular organisational form is necessarily universal. However, as all human life must take place within a society, certain organisational problems always occur. We will mention only two of the most obvious and important.

Any social system must recruit new members. It may seem that in the case of a society this is simply a biological matter, but it is not. *Legitimate reproduction* is very much a social event. Infants must be given a legitimate status and a position in the social system. Widespread use of contraception indicates that even the desire for children is a social product and that reproduction is too important to be left to organismic factors alone.

Another organisation specific problem which is universal is the development and maintenance of *Core Values*. These help people to come to terms with their social and non-social environments. These environments are difficult to control, and the introduction of general principles which create order out of chaos may make them more predictable and provide guidelines for dealing with them. Hence, core values are related to a fundamental problem of human existence, namely the need for common understanding and meaning. These values tend to be very general but form the basis for the derivation of specific norms. They should not be confused with the more general term 'culture'. They are orientated to the solution of specific tasks, and require specific institutions for their development and maintenance.

9. Perhaps Parsons's is the best known scheme, with its categories of goal attainment, adaptation, integration and latent pattern maintenance.

10. Gouldner, A. W., and Gouldner, H. P., *Modern Society: an Introduction to the Study of Human Interaction* (London, Harcourt, Brace and World, 1963).

11. Nisbett, Robert A., *The Social Bond* (New York, Alfred Knopf, 1970).

12. Lieberman has shown that workers who are promoted to foremen become more favourable to the management, but that if they return to the shop floor, their old attitudes return too. Thus, it is not just that people with particular views find the right role for these views but that the roles they hold help form their views. See Lieberman, S., 'The Effects of Changes in Roles on the Attitudes of Role Occupants' in Smelser, N. J., and Smelser, W. T. (Eds.), *Personality and Social Systems* (New York, Wiley, 1970).

13. For example, people in the same class but in different sections of the labour market, such as managers in financial institutions and their counterparts in manufacturing industry, differ in many of their personal and interpersonal characteristics, such as their feelings of powerlessness with respect to their control of society. See Hopper, Earl, 'Relative Deprivation, Occupational Status, and Occupation "Situs": The Theoretical and Empirical Application of a Neglected Concept', in Warner, M., (Ed.), *The Sociology of the Workplace* (London, Allen & Unwin, 1973).

14. For example, Young, M., and Willmott, P., 'Social Grading by Manual Workers', in *British Journal of Sociology* (Dec. 1956).

15. Societies which have tried to replace the family with other institutions have often returned to more traditional family structures. This has been so in Russia and in the case of some of the Israeli kibbutzim.

16. The degree to which interaction patterns are integrated may be

viewed at several levels of analysis. For example, one can refer to the degree to which a person's many roles are integrated. At another level, one can refer to the degree to which the institutions of a society are integrated with other institutions.

17. Even an inorganic system like a building, which seems to be in a state of 'static equilibrium', is open to environmental influences which can make it disintegrate in time.

18. The annual change cycle of the Nuer in which they accommodate to seasonal climatic changes through structural changes in their society is an example of this type of fluctuation. Evans-Pritchard, E. E., *The Nuer* (Oxford, Oxford University Press, 1940).

19. The dimension 'simple-complex' has often been viewed as a developmental sequence, and any change towards complexity has been called 'development', and changes towards simplicity, 'regression'. However, this treatment is based on an organismic analogy and must be used with great caution. Social systems are not organisms and do not evince natural laws of growth or determination. Hence, the term 'stages or phases of development' may be used as a description, but does not denote an inevitable evolutionary process. (The theoretical weaknesses of social evolutionism have been discussed at length elsewhere. For example, Cohen, P. S., *Modern Social Theory*, London, Heinemann, 1968.) A more serious difficulty is that 'development' has been used to connote adulthood, which is felt to be 'better' and more mature, and 'regression' to connote 'childhood' which is 'worse' and more immature. However, simplicity or complexity should not be interpreted in this way, as illustrated by the following examples.

In a tribal society which has matrilineal kinship and patrilocal residence, males from different kin groups are not subject to the same structure of authority and power. As a result, it may be difficult to form stable work groups. This problem can be solved by adopting a different form of organisation, for example, a system of patrilineal descent and patrilocal residence. However, this is not a move to greater complexity. Alternatively, the problem may be solved by a structural differentiation which separates work from more general domestic affairs and creates a more complex system of authority and power. This increased complexity would be described as 'development'. Yet another solution would be for work to become less cooperative so that members become more economically self-sufficient. This increased simplicity would be described as 'regression'. It is difficult to understand in what ways the development of a more complex arrangement is 'better' than the other two. It may be better, but this assessment is an empirical matter, one which involves the study of many of its ramifications, both planned and unanticipated. A similar example can be drawn from industrial societies in which the structure of the family has become simpler, and the family has been divested of many of its functions. Conjugal role relationships have become more diffuse and overlapping. This change could be termed a 'regression' because it is a move to greater simplicity, but many would prefer to call it a 'development' to a 'better' and more 'mature' type of relationship. Clearly, the problems involved in the term 'development' are so great that we prefer not to use it in the following discussion of simple and complex societies.

20. Interestingly enough, the lack of solidarity produced by a system of egoistic norms may actually contribute to the cohesion of a society with an organically integrated interaction system, e.g., through the constraints of universalistic norms of achievement and norms of affective neutrality which facilitate bureaucratisation. Such latent processes and, to a lesser extent, those connected with altruistic norms which give rise, for example, to nationalistic sentiments, are also likely to play their part in the cohesion of complex societies. But they tend to be much less important than is the case in their relatively simple, mechanically organised counterparts, and perhaps are of importance only under conditions of severe crisis for the whole society, such as a war.

21. This view is consistent with the distinction between system integration and social integration introduced by Lockwood. See Lockwood, D., 'Social Integration and System Integration', in Zollschan, G. K., and Hirsch, W. (Eds.), *Explorations in Social Change* (London, Houghton Mifflin, 1964), pp. 244–57.

22. Gouldner, A. W., 'Autonomy and Reciprocity in Functional Theory', in Gross, L. (Ed.), *Symposium on Sociological Theory* (New York, Row Peterson, 1959), pp. 241–70.

23. The careful regulation of part of life and the lack of regulation elsewhere may be a source of distress to the individual who only 'knows how to behave' in a narrow range of circumstances. Traditional and simple societies have less of this 'freedom' and less of the anxiety that goes with it.

The specificity of complex societies and the diffuseness of simple societies has been used as the basis of a classification of societies. For example, complex societies can be categorised as universalistic, achievement-orientated and emotionally neutral whereas simple societies are particularistic, ascriptive and affective. See Parsons, T., *The Social System* (London, Routledge and Kegan Paul, 1951). However, complex societies do contain segments in which diffuse elements dominate. For example, the English upper class is ascriptive and particularistic. Such 'anachronisms' seem to be remarkably powerful in complex societies and indeed seem also to develop in new élites.

24. Perhaps we should mention once again that the present systems approach treats the personalities of members of the system as its psychological environment.

25. Closure can, however, prevent the absorption of useful phenomena such as new knowledge.

26. Awareness of vulnerability to any kind of environment may stimulate actions which attempt to increase the degree of closure.

27. Cooley, C. H., *Social Organisation* (New York, Scribners 1909). Our approach to groups is similar to Cooley's discussion of 'primary' groups. However, we regard his notion of a 'secondary' group, which includes any social form other than a primary group, to be a residual category of little explanatory value, especially as some of these collectivities, such as a church or even a nation, can become highly internalised despite their high degree of institutionalisation. In simple societies, there are very few collectivities which can be internalised. For example, there may only be kinship units and the tribe. In complex society there are many, ranging from simple family units to the nation. Some of these will be institutionalised, the larger and more complex of which will contain others that may or may not themselves be institutionalised. For example, the nation includes churches, schools and families, which are institutionalised, as well as play groups which are not. Further, churches contain families, and schools contain play groups. All these collectivities can be internalised. Which collectivity is identified by the individual as 'we' at any time depends on various factors. For example, in war the nation may become more prominent than the family, and in inter-school athletic competitions the school team becomes more important than the house team.

28. Cartwright, D., and Zander, A., *Group Dynamics* (New York, Row Peterson, 1953).

29. Homans, G. C., *The Human Group* (New York, Harcourt, Brace, 1950).

30. This is why the family is such an important prototype for all groups.

31. The plausibility of considering groups as sets of people is related to the fact that groups are very open to their psychological environment. Hence, psychologies of various kinds have more to offer to the understanding of groups than of societal social systems, as evidenced by such banal phrases as the 'sane society'.

32. Tönnies introduced this dichotomy to distinguish 'community'

from 'society'. Many other dichotomies have also been introduced, e.g., Durkheim's mechanical and organic solidarity.

33. In support of this view, Pierre Turquet points out that each player
in a chess game has 16 men, and he considers that this may be the
largest number of people that an individual can keep consciously
in mind at one time (Address to the British Association of Psychotherapists Training Course in Group Psychotherapy, 1972).

34. Berelson & Steiner, *Human Behaviour* (New York, Harcourt, Brace
and World, 1964).

35. Boocock, S. S., 'Towards a Sociology of Learning', in *Sociology of
Education*, 39 (1966), pp. 1–45.

36. *The Sociology of Georg Simmel*, edited and translated by Kurt Wolff
(New York, The Free Press, 1950).

37. A review of the empirical evidence for Simmel's work is given in
Caplow, T., *Two Against One: Coalitions in Triads* (Englewood
Cliffs, Prentice-Hall, 1968).

38. Asch, S. E., *Social Psychology* (Englewood Cliffs, Prentice-Hall,
1952).

39. Bales, Robert F., and Borgatta, Edgar F., 'Size of Group as a
Factor in the Interaction Profile' in Paul Hare, et al. (Eds.), *Small
Groups: Studies in Social Interaction* (Glencoe, The Free Press, 1955).

40. Bales et al. believe that the number of individuals a group member
can take into account at one time is between 5 and 7. However,
the number varies with age. 'Increasing maturity of the personality
associated with age permits effective participation in larger groups.
In the early stages of growth the number of children observed in
play groups varies with the age of the child. Pre-school children
tend to play first individually, although in parallel, then in pairs
and then in larger groups.' Bales, Robert F., et al., 'Structure and
Dynamics of small Groups: A Review of Four Variables', in
Joseph B. Gittler (Ed.), *Review of Sociology: Analysis of a Decade*
(New York, Wiley, 1957). Those who favour large-group therapy
for all patients regardless of their level of emotional maturity
would be well advised to consider this finding.

41. Bales and Borgatta, op. cit.

42. Some of the contributions to this debate are: Weber on bureaucracy, in Gerth, H. H., and Wright Mills, C. (Eds.), *From Max
Weber* (London, Oxford Univ. Press, 1948); Robert Michels on
oligarchy, see his *Political Parties* (New York, Collier-Macmillan,
1962); Simmel on Socialism in *The Sociology of Georg Simmel*,
op. cit. Blau has summarised modern studies on bureaucracy in
Blau, P. M., *Bureaucracy in Modern Society* (New York, Random
House, 1965), and Blau and Schoenherr have summarised the
literature on the effects of the size, see Blau, P. M., and Schoenherr,

R. A., *The Structure of Organisations* (New York, Basic Books, 1971).

43. Equally it is possible that psychotherapists do not wish to see them. The economic pressures within hospitals which press for the development of therapy within large groups may prevent a systematic assessment of their merits.

44. We would argue that no dyad can exist without a social context which contains at least one other person. No two people can maintain a relationship without the shared symbols of the group, which has a prior existence. It may be misleading to call any social form 'elemental'. However, it is consistent with the sociological perspective that the most elemental form is the triad.

45. We do not intend to enter the debate about specific therapeutic techniques which involve only the interpretation of transference phenomena and exclude external material from their interpretations.

46. Springmann, R. R., 'The application of interpretations in large groups', *Int. J. Group Psychotherapy*. (In the press.)

47. Hopper, Earl, 'Some Effects of Variations in Supervisory Style: A Sociological Analysis', *B.J.S.* (September 1965).

48. MacGregor, F. C. *Social Science in Nursing* (New York, Russell Sage, 1960).

49. Edelson, M., *Sociotherapy and Psychotherapy* (London, The University of Chicago Press, 1970).

6. The large group as a medium for sociotherapy – J. Stuart Whiteley

1. Bion, W. R., *Experiences in Groups* (London, Tavistock Publications, 1961).

2. Whitaker, D. S., and Lieberman, M. A., *Psychotheraphy through the Group Process* (London, Tavistock Publications, 1965).

3. Edelson, M., *Sociotherapy and Psychotherapy* (London, University of Chicago Press, 1970).

4. Clark, A. W., and Yeomans, N. T., *Frazer House, Theory, Practice and Evaluation of a Therapeutic Community* (New York, Springer Pub. Co., 1969).

5. Whiteley, S., Briggs, D. and Turner, M., *Dealing with Deviants* (London, Hogarth Press, 1972).

6. Main, T. F., 'The Hospital as a Therapeutic Institution', in *Bull. Menn: Clinic.* Vol. 10. (1946), pp. 66–70.

7. Foulkes, S. H., *Therapeutic Group Analysis* (London, Allen and Unwin, 1964).

8. Jones, Maxwell, 'Rehabilitation of Forces Neurosis Patients to Civilian Life', in *B.M.J.* 1:533 (1946).

9. Foulkes, S. H., op. cit. (1964).
10. Rapoport, R., *Community as Doctor* (London, Tavistock Publications, 1960).
11. Clark, D. H., 'The Therapeutic Community Concept, Practice and Future', in *Brit. J. Psych.*, Vol. 111, No. 479 (1965).
12. Clark, A. W., has described considerably larger groups of up to 400 in Frazer House, Australia, with a wide-ranging diagnostic mix in which it is difficult to conceptualise unifying themes. See Clark, A. W., and Yeomans, N. T., *Frazer House,* op. cit.
13. Manning, N., Unpublished research at Henderson Hospital, 1973.
14. Matza, D., *Becoming Deviant* (New Jersey, Prentice-Hall, 1969).
15. Whiteley, J. S., 'Coming to terms with Deviance: Opportunities in the Criminal Justice Act', in *Howard Journal of Penology,* Vol. XIII, No. 4 (1973).
16. Whiteley, J. S., 'The Response of Psychopaths to a Therapeutic Community', in *Brit. J. of Psych.*, Vol. 116, No. 534 (1970).
17. Schiff, S. B., and Glassman, S. M., 'Large and Small Group Therapy in a State Mental Health Center', in *Int. J. of Group Psychotherapy,* Vol. XIX, No. 2 (1969).
18. Cook, G., Unpublished research at Henderson Hospital, 1972.
19. Manning, N., Unpublished research at Henderson Hospital, 1973.
20. Whiteley, J. S., and Zlatic, M., 'A Re-appraisal of Staff Attitudes to the Therapeutic Community', in *Brit. J. Soc. Psychiat,* Vol. 3, No. 2 (1972).

7. Psychotherapy in the large group – Rafael Springmann

1. This chapter is based on two papers of mine, 'A Large Group' and 'The Application of Interpretations in Large Groups.' I would like to express gratitude to the editors of *International Journal of Group Psychotheraphy* for allowing me to reuse the material.

   I would also like to express my gratitude to H. Ezriel, M.D. who set me on a new course, and to A.Z., who helped solve many an embarrassing situation by whispering the correct word at the right moment.
2. Ezriel, H., 'The role of Transference in Psychoanalytic and other Approaches to Group Treatment', in *Acta Psychotherapeutica,* Supplementum of Vol. 7 (1959).
3. Strachey, J., 'Nature of Therapeutic Action of Psycho-Analysis', in *Int. J. Psych. Anal.*, 15 (1934).
4. Ezriel, H., 'Experimentation within the Psycho-Analytic Session', in *Brit. J. Phil. Sci.,* 7, 25 (1956).
5. Springmann, R. R., 'The Application of Interpretations in Large Group', in *Int. Journal of Group Psychoth.* (1974).
6. Bion, W. R., 'Group Dynamics; A Review', in Klein, Melanie

(Ed.), *New Directions in Psycho-Analysis* (London, Tavistock Publications, 1955).

8. **The large group in training – Robin Skynner**
   1. I wish to thank the Editor of *Group Analysis* for permission to reproduce the account of the large group at the Institute of Group Analysis course, and also Dr D. Bennett and the staff of the Maudsley Day Hospital for permision to describe the development of the staff group there. However, the views are my own and are not necessarily shared by all those who took part.
   2. Irvine, E., 'The Use of Small Group Discussions in the Teaching of Human Relations and Mental Health', in *Brit. J. Psychiat. Social Work*, 5, 3 (1959).
   3. Caplan, G., *Principles of Preventive Psychiatry* (London, Tavistock, 1964).
   4. Gosling, R., Miller, D. H., Turquet, P. M., and Woodhouse, D., *The Use of Small Groups in Training* (London, Codicote, 1967).
   5. Balint, M., *The Doctor, The Patient and his Illness* (London, Pitman Medical, 1957).
   6. Bion, W., *Experiences in Groups* (London, Tavistock, 1961).
   7. Ezriel, H., 'A Psychoanalytic Approach to Group Treatment', in *Brit. J. Med. Psychol.*, 23, 59 (1950).
   8. Foulkes, S. H., *Introduction to Group Analytic Psychotherapy* (London, Heinemann, 1948); *Therapeutic Group Analysis* (London, Allen and Unwin, 1964); and Foulkes, S. H., and Anthony, E. J., *Group Psychotherapy: The Psychoanalytic Approach* (London, Penguin, 1965).
   9. Skynner, A. C. R., 'Group-Analytic Themes in Training and Case-Discussion Groups', Selected Lectures, 6th Int. Congress of Psychother. (Basle and New York, Karger, 1964); 'A Family of Family Casework Agencies', in *Int. J. Group Psychother.*, 18, 352 (1968); 'An Experiment in Group Consultation with the Staff of a Comprehensive School', in *Group Process*. 6, 99 (1974).
   10. Rice, A. K., *Learning for Leadership* (London, Tavistock Press, 1965).
   11. Rioch, M. J., 'Group Relations: Rationale and Techniques', in *Int. J. Group Psychother.*, 20, 340 (1970).
   12. Menninger has recently described the effect of such conferences on the functioning of an institution. See Menninger, R. W., 'The Impact of Group Relations Conferences on Organisational Growth', in *Int. J. Group Psychother.*, 22, 415 (1972).
   13. Bennett, D., 'The Day Hospital' in Petrilowitsch, N., and Flegel, H. (Eds.), *Social Psychiatry*, Top. Probl. Psychiat. Neurol., Vol. 9, pp. 4–18 (Karger, Basle/New York, 1969).

14. Jones, M., *Social Psychiatry* (London, Tavistock, 1952); and *Social Psychiatry in Practice* (London, Penguin Books, 1968).
15. Menzies, I. E. P., *The Functioning of Social Systems as a Defence Against Anxiety* (London, Tavistock Pamphlet No. 3, 1961).
16. Harrington, J., 'Much Ado About Milieu' *Laval Medical*, 41, 814 (1970); Stauble, W. J., 'Evaluation of Psychiatric Services', *Canad. Psychiat. Assn. J.*, 16, 197 (1971); and Christ, J., 'Comment on "A Passing Glance at the Therapeutic Community in 1964" by Maxwell Jones,' in *Int. J. Group Psychother.*, 15, 5 (1965).
17. Curry, A. E., 'Large Therapeutic Groups: A Critique and Appraisal of Selected Literature', in *Int. J. Group Psychother.*, 17, 536 (1967).
18. Schiff, S. B., and Glassman, S. M., 'Large and Small Group Therapy in a State Mental Health Center', in *Int. J. Group Psychother.*, 19, 150 (1969).
19. Christ, J., op. cit. (1965).
20. Jones, M., 'A Passing Glance at the Therapeutic Community in 1964', in *Int. J. Group Psychother.*, 15, 5 (1965).
21. Skynner, A. C. R., 'An Experiment in Group Consultation with the Staff of a Comprehensive School', op. cit.
22. Skynner, A. C. R., 'Implications of Recent Work in Conjoint Family Therapy for Group-Analytic Theory', in *Group Analysis,* 5, 153 (1972).

9. Large groups in natural settings – Myles Hopper

1. Mr William Duggan, research assistant to the director of the project, has contributed to the preparation of this article through his site visits and field notes and has prepared drafts of several sections containing data about the natural settings. His assistance is gratefully acknowledged.
2. Space does not permit the inclusion of ethnographic data. The analysis of large-group phenomena in this paper is dependent upon a discussion of the natural setting as a general milieu rather than on the specific character of any one community. Any deeper examination of the process and outcome in the project sites would, of course, necessitate more elaborate presentations of ethnographic material. At present, we are providing only the general framework for our selection procedure.

10. Large groups in industry – Trevor Mumby

1. Guest, R. H., *Organisational Change: The Effect of Successful Leadership* (Homewood, Ill, The Dorsey Press, 1962).
2. Storr, A., *Sexual Deviation* (London, Penguin, 1964).
3. Harrison, K., in Cooper, C. (Ed.), *Group Training for Individual and Organisational Development* (New York, Karger, 1973).

4. Tofler, A., *Future Shock* (London, Pan Books, 1970).
5. Harrison, R., 'Understanding Your Organisation's Character', in *Harvard Business Review* (May/June 1972).
6. Schein, E. H., and Bennis, W. G., *Personal and Organisational Change Through Group Methods: The Laboratory Approach* (New York, Wiley, 1965).
7. Hampden-Turner, C., *Radical Man* (London, Duckworth, 1971), p. 182.
8. de Maré, P. B., *Perspectives in Group Psychotherapy. A Theoretical Background* (London, Allen & Unwin, 1972).
9. Blake, R. R., and Mouton, J., *The Managerial Grid* (Gulf Publishing Co, 1965).
10. Mumby, Trevor, 'The impact of self-development training on a sales force.' Unpublished M.Sc. dissertation.
11. Humble, J., *Social Responsibility Audit. A Management Tool for Survival* (Foundation for Business Responsibilities, 1973).
12. de Maré, P. B., op. cit. (1972).
13. Rogers, C., Quotation by Einstein used in *Freedom to Learn* (New York, Bobs-Merrill, 1969).

Overview – Malcolm Pines

1. Milgram, S., and Toch, H., 'Collective Behaviour' in Lindzey, G., and Aronson, E. (Eds.), *Handbook of Social Psychology* (New York, Addison-Wesley, 1969), Vol. 4; Greenacre, Phyllis, 'Crowds and Crisis. Psychoanalytic Considerations', in *The Psychoanalytic Study of the Child* 27 (New York, Quadrangle Books, 1972); and Canetti, Elias, *Crowds and Power* (Harmondsworth, Penguin Books, 1973).
2. Stanton, A., and Schwartz, M. S., *The Mental Hospital* (New York, Basic Books, 1950).
3. Nisbet, R. A., *The Sociological Tradition* (London, Heinemann Educational Books, 1970).
4. Nisbet, op. cit.
5. Martin, Jay, *The Dialectical Imagination* (London, Heinemann Educational Books, 1973).
6. Foulkes, S. H., *Therapeutic Group Analysis* (London, Allen & Unwin, 1964).
7. Psychoanalytic studies and speculations as to the origins and experience of grasping hold of reality underpin my theoretical approach. In addition, I refer to the 'cognitive unconscious' of Piaget and other work on areas of infantile development. See Piaget, J., 'The Affective Unconscious and the Cognitive Unconscious' in *Journal American Psychoanalytic Assn*, 21, 249–61 (1973).

8. Hamburg, P. A., Adams, J., in *Arch. Gen. Psychiatry*, 17, 277–84 (1967).
9. Shands, M. C., *Thinking and Psychotherapy* (Harvard University Press, 1960).
10. Scheidlinger, S., 'Identification, The Sense of Belonging and Identity in Small Groups', in *Int. J. Group Psychother.*, 14, 291–306 (1964).
11. Scheidlinger insists on the importance of differentiating group formative regression, based on Freud's original discussion of identifications in large groups with therapeutic regression centred on transference in small therapy groups. Scheidlinger further differentiates between two broader group-process levels, a contemporaneous-dynamic and a genetic-regressive. See Scheidlinger, S., 'The Concept of Regression in Group Psychotherapy' in *Int. J. of Group Psychother.*, 18, 3–20 (1968), and Freud, S., *Group Psychotherapy and the Analysis of the Ego* (1921) Standard Edition, Vol. 18 (London, Hogarth Press, 1955).
12. Kohut, H., *The Analysis of Self* (New York, Int. Universities Press, 1971).
13. Kohut, H., 'Narcissism and Narcissistic Rage', in *The Psychoanalytic study of the child*, 27 (New York, Quadrangle Books, 1973).
14. Shands, M. C., *Thinking and Psychotherapy* (Harvard University Press, 1960).
15. Spiegel, L., 'The Self, Reality and Perception,' *Annals N.Y. Academy of Sciences*; and Spiegel, L., 'The Self, the Sense of Self and Perception', in *Psychoanalytic Study of the Child* 14, 81–109 (New York, Int. Universities Press, 1959).
16. Spiegel, L., op. cit. (1959).
17. Grinker, Roy (Sr), 'Conceptual Progress in Psychoanalysis' in Marmor, J. (Ed.), *Modern Psychoanalysis* (New York, Basic Books, 1968).
18. Shands, M. C., op. cit. (1960).
19. Charney, I. W., 'Regression and Reorganisation in the "Isolation Treatment" of Children', in *J. Child Psychol. Psychiat.*, 4, 47–60 (1963).
20. Rinsley, D. B., 'The Adolescent Inpatient, Patterns of Depersonification', in *Psychiat. Quart.*, 45, 1–20 (1971).
21. Masterson, J. F., *Treatment of the Borderline Adolescent: A Developmental Approach* (New York, Wiley Interscience 1972).
22. Piaget, J., op. cit. (1973).
23. Piaget points out that this applies no less to the process of development of scientific thought, than it does to the individual's developmental stages. Scientific thought itself obeys the laws of certain cognitive structures before we become consciously aware of them.

Thus, mathematical reasoning was used by Euclid and by Aristotle without their being conscious of the whole ensemble of structures used, which we have only become aware of through the nineteenth-century study of the logic of relations (Galileo).

24. Trigant Burrow, in *The Social Basis of Consciousness:* 'I am convinced that an adjustment of consciousness . . . will ultimately demand that we bring to both the very origins of our mental and social systems of *"thinking"*, that we challenge our customary values of mental adaptation at their very foundation . . . that shall challenge in every detail the fixed pattern of an arbitrary and unconscious position of absolutism as contrasted with the fluent evaluation that alone pertain to a basis of conscious relativity.' (London, Kegan Paul, 1927), pp. 226–7.

25. Money-Kyrle, R., 'Varieties of Group Formation': in Rohem (Ed.), *Psychoanalysis and Social Science,* Vol. 2 (1950), pp. 313–29.

26. Shands, M. C., op. cit. (1960); Piaget, J., op. cit. (1973).

27. Edelson, Marshall, *Psychotherapy and Sociotherapy* (University of Chicago Press, 1970).

28. Mahler, Margaret, *On Human Symbiosis and the Vicissitudes of Individuals* (London, Hogarth Press, 1969).

29. Main, T. F., 'The Hospital as a Therapeutic Institution', in *Bull. Menn. Clin.,* 10, 66 (1946).

30. Foulkes, S. M., *Group Analytic Psychotherapy* (London, Heinemann, 1948).

31. Abrams, G. W., 'Defining Milieu Therapy', *Arch. Gen. Psychiatr.,* 21, 553–60 (1969).

32. Stotland, E., and Kobler, A. L., *Life and Death of a Mental Hospital* (Seattle, University of Washington Press, 1965).

33. Robinson, D., *Patients, Practitioners and Medical Care* (London, Heinemann Medical Books, 1973).

34. Parsons, Talcott, 'Illness and the Role of the Physician', *Am. J. Orthopsychiat.* 21, 452–60 (1951).

35. Rickman, J., 'The Factor of Number in Individual and Group Dynamics' (1950), in *Selected Contributions to Psychoanalysis* (London, Hogarth Press, 1957).

36. Daniels, D. N., and Rubin, R. S., 'The Community Meeting', *Arch. Gen. Psychiatr.,* 18, 60–75 (1968).

37. Watzlawich, P., Beavin, J., Jackson, D., *Pragmatics of Human Communication* (London, Faber & Faber, 1968); also Shands, M. C., op. cit. (1960).

38. In terms of Szasz and Hollander's three basic models of the physician/patient relationship the model of guidance cooperation (parent/child) has been replaced by that of mutual participation (adult/adult). See Szasz, T., and Hollander, M. M., 'A Contri-

bution to the Philosophy of Medicine', *A.M.A. Archives of Interna Medicine,* 97, 585 (1956).

39. Zetzel, E., *The Capacity for Emotional Growth* (London, Hogarth Press, 1970).
40. Grinker, Roy, op. cit. (1968); Spiegel, J., *Transactions, The Interplay between Individual, Family and Society* (New York, Science House, 1971).
41. Zetzel, E., op. cit. (1970).
42. Simmel, E., 'Psychoanalytic Treatment in a Clinic', *Int. J. Psychoanal.,* 10 (1929).
43. Stanton, A., and Schwartz, M. S., *The Mental Hospital* (New York, Basic Books, 1954).
44. Edelson, M., *Psychotherapy and Sociotherapy* (University of Chicago Press, 1970); Edelson, M., *The Practice of Sociotherapy* (Yale, 1970).
45. Shands, M. C., op. cit. (1960); Zetzel, E., op. cit. (1970).
46. James, William, *The Principles of Psychology.*
47. Parsons, T., op. cit. (1951).
48. ibid.
49. de Maré, P. B., *Perspectives in Group Psychotherapy* (London, Allen & Unwin, 1972).
50. Canetti, Elias, op. cit. (1973).
51. Nisbet, R. A., *The Sociological Tradition* (London, Heinemann Educational Books, 1970).

Index

experience-centred, 42–44
four processes, 194–95
functioning, 23, 247
fusion words, 100
group-dynamic features, 152
history, 149–50
interactions in, 185
leadership, 25–9, 250
location of responsibility in, 131
main approaches to the, 19
manner of talking in, 158
meaning of silence in the, 111,
 119
meetings, 68–74, 87, 202–7
members' search for suitable
 model in, 132
mindlessness, 153
minimal structure, 50–51
multi-body psychology of, 86
in natural settings, 252–71
non-interpretive therapeutic
 interventions in, 84
particular qualities, 194
polarisation, 100
politics, 145–58
problem-centred, 41–42, 44
problems, 33–56
psychodynamics, 57–86
psychology, 281, 293
psychotherapeutic potential of
 the, 22, 23, 306
psychotherapy in, 212–26
psychotic mechanisms in, 24–5,
 52–3, 55
the question of abstinence in,
 49–50
response location in, 105
role, 150–58
selection in, 48
seating, 50, 88–9
the 'singleton' in, 93–108
size, 51–2, 88, 180–88
as social system, 160, 162
sociological view of, 159–89
staff in, 209–11
struggle in domination in, 92
sub-grouping, 24, 48–9, 185
task, 89–90
in a therapeutic community
 setting, 206–207
therapy, 41–7, 151, 154, 197,
 198, 305
therapy-centred, 44–7

thinking, 146
threats to identity in the, 87–144
in training, 227–51
two categories involved in, 19
and violence, 125–38
Leadership, 25–9
 multiple, 250–51
 struggle, 233–34
Le Bon, 17, 291
 Psychology of Crowds (1895), 17
Leiberman, M. A., 207
 Focal Conflict Theory, 194
Leicester Conferences, 19, 87
Leverhulme, Lord, 273
Lévi-Strauss, Claude, 145, 155
Lewin, Kurt, 18
London, 14, 26
Lumpenproletariat state, 139, *see also*
 M.I. state

Macneice, Louis, 99
Main, Tom, 18, 44, 57–86, 292,
 294, 295, 301, 302, 303, 306
 'The Hospital as a Therapeutic
 Institution', 18
 Northfield experiments, 197, 198
Manning, N., 206, 210
Mark, Sir Robert, 40
Marsh, Cody, 149
Masterson, J. F., 299
Matza, D., 208
Maudsley Hospital, 18
 Day Hospital at the, 234, 235
 postgraduate training complex,
 234
 Rehabilitation Unit, 240
Medical team, psychotherapeutic
 function, 200
'Membership individual' (M.I.),
 109, 119, 120, 123, 127, 131,
 142, 144
 the boundary between I.M. and,
 124
 the I.M. conversion into a, 139
 state, 97, 107, 140
 status, 124, 138
 threat of annihilation in
 becoming a, 95
Mental, health, 218, 228, 301, 302,
 308
 illness, 15, 301, 302, 303
 splitting, 59